Western Involvement in Nkrumah's Downfall

Godfrey Mwakikagile

Copyright © 2015 Godfrey Mwakikagile
All rights reserved.

Western Involvement in Nkrumah's Downfall

Godfrey Mwakikagile

First Edition

ISBN 978-9987-16-004-4

New Africa Press
Dar es Salaam, Tanzania

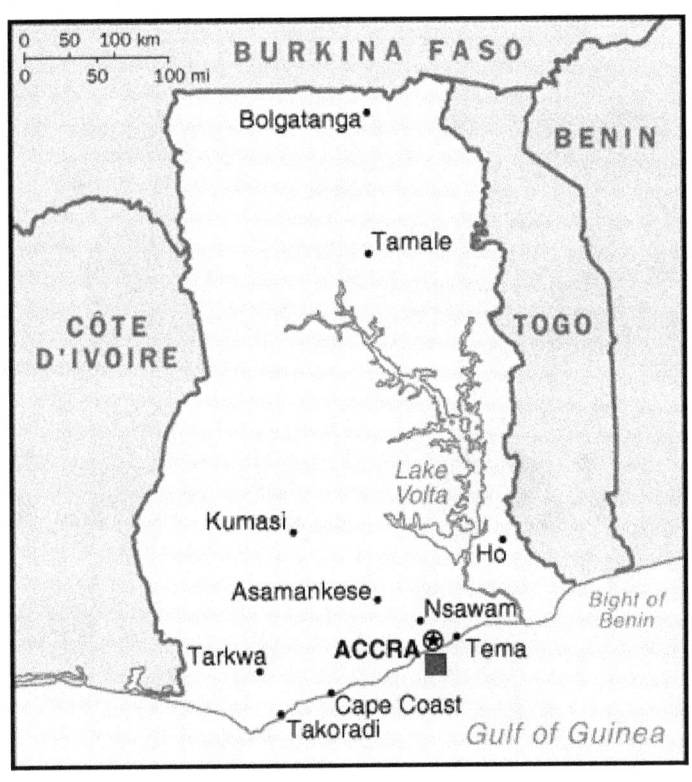

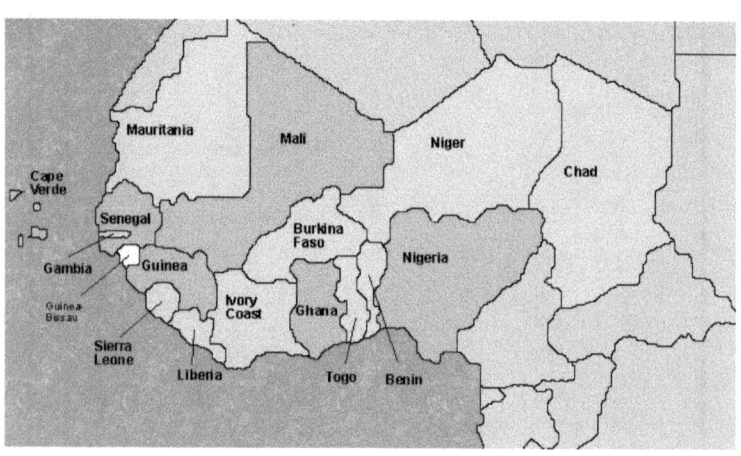

Kwame Nkrumah

Nkrumah

Nkrumah with Nyerere

Nkrumah with Sékou Touré

Nkrumah, 21 September 1909 – 27 April 1972

Introduction

DECLASSIFIED DOCUMENTS show that Western governments led by the United States played a major role in orchestrating the military coup which led to the downfall of Ghana's first president, Kwame Nkrumah, who was also the first leader to lead an African country – south of the Sahara – to independence.

There is also enough circumstantial evidence showing that the United States government was not just implicated but played a significant role in creating conditions which led to the coup and actively participated in Nkrumah's ouster even though the CIA *deliberately* did not leave a paper trail to document its involvement.

The circumstantial evidence also comes from many statements made by some of the former American ambassadors to Ghana in interviews decades after Nkrumah was overthrown. They are reprinted as an appendix to this book.

Although conditions within Ghana itself created a climate conducive to the execution of a successful military coup, Western powers did play a big role in exacerbating those conditions. It is also important to understand that the conditions themselves may not have been enough to enable the soldiers to overthrow Nkrumah had Western governments and their intelligence agencies not been actively involved in fanning the flames and in supporting Nkrumah's opponents in their concerted effort to overthrow him. Perhaps that is what prompted one of the coup leaders, Major Akwasi Afrifa, to say they probably would not have succeeded in overthrowing Nkrumah if he was still in Ghana when the coup was launched.

They waited until he was out of the country in order to carry out a successful coup against him. In fact, the presidential guard at Flagstaff House put up stiff resistance against the coup makers. There were many casualties on both sides. The guards were ready to die for Nkrumah and many of them did. As Kwame Botwe-Asamoah states in his book, *Kwame Nkrumah's Politico-Cultural Thought and Politics: An African-Centered Paradigm for the Second Phase of the African Revolution*:

"The C.I.A-sponsored military coup on February 24, 1966, was the result of the systematic campaign against Nkrumah's government, especially coming after the formal opening of the Akosombo dam. According to Retired Colonel Oteng, the coup makers might not have succeeded had his counterpart at the Ghana Broadcasting Station not been pressured to surrender.

Until the arrival of the Commander of the POGR (President's Own Guard Regiment), Colonel Zanleringu, Colonel Oteng was the most senior officer on duty at the time of the coup, with his men bent on defending Nkrumah's government. Later, under the command of Colonel Zanleringu, the small band of the soldiers fought and defended the Flagstaff House, the official residence of President Kwame Nkrumah. But as Colonel Oteng further explained, they surrendered at the suggestion of the Commander of the POGR at ten o'clock on the morning of February 24, 1966. With the announcement on Ghana's radio that Nkrumah's government had been overthrown by Ghana Armed Forces, no commander of any military unit could have successfully mobilized his forces to resist the takeover. This has been the case with all military coups overthrowing civilian governments in Ghana.

With the C.I.A.-sponsored military action coup of 1966, the great promises of the country's Seven-Year Development Plan that would have totally transformed Ghana's social, economic, industrial, agricultural, educational and cultural programs came to a sudden halt.

Perhaps, had the humiliation of the Asantes by the capture and deportation of Prempeh I, and the subsequent Yaa Asantewa war, for instance, been presented on the stage or turned into a motion picture, Major Afrifa perhaps would have been the first to support Nkrumah's diplomatic action against Britain over Ian Smith's unilateral declaration of independence in Zimbabwe in 1965." – (Kwame Botwe-Asamoah, *Kwame Nkrumah's Politico-Cultural Thought and Politics: An African-Centered Paradigm for the Second Phase of the African Revolution*, New York: Routledge, 2005, p. 219. For a contrasting view, see Obed Yao Asamoah, *The Political History of Ghana (1950 – 2013): The Experience of a Non-Conformist*, Bloomington, Indiana, USA: AuthorHouse, 2014).

It is not the aim of this book to deny the existence of strong opposition to Nkrumah's authoritarian rule but to provide a balanced account of what happened during that turbulent period.

There was very strong opposition to Nkrumah's leadership, especially among the elite. And there was mass discontent among ordinary people, mainly in urban centres, who felt economic hardship – more than their rural counterparts did – when the cost of living kept on rising and economic conditions continued to deteriorate.

It was also mostly the urban residents, with access to

the media, who felt they were being deprived of free expression under Nkrumah's regime which, as a one-party state, did not tolerate dissent.

People in towns and cities have in general felt that they are more enlightened and are more aware of what goes on – especially what the government does, good and bad – than their brethren in the rural areas are. They are therefore the most vocal opponents of the government when leaders do not fulfill their promises and when living conditions deteriorate; which can be very hard for urban residents because of the high cost of living, unlike in the rural areas where most people don't have to buy food, pay rent, water and electric bills and so on.

All that militated against Nkrumah in spite of his genuine effort to pursue and implement economic policies which would have enabled Ghana to achieve rapid industrialisation. And he did succeed in many areas – infrastructure development among many other things – although his achievements are ignored or dismissed by his critics who contend that Nkrumah's policies bankrupted Ghana and therefore his ouster was justified.

Yet it was Nkrumah who laid the foundation for modern-day Ghana – all the schools, factories, tarmac roads, the Akosombo dam, a modern harbour at Tema, bridges and power installations, various institutions and much more, which he built and which did not exist before he came to power. And he achieved all that within only a few years – fewer than ten.

What is also deliberately ignored or overlooked by his critics and other people who don't know about the other side – what the United States and her Western allies did – is the role external forces played in Nkrumah's ouster. Even if he did not have enemies in Ghana, the United States still would have worked on plans to get rid of him because the Americans considered him to be a threat to American interests in Africa.

My work attempts to construct a proportional

perspective on what happened in Ghana during that time, which is impossible to do if Western involvement, especially by the CIA, in Nkrumah's downfall is not taken into account.

Western conspiracies against Nkrumah and his downfall

NINETEEN SIXTY SIX was one of the most tragic years in the history of post-colonial Africa. Besides the upheavals – two military coups, political assassinations and massacres of tens of thousands of people – which took place in Nigeria, the continent's largest nation in terms of population and a potential Third World power, it was also in the same year that one of Africa's most prominent leaders, Kwame Nkrumah, was overthrown in a military coup.

Widely acknowledged as the strongest proponent of immediate continental unification under one government, and an embodiment of Pan-Africanism, Nkrumah blazed the trail for the African independence movement when he led Ghana to become the first African country south of the Sahara to emerge from colonial rule.

The coup, engineered and masterminded by the CIA, took place on 24 February 1966. It marked the end of the political career of probably the most influential African leader.

When Dr. Nkrumah's reign came to an abrupt end,

several reasons were given for his ouster. His critics accused him of dictatorship. But that is not why the CIA orchestrated his downfall.

The United States has always supported and propped up dictators around the world, including some in Africa such as Mobutu Sese Seko for 32 years, as long as the despots serve American and Western interests. Nkrumah did not and incurred the wrath of the United States and other Western governments.

The United States was no more interested in helping the people of Ghana establish democracy than they were in helping the people of Iraq and Afghanistan establish democracy when she invaded those countries.

In the case of Iraq, it was oil more than anything else that triggered the invasion. In the case of Afghanistan, the invasion was "justified" by the Americans on grounds of national security to neutralise terrorists who were radical Islamists.

Other geopolitical interests of the United States were at stake. Yet, in both cases, American leaders claimed they wanted to help the people in those two countries establish democracy.

If the United States wanted to help the people who live under dictatorial regimes institute democracy, she would have helped to overthrow *all* dictators, not just some.

In Africa, the United States supported not only Mobutu but the apartheid regime of South Africa. It was a tyrannical regime. For some inexplicable reason, American leaders felt that black people and other non-whites in South Africa did not want to live under democracy, although the majority of South Africans made it clear that they did not want to live under apartheid or to be denied basic human rights.

Yet, the United States found it necessary to overthrow a democratically elected government in Ghana under Nkrumah on the spurious grounds that it was helping to establish democracy in that country. Why in Ghana and not in South Africa, in Zaire under Mobutu, in Rhodesia and in the Portuguese colonies of Angola, Mozambique and Guinea Bissau if the United States was really interested in helping Africans establish democracy?

The plot against Nkrumah by the United States must be looked at in the larger context of American imperialist designs to dominate and exploit African countries, and to neutralise leaders whom they considered to be hostile to American geopolitical and economic interests which included keeping white minority regimes in power in the countries of southern Africa, especially the citadel of white supremacy on the continent, apartheid South Africa, which helped the other white minority rulers in the region in their military campaigns against the African nationalist forces; which explains why a leader like President Julius Nyerere of Tanzania was also targeted for elimination because he was the strongest supporter of the liberation movements in the region.

American policy towards Africa was also dictated by Cold War imperatives to secure and install friendly regimes which could be manipulated at will – what Nkrumah called "client states" – to serve American interests.

Although other Western powers, especially the United Kingdom and West Germany, were involved in the plot to overthrow Nkrumah even if it meant assassinating him, it was the United States which was the driving force behind this nefarious scheme. In fact, meetings were held in Washington, D.C., attended by American, British and German officials to coordinate efforts to undermine Nkrumah. As Opoku Agyeman, a Ghanaian professor of political science at Montclair State University – he also taught at the University of California-Berkeley, Cornell University, the University of the West Indies, and the University of Dar es Salaam in Tanzania – states in his book, *The Failure of Grassroots Pan-Africanism*:

"L. Martin had written in 1962 that 'only when vital U.S. defense positions are endangered by the inimical behavior of countries unmistakably allied with the Sino-Soviet bloc should it be necessary to consider direct interference and, possibly, to take military action against them.'[276]

Then in 1964, a U.S. State Department report mentioned five 'danger spots where Communism had supposedly made considerable headway,' and which, by implication, might become proper targets of U.S. 'direct interference.' These were Zanzibar, Algeria, Ghana, Mali, and 'Southern Africa.'[277] While there is no evidence that the United States had anything to do with the ousters of Modibo Keita and Ben Bella, Tanzania (embracing Zanzibar) became the object of an abortive U.S.-sponsored military coup d'etat in November 1964.[278]

Meanwhile, by 1965, Accra, the capital of Ghana and the headquarters of AATUF (All-African Trade Union Federation formed in November 1959, urged by Nkrumah), had replaced Algiers in Western thinking as 'the Communists' favorite place for front organization meetings.'[279] That Irving Brown, the man straddling American unionism and the CIA might have employed his considerable talents in disseminating this view and thereby stirring the CIA to action is not at all inconceivable.

At any rate, the overthrow of Nkrumah – and therefore the AATUF from Accra – was only a few weeks away. Nkrumah was a subject of discussion 'at the highest NATO level' during 1965. From the end of that year, as Ruth First wrote, the United States, Britain, and West Germany were all 'preoccupied with the matter of how to get rid of him.'[280] That eventually the Americans were responsible for the February 1966 military coup in Ghana is now well established.[281] *The New York Times* would report, concerning the reason behind the CIA-backed coup, that Nkrumah 'had angered the US by maintaining close ties to the East.'[282]

In many ways, the overthrow of Nkrumah was tantamount to the overthrow of the AATUF. The Western trade union movement jubilated on that account." – (Opoku Agyeman, *The Failure of Grassroots Pan-Africanism: The Case of the All-African Trade Union Federation*, New York: Lexington Books, 2003, pp. 241 – 242. See also Godfrey Mwakikagile, *Statecraft and Nation Building in Africa: A Post-colonial Study*, Dar es Salaam: New Africa Press, 2014, p. 281; G. Mwakikagile, *Nyerere and Africa: End of an Era*, Pretoria: New Africa Press, 2010, p. 312:

"The ouster of Dr. Milton Obote had striking similarities to the coup against President Kwame Nkrumah of Ghana five years earlier on February 24, 1966. Both leaders were ardent Pan-Africanists and strong supporters of liberation movements in Africa. Both antagonized the West because of their Pan-African militancy and the socialist policies they pursued. And both were overthrown – with Western help including the CIA – when they were outside their countries: Nkrumah, while on his way on a peace mission to Hanoi at the invitation of Vietnamese President Ho Chin Mihn to help end the Vietnam war (and in pursuit of Nkrumah's ambition to make Africa an important player on the global scene and in major international affairs); and Obote, when he was at the Commonwealth conference in Singapore where he had gone, at the urging of President Julius Nyerere, to make a strong case against Britain because of her insistence on selling arms to apartheid South Africa and her unwillingness to take stern measures against the apartheid regime and the white minority government in Rhodesia").

Western governments, especially the United States which masterminded the coup through the CIA, also celebrated Nkrumah's ouster. One of the American officials involved in planning the coup against Nkrumah was Robert Komer who was known for his passion and dedication to whatever he was assigned to do, including a notoriously brutal operation in Vietnam during the Vietnam war. As Alex Abella states in his book, *Soldiers of Reason: The RAND Corporation and the Rise of the American Empire*:

"Operation Phoenix (was) a notorious campaign that culminated in the outright execution of tens of thousands of Vietnamese.

The main RAND character in Operation Phoenix was Robert W. Komer, a man of fierce passions and keen intellect. Komer was known as 'Blowtorch Bob,' a nickname given to him by U.S. Ambassador Henry Cabot Lodge, who said that arguing with Komer was like having a blowtorch aimed at the seat of your pants. Yet, with his normally mild demeanor, horn-rimmed glasses, and briar pipe, Komer could also pass for what spy novelist John le Carré called an 'intellocrat.'

As a National Security Council staffer in the mid-1960s, Komer was involved in the planning of a successful military coup against the Socialist regime of President Kwame Nkrumah of Ghana, West Africa.

In 1966, as the U.S.-led war in Southeast Asia escalated, President Johnson named Komer special assistant in charge of 'direction, coordination, and supervision of all U.S. non-military programs for peaceful construction relating to Vietnam.'

Komer's mission was to win control of the hearts and minds of the Vietnamese through pacification, a program that in theory used information, propaganda, and judicious amounts of force to accomplish its objective. When Komer told Johnson he didn't have much experience in the field, the president replied, 'Well, maybe what we need is some fresh meat.' In an interview years later, Komer was still amazed at Johnson's choice of words. 'That's what he said. Not fresh blood but fresh meat.'

Future CIA director William Colby would later

describe Komer as 'statistics crazy and aggressively optimistic,' urging Vietnam experts to set measurable goals and standards of achievement for the conflict instead of settling for broad philosophical discussions. Komer, who shared the RAND devotion to numerical rationality, was also someone whose antennae were supremely sensitive to Johnson's needs. And what Johnson needed at the time were figures to back up his claims that America was winning. An aide to Johnson said that if Komer had been asked how many people were influenced by Vietcong propaganda, he would have replied within '13 hours and 20 minutes' with a top-secret cable 'definitely stating: 2,634,201.11.'" – (Alex Abella, *Soldiers of Reason: The RAND Corporation and the Rise of the American Empire*, Boston: Houghton Mifflin Harcourt, 2008, pp. 180 – 181).

He had such devotion to a cause, including Nkrumah's ouster.

There had been denials through the years about American involvement in Nkrumah's ouster. But years later, evidence emerged showing that the American government, including President Lyndon Johnson himself, and the CIA, planned the coup. The US State Department even released declassified material which clearly implicated and confirmed American involvement in Nkrumah's downfall. As Vivienne Jabri, a professor of international politics at King's College, London, states in her book, *The Postcolonial Subject: Claiming Politics/Governing Others in Late Modernity*:

"For Kwame Nkrumah, the decolonisation process had to encompass not just the institutions of the state, but the political economy and African consciousness itself.

Western hostility towards Nkrumah was exactly directed at disrupting his efforts to combat what he called 'neo-colonialism,' his support for liberation struggles across the continent and globally, and his proposal, according to David Birmingham (1998), to allow the establishment of a Soviet airbase in Ghana.

Indeed in 1999, the Historian's Office of the US State Department published declassified intelligence reports relating to American activities in Africa, including plans to overthrow Nkrumah. In a case reminiscent of the overthrow of Mossadeq in Iran and the reinstatement of the Shah and the Pahlavi dynasty in 1952, an event instilled in the Iranian mind, the 8-point 'proposed Action Programme for Ghana,' drawn up by William Trimble, the Director of the Office of West African Affairs in February 1964, stated:

'Intensive efforts should be made through psychological warfare and other means to diminish support for Nkrumah within Ghana and nurture the conviction among the Ghanaian people that their country's welfare and independence necessitate his removal.'

The US Secretary of State at the time, Dean Rusk, along with CIA Director John McCone, explored the potential of particular generals in the Ghana military as authors of an envisaged coup d'etat that would overthrow Nkrumah, and this coming in parallel with considerations of ending US support for large infrastructural projects in Ghana initiated during the Kennedy Administration." – (Vivienne Jabri, *The Postcolonial Subject: Claiming Politics/Governing Others in Late Modernity*, Abington, Oxon, OX, UK: Rotledge, 2013, pp. 159 – 160).

Kwame Badu Antwi-Boasiako and Okyere Bonna also state in their book, *Traditional Institutions and Public Administration in Democratic Africa*:

"Despite the initial denial of America's (CIA) involvement in financially supporting the overthrow of democratically elected governments in Africa, studies show that America was fully behind the February 24, 1966, coup in Ghana, which ousted President Kwame

Nkrumah....

Today, General J.A. Ankrah's picture together with American president L.B. Johnson is displayed at the latter's library in Austin, Texas, USA, when the former paid a visit to the US to report the successful operation of the 1966 coup....In yet another denial, America is believed to have coordinated, together with Belgium, the assassination of Patrice Lumumba, which brought a military dictator, Mobutu Sese Seko, to power who ruled for decades in the interest of America....

These examples and many others not mentioned here, show that postcolonial African leaders served under the mercy of the superpowers. And those leaders who failed to bow to the dictates of these powers were forcefully removed from office against the will of the people." – (Kwame Badu Antwi-Boasiako and Okyere Bonna, *Traditional Institutions and Public Administration in Democratic Africa*, Bloomington, Indiana, USA: Xlibris, 2009, p. 55. See also, cited by Kwame Badu Antwi-Boasiako and Okyere Bonna, Olajide Aluko, "After Nkrumah: Continuity and Change in Ghana's Foreign Policy Issue," *A Journal of Opinion*, 5 (1), 1975, pp. 55 – 62).

There are those who contend that there was such strong opposition to Nkrumah's rule within Ghana itself that external intervention – especially by the United States – did not play an important role, if any, in overthrowing Nkrumah.

What is overlooked is the fact that the United States had been working on covert operations to oust Nkrumah long before Ghanaian soldiers and police officers overthrew him in 1966. The United also offered and provided support to major political figures in Ghana who were opposed to or who had fallen out with Nkrumah. One example was Komla Gbedemah, former finance minister and former vice-chairman (under Nkrumah) of the ruling

Convention People's Party (CPP), who also was the second most powerful man in Ghana when he was a member of Nkrumah's cabinet.

He had also been Nkrumah's friend for a long time since colonial days when they were together campaigning for independence. They were members of the United Gold Coast Convention (UGCC), the largest and oldest political party in the country led by Dr. J.B. Danquah. Nkrumah was the party's general secretary.

The two friends left the UGCC and formed a rival party, the Convention People's Party (CPP) which, unlike the UGCC, appealed to the masses and demanded "Independence Now."

Komla Gbedemah, 17 June 1913 - 11 July 1998

Another major political figure who was supported by the United States for years long before the coup took place was Dr. Danquah, leader of the opposition who lost the election to Nkrumah.

Professor Roger Gocking, while not entirely ignoring CIA's participation in Nkrumah's ouster seems to downplay that, while also conceding that the United States was already supporting Nkrumah's opponents long before he was overthrown. As he states in his book, *The History of Ghana*:

"In keeping with the cold-war mentality of the 1960s, it was easy for him (Nkrumah) to single out Western intelligence sources led by the U.S. Central Intelligence Agency (CIA) as one of the main forces behind the coup.

Indeed, there was a history of such subversion. As early as 1961 CIA agents had been in touch with Komla Gbedemah in Togo (where he fled and sought refuge) after Nkrumah had ousted him from power and had offered the former financial minister help in seizing power. The agency had also offered financial assistance to J.B. Danquah in 1962.

Revelations about the CIA's subversive activities in Africa in general had become common knowledge, and in 1962 Nkrumah, according to the US embassy officials in Ghana, 'was 'pathologically obsessed' with the CIA and was passing out copies of Andrew Tully's exposé, *CIA: The Inside Story*, on an indiscriminate basis.' The Kulungugu assassination attempt and the obvious connection of the plotters to Togo reinforced these feelings.

In the last years of the regime an 'atmosphere of intrigue and distrust...increased in intensity.' In 1965 even his long-serving British secretary, Erica Powell, who had transcribed Nkrumah's autobiography, was suspected of being a foreign agent.

However, there was obviously too much local support for the coup even those on the left to accept totally this CIA-engendered explanation of events." – (Roger Gockling, *The History of Ghana*, Westport, Connecticut, USA: Greenwood Press, p. 139).

This explanation, of the the major role the CIA played

in Nkrumah's downfall, does not come just from the ideological left or from Nkrumah's supporters alone, as Gockling claims or implies.

J.B. Danquah, 18 December 1895 - 4 February 1965

The American government itself, in the declassified documents it released to the public in November 1999, clearly shows that American leaders – including President Lyndon B. Johnson himself, the CIA director and other high-ranking government officials together with their British and West German counterparts – sanctioned and supported the coup against Nkrumah which was carried out with a lot of support from the CIA. The brain behind the coup was none other than the CIA station chief in Accra, Howard T. Bane, who was greatly honoured by his superiors at the CIA headquarters and by officials in the

Johnson administration for doing an excellent job soon after Nkrumah was overthrown.

The French also wanted Nkrumah to be overthrown. They saw him as a threat to their interests in Francophone Africa, especially their main satellite, the Ivory Coast, which was securely anchored in the French orbit and bordered Ghana.

It was a major Western conspiracy against Nkrumah, not just a figment of the imagination among Nkrumah's supporters. And the evidence against the United States especially, as the major sponsor of the coup, is more than anecdotal. There is plenty of such evidence provided by the American government itself in its declassified documents. There is, of course, no question that it was the Ghanaians themselves – the army and police officers opposed to Nkrumah – who carried out the coup, although there are those who still contend that there is no direct evidence linking the CIA to the coup, in spite of such evidence being available to the public. As Professor Carlson Anyangwe states in his book, *Revolutionary Overthrow of Constitutional Orders in Africa*:

"On 24 February 1966, Generals Harlley, Kotoka, Afrifa, Ocran and Ankrah overthrew Kwame Nkrumah in a military coup and seized power....It is believed by many political analysts that the United States Central Intelligence Agency participated in the coup against Nkrumah, but others claim that the evidence pointing to CIA involvement is anecdotal." – (Carlson Anyangwe, *Revolutionary Overthrow of Constitutional Orders in Africa*, Bamenda, Cameroon: Laanga Research & Publishing common Initiative Group (RPCIG), 2012, p. 143).

Even the anecdotal evidence itself is reinforced by other evidence linking the CIA to the coup. Besides declassified material pointing to the CIA, there are also books written by former CIA agents such as John Stockwell (*In Search of Enemies: A CIA Story*), Philip Agee (*Inside the Company: CIA Diary*), and Ralph McGee (*Deadly Deceits: My 25 Years in the CIA*) about American covert operations overseas to undermine foreign governments. One of those governments was Ghana's under Nkrumah.

Stockwell, head of the CIA task force in Angola, has also written and given lectures about CIA covert operations in Ghana – besides Angola – and the role the CIA played in overthrowing Nkrumah.

Agee also wrote a book focusing on CIA activities in Africa entitled, *Dirty Work: The CIA in Africa*.

American involvement in undermining African leaders whom the United States considers to be against her interests is underscored by William Blum:

"After his June 4 Cairo speech, President Obama was much praised for mentioning the 1953 CIA overthrow of Iranian prime minister Mohammed Mossadegh. But in his talk in Ghana on July 11 he failed to mention the CIA coup that ousted Ghanian president Kwame Nkrumah in 1966, referring to him only as a 'giant' among African leaders.

The Mossadegh coup is one of the most well-known CIA covert actions. Obama could not easily get away without mentioning it in a talk in the Middle East looking to mend fences. But the Nkrumah ouster is one of the least known; indeed, not a single print or broadcast news report in the American mainstream media saw fit to mention it at the time of the president's talk. Like it never happened.

And the next time you hear that Africa can't produce good leaders, people who are committed to the welfare of the masses of their people, think of Nkrumah and his fate. And think of Patrice Lumumba, overthrown in the Congo 1960-61 with the help of the United States; Agostinho Neto of Angola, against whom Washington waged war in the 1970s, making it impossible for him to institute progressive changes; Samora Machel of Mozambique against whom the CIA supported a counter-revolution in the 1970s-80s period; and Nelson Mandela of South Africa (now married to Machel's widow), who spent 28 years in prison thanks to the CIA." – (William Blum, "The Anti-Empire Report #72," 4 August 2009).

Blum also explains how the CIA undermined Nkrumah. In a chapter entitled, "Kwame Nkrumah steps out of line," in his book, *Killing Hope: US Military and CIA Interventions Since World War II*, he states:

"In October of the year 1965, Kwame Nkrumah, the President of Ghana, published his famous-to-be book, *Neo-Colonialism–The Last State of Imperialism*, dedicated to 'the Freedom Fighters of Africa, living and dead.'
In the book, Nkrumah accused the CIA of being behind numerous setbacks and crises in the Third World and Eastern Europe. He later wrote that 'the American Government sent me a note of protest, and promptly refused Ghana $35 million of 'aid.' Four months later he was overthrown in a CIA-backed military coup.
....Though he spoke out boldly against neo-colonialism, he was unable, ultimately, to keep Ghana from falling under the sway of the multinationals. When he attempted to lessen his country's dependence on the West by strengthening economic and military ties to the Soviet Union, China and East Germany, he effectively sealed his fate.
The United States wanted him out. Great Britain, the former colonial power in Ghana when it was known as the Gold Coast, wanted him out. France and West Germany wanted him out. Those Ghanaians who carried out the coup suffered from no doubts that a move against Nkrumah would be supported by the Western powers.
At the time of the coup, the Soviet press charged that the CIA had been involved, and in 1972 *The Daily*

Telegraph, the conservative London newspaper, reported that 'By 1965 the Accra [capital of Ghana] CIA Station had two-score active operators, distributing largesse among President Nkrumah's secret adversaries.' By February, 1966, the report continued, the CIA had its plans ready to end Nkrumah's regime: 'The patient and assiduous work of the Accra station was fully rewarded.'

It wasn't until 1978, however, that the story 'broke' in the United States. Former CIA officer John Stockwell, who had spent most of his career in Africa, published a book in which he revealed the Agency's complicity. Shortly afterwards, *The New York Times*, quoting 'first-hand intelligence sources,' corroborated that the CIA had advised and supported the dissident Ghanaian army officers.

Stockwell disclosed that the CIA station in Accra 'was given a generous budget, and maintained intimate contact with the plotters as the coup was hatched. So close was the station's involvement that it was able to coordinate the recovery of some classified Soviet military equipment by the United States as the coup took place.'

The CIA station had also proposed to headquarters in Washington that a small squad of paramilitary experts, members of the agency's Special Operations Group, be on hand at the moment of the coup, with their faces blacked, storm the Chinese Embassy, kill everyone inside, steal their secret records, and blow up the building to cover the fact.

'This proposal was squashed,' Stockwell wrote, 'but inside CIA headquarters the Accra station was given full, if unofficial credit for the eventual coup, in which eight Soviet advisers were killed.' The Soviet Union categorically denied that any of its advisers had been killed.

Other intelligence sources who were in Ghana at the time of the coup have taken issue with Stockwell's view that the CIA deserved full credit for Nkrumah's downfall.

But they considered the Agency's role to have been pivotal, and at least some officials in Washington apparently agreed, for the CIA station chief in Accra, Howard T. Bane, was quickly promoted to a senior position in the agency.

'When he was successful,' one of the *New York Times* sources said of Bane, 'everyone in the African division knew it. If it had failed, he would have been transferred and no CIA involvement revealed.'

Bane, nevertheless, was enraged by the CIA's high-level decision not to permit the raid on the Chinese Embassy, at the time the Peking government's only embassy in Africa. 'They didn't have the guts to do it,' he subsequently told an associate." – (William Blum, *Killing Hope: US Military and CIA Interventions Since World War II*, London: Zed Books, 2003, pp. 198 – 199).

Blum goes on to state:

"After the coup, the CIA made a payment of 'at least $100,000' to the new Ghanaian regime for the confiscated Soviet material, one item of which was a cigarette lighter that also functioned as a camera.

The Ghanaian leaders soon expelled large numbers of Russians as well as Chinese and East Germans. Virtually all state-owned industries were allowed to pass into private hands. In short order the channels of aid, previously clogged, opened wide, and credit, food and development projects flowed in from the United States, the European powers, and the International Monetary Fund. Washington, for example, three weeks after the coup, approved substantial emergency food assistance in response to an urgent request from Ghana. A food request from Nkrumah four months earlier had been turned down. One month after his ouster, the international price of cocoa – Ghana's economic lifeblood – had risen 14 percent.

The CIA's reluctance to approve action at the Chinese

Embassy may have stemmed from the fact that the National Security Council had specifically refused to authorize the Agency's involvement in the coup at all.

This was...not the first instance of the CIA taking American foreign policy into its own hands. On such occasions, the *modus operandi* calls for putting as little into writing as feasible, or keeping records out of official CIA files, thus making them immune to Freedom of Information disclosures or congressional investigations; technically the records do not exist, legally they can be destroyed at any time. This was the case with the Ghanaian coup and may explain why more details of the CIA role have never been revealed.

The American right-wing view of what happened

According to John Barron, the *Readers Digest's* resident KGB expert, Nkrumah was overthrown by only native insurgents, the only foreigners in the picture being 11 KGB officers who were found in Nkrumah's headquarters and summarily executed.

The Soviet Union didn't say a word about this, he wrote, because they didn't want 'the world to know that KGB officers were actually sitting in the Ghanaian President's office running the country.'

Barron offers no evidence at all to support his claim of the KGB running the country, nor does he explain why the new government didn't publicize this very interesting fact.

He goes on to write of 'the copious secret files of the Nkrumah regime' which were discovered and then studied and analyzed. The files revealed, he says, that 'the KGB had converted Ghana into one vast base of subversion, which the Soviet Union fully intended to use to capture the continent of Africa.'

For reasons best known to himself perhaps, Barron fails to offer the reader a single quotation from any of the copious secret files to support his allegations." – (Ibid., pp. 199 – 200).

Several factors converged through the years Nkrumah was in power which made him a target for coups by both internal and external forces.

Lyndon B. Johnson
27 August 1908 - 22 January 1973

His Pan-African militancy, relentless support for African liberation movements, and his quest for genuine political and economic independence not only for Ghana but for the entire African continent antagonised the West; prompting Lyndon Johnson who was the American president when Nkrumah also was in office to say that Nkrumah – among all African leaders – was the biggest threat to American interests in Africa. He inspired, educated and influenced others by example. And the United States was not going to tolerate that.

Nkrumah also infuriated the United States government by tying to intervene in Vietnam in order to end the Vietnam war. American leaders saw it as their domain of foreign policy, a region vital to American interests where the United States was trying to contain communism. An attempt by anyone – let alone an African leader from a weak and backward continent – to encroach on what they considered to be their turf, was not only an insult to the United States; it virtually amounted to an invasion of America's sphere of influence. It was the last thing American leaders wanted to see – someone from a small Third World country strolling on the international stage, trying to be an international statesman as if he represented a world power. As Dr. John Prados, a renowned national security analyst at the National Security Archive, George Washington University, states in his book, *Safe for Democracy: The Secret Wars of the CIA*:

"Kwame Nkrumah strove for a role on the world stage, trying to be a peacemaker and help end the Vietnam War. This annoyed Washington, especially when Nkrumah tried to intercede between the British and Guyana's Cheddi Jagan. He also made unwelcome overtures in the Middle East.

In the summer of 1965 Nkrumah sent diplomatic envoys to North Vietnam, suggesting that he himself visit early the following year. He tacked on visits to Burma and the People's Republic of China. According to CIA political operative Miles Copeland, under whom the agency had begun an effort to plant astrologers on world leaders known to favor the occult, a CIA occult agent may have had a role in convincing Nkrumah to plan the trip.

In 1965 Nkrumah published a book, *Neo-Colonialism: The Last Stage of Imperialism*, which must have raised hackles in Washington. Then came an overt move toward Moscow – Nkrumah accepted Soviet arms and training for his presidential guard. The last straw may have come when the CIA reported that a Soviet arms shipment was on its way to Ghana." – (John Prados, *Safe for Democracy: The Secret Wars of the CIA*, Chicago: Ivan R. Dee, Publisher,

2006, pp. 328 – 329).

A lot has been said about Nkrumah's assumption of dictatorial powers; it is also often cited as one of the main reasons he was overthrown.

It is true that assumption of virtual dictatorial powers by Nkrumah solidified opposition to his rule in Ghana. Yet, it was the people of Ghana themselves who, in a national referendum in July 1964, voted to transform Ghana into a one-party socialist state. The parliament also approved the establishment of a one-arty state.

The establishment of authoritarian rule and the introduction of the Preventive Detention Act by Nkrumah to keep a tight reign on some of his opponents who were his political enemies determined to destroy him also should be viewed in its proper historical context; all those measures were passed by parliament, not by decree issued by Nkrumah.

Curtailment or abrogation of freedom is deplorable. But those who criticise Nkrumah for muzzling his critics and for detaining his political enemies by using the Preventive Detention Act should also concede that Nkrumah was compelled to invoke such powers – even if he may have exceeded or violated his mandate in some cases – because of constant threats to his life.

He had been shot at; also bombs had been planted on different occasions to blow him up and his entourage. Even some members of his own security forces tried to kill him.

He survived several assassination attempts by his enemies within Ghana who worked in collusion with external forces, especially with the CIA, to eliminate him.

Under those circumstances, it is not difficult to understand why he had to take draconian measures to protect himself and his government.

That does not justify dictatorship. But it puts things in proper perspective in the context of Ghana under

Nkrumah. He was forced to live in a state of emergency and under very difficult conditions created by his enemies including the CIA and other Western intelligence services.

Yet, his critics don't blame the CIA for threatening his life. And they don't blame some of his fellow countrymen who tried to kill him for creating such a climate – of fear and insecurity.

That partly explains why he turned East, a move which angered the United States and other Western powers, although they themselves were, to some extent, responsible for that.

Despite his own ideological inclinations – socialist and Marxist-Leninist – which aligned him with the Sino-Soviet bloc, security concerns forced Nkrumah to seek help from the Soviets. The West had already turned against him and was plotting to overthrow and even assassinate him.

He was vindicated only a few years later when he was overthrown by the same powers he feared were plotting to oust and kill him. As Christopher Andrew, although from a different perspective, states in his book, *Defend the Realm: The Authorized History of MI5*:

"After an assassination attempt against him in 1962 Nkrumah became obsessed by the belief that the Agency (the CIA) was plotting his overthrow, gave visitors copies of a book denouncing CIA conspiracies, and accepted a Soviet offer to send a KGB officer to give advice on his personal security. Other officers from the KGB and the East German Stasi followed to train a new National Security Service which ran a large network of informers (a particular specialty of the Stasi).

In November 1963 Thomson (John Thomson, a British intelligence officer and the first Security Liaison Officer (SLO) in independent Ghana) reported that the head of the Special Branch, J.W.K. Harlley, and his deputy, A.K. Deku, had told him they were convinced Nkrumah was turning Ghana into a Soviet satellite.

In January 1964 a Ghanaian policeman fired at Nkrumah, causing him only minor injury but killing a security guard....On 24 February 1966 Harlley succeeded in organizing a combined military and police coup which overthrew the Nkrumah regime.

Next day Sir Arthur Snelling of the Commonwealth Relations Office rang the DG (Director General of the British security service), Furnival Jones, to ask him to despatch Thomson urgently to Ghana. Arriving in Accra on the 28th, Thomson was welcomed with open arms by Harlley, who was now deputy chairman of the National Liberation Council (NLC). After a brief tirade from Harlley upbraiding Her Majesty's Government (HMG) for having abandoned him in 1963 and put his life in danger, as well as failing to supply the equipment he had asked for in 1965, the two men settled their differences and renewed their friendship over a bottle of brandy.

Thomson went on to be welcomed by, and deliver unofficial congratulations to, the NLC chairman, General Ankrah, and the other NLC members.

On 2 March, following a favourable report from Thomson, Britain formally recognized the new Ghanaian regime, establishing full diplomatic relations three days later. This was the only occasion on which a Security Service officer was charged by HMG with making the first contact with a new government which had seized power in a coup *coup d'etat*." – (Christopher Andrew, *Defend the Realm: The Authorized History of MI5*, New York: Alfred A. Knopf, 2009, pp. 470, and 471).

It is obvious why the British government was excited about Nkrumah's ouster and congratulated the coup makers soon after the coup. Britain had participated in the planning of the coup, together with the United States and West Germany. It also explains why Britain recognised the new military government after only a few days after Nkrumah's downfall.

Five years later, Britain did the same thing when Idi Amin overthrew Dr. Milton Obote in Uganda in January 1971 and became the first country to recognise Amin's regime. The British congratulated Idi Amin for seizing power. It was also the British, together with the Israelis, who were behind the coup which ousted Obote who was also a close friend of Nkrumah.

Emmanuel Kotoka in February 1966
(26 October 1926 – 17 April 1967)

Nkrumah himself had earlier, even before the 1966 military coup, survived coup attempts. Akwasi Afrifa was one of the solders who attempted to overthrow him in 1962 and 1964 but security forces neutralised those attempts.

There had been other attempts to undermine Nkrumah's government. And there were a number of army and police officers who were against his government for various reasons including tribalism, personal grudges against Nkrumah after he relieved some of them of their duties, and complaints about their mistreatment at the hands of Nkrumah and his colleagues in the government; although tribalism did not play a major role in the 1966 coup – it was far outweighed by CIA participation, the driving force behind the coup. The coup leaders came from different tribes: Ashanti, Ewe, Fanti, and Ga.

Joseph Arthur Ankrah who became Ghana's first military head of state was a Ga. His successor and one of the leaders of the coup, Akwasi Amankwaa Afrifa, was an Ashanti.

Emmanuel Kwasi Kotoka, the leader of the coup who was supported in the military takeover by his friend Afrifa and became chief of defence staff, was an Ewe. John Willie Kofi Harlley, who was the inspector-general of police during the coup and became minister of foreign affairs in the first military government, was also an Ewe.

Albert Kwesi Ocran, who became army chief of staff in the military government after the coup, was a Fanti. He was, at this writing, the only living member of the four coup makers.

Kotoka died first in an attempted counter-coup on 17 April 1967.

The counter-coup, launched by three junior army officers – Samuel Arthur, Moses Yeboah who shot and killed Kotoka; and Osei-Poku, all lieutenants and supported by a number of senior army officers – was reportedly intended to reinstate Nkrumah.

Still, tribalism may have played a role – although a secondary role – in the coup against Nkrumah, dubbed "Operation Cold Chop." As Professor Harcourt Fuller states in his book, *Building the Ghanaian Nation-State: Kwame Nkrumah's Symbolic Nationalism*:

"In exile, Nkrumah had lots of time to reassess his time in power and ponder the factors that led to his downfall. For one, he blamed the resilience of what he saw as 'tribalism' in national politics as culpable for the coup that removed him from power.

As a nationalist, Nkrumah tried to downplay tribalism in Ghanaian politics and stressed regional and tribal unity as necessary for nation-building. Having fought an uphill battle against traditional chiefs – particularly the Asantes – before and after independence, he also recognized that there had always been a close Ewe-Asante relationship, exemplified by the tribal alliance between Harlley (an Ewe), Kotoka (an Ewe), and Afrifa (an Asante) who headed the coup against him.

In his memoirs, however, Nkrumah admitted some failure in his attempts to eliminate the scourge of tribalism that threatened to undermine his nation-building policies and ideals:

'I had to combat not only tribalism but the African tradition that a man's first duty was to his family group and that therefore nepotism was the highest of all virtues. While I believe we had largely eliminated tribalism as an active force, its by-products and those of the family system were still with us. I could not have chosen my government without some regard to tribal origins and even, within the Party itself, there was at times a tendency to condemn or recommend some individual on the basis of his tribal or family origin.'

Nkrumah also blamed the coup in Ghana and others throughout Africa on 'neocolonialists' – primarily British, American, and West German – and the small domestic 'reactionary elements' that desired to 'sabotage our great struggle for economic independence, and our efforts in the African Revolution to achieve the total liberation of the continent and a Union Government of Africa.'

Chiefly among the 'reactionary elements' in Ghana were certain members of the armed forces. Nkrumah alleged that, since he became Head of Government

Business in 1951 and during his presidency, he had been the target of certain branches of the police, military, opposition leaders, and neocolonialist hostilities and conspiracies to assassinate him six times. Of the eight leaders of the NLC (National Liberation Council) who ousted Nkrumah, four were members of the army and four from the police force; all of them were trained in Britain. Consequently, he accused them of having a colonial, elitist mentality and of being prone to insubordination and rebellion.

At the time of the coup, Nkrumah had not yet confirmed Colonel E.K. Kotoka's appointment as commander of the Second Infantry Brigade Group of the Kumasi garrison. Nkrumah further asserts that in 1965, he was forced to dismiss Ankrah for being 'lazy, incompetent and unreliable' and for plotting with others to overthrow his government." – (Harcourt Fuller, *Building the Ghanaian Nation-State: Kwame Nkrumah's Symbolic Nationalism*, New York: Palgrave Macmillan, 2014, pp. 163 – 164).

Fuller goes on to state:

"(Roger) Gocking corroborates some of Nkrumah's claims. He asserts that the military had numerous reasons to stage a coup against Nkrumah, chief among which were Nkrumah's treatment of army officials over the years. Major Afrifa, who had served in the Congo Crisis, lamented the death of 43 Ghanaian soldiers in the conflict, which he blamed on Nkrumah. Thus on at least two occasions, in 1962 and 1964, Africa considered using military force against the regime, but Nkrumah's security detail and other factors prevented a coup from taking place then. Moreover, Nkrumah's 'dismissal of the army's commanders in 1965 all seemed to point to his determination to bring the military under his direct control.'

Those dismissed from their positions that year included commander of the army, Lieutenant General J.A. Ankrah, as well as Commissioner of Police J.W. K. Harlley. After the coup, Ankrah installed himself as chairman while Harlley served as deputy chairman of the NLC. Major Afrifa and Colonel Kotoka also 'played major roles in planning the coup.'" – (Ibid., p. 164).

Joseph A. Ankrah, 18 August 1915 – 25 November 1992

John Willie Kofi (J.W.K.) Harlley, 9 May 1919 – c. 1980s

Nkrumah and his supporters made a number of attempts to overthrow the new military government but failed to do so. Plans for the counter-coups were made in Ghana and in Conakry, Guinea, where Nkrumah was living in exile. However, the only serious attempt to seize power from the new military rulers was the April 1967 abortive coup in which Kotoka was killed.

Brazen attempts on Nkrumah's life clearly showed that

he had enemies who were determined to get rid of him. His enemies had even penetrated his security at Flagstaff House. As Dr. Obed Yao Asamoah states in his book, *The Political History of Ghana (1950 – 2013): The Experience of a Non-Conformist*:

"As early as 1958, a coup plot was allegedly hatched by R.R. Amponsah, M.K. Apaloo, opposition MPs, and Captain Ahwaitey.

The R.R. Amponsah affair was followed by the railway strike in 1961, which the government saw as an attempt to overthrow it, masterminded by the opposition and disgruntled elements of the CPP (the ruling Convention People's Party)....

The next effort to overthrow the government was the attempt to assassinate Nkrumah at Kulungugu, a village on the border of Ghana and Upper Volta (now Burkina Faso) near Bawku in August 1962.

On Nkrumah's return from a meeting with (President) Maurice Yameogo of Upper Volta concerning the unity of African groupings, a bomb which had been planted along the route exploded. Nkrumah was fortunate to escape injury, but a schoolboy was killed and fifty-six people were injured (it was a seven-year-old school girl, carrying a bouquet of flowers she was getting ready to present to Nkrumah and in which the bomb was hidden, who was killed together with several other people).

Some elements of the press attempted to link the incident to the UK, which aroused the concern of the British High Commission and was deprecated by the Ghana government.

This explosion heralded a series of other bombings, killing and causing injury to many. One soldier, W.O. Edward Tettey, an explosives expert, was placed under close arrest on 10 September 1962 for giving a misleading report on the Kulungugu explosion. While under questioning after a subsequent explosion, he apparently jumped from the fourth floor of the Police Headquarters building and later died at the Military Hospital.

In Accra, bombings among crowds killed fifteen and injured two hundred and fifty-six people, according to police, and provoked a declaration of a state of emergency in the Accra-Tema area. Processions were banned, a curfew was imposed, and the police were given special powers to search house to house with soldiers and to stop and search vehicles. But more bombs went off in processions in celebration of the Founder's Day – Nkrumah's birthday – in September 1962. Nehru cancelled a planned visit to Ghana likely because of the violence....

In October 1962, the police offered a £5,000 reward for information leading to the arrest and conviction of the bombers, yet in early 1963, another bomb went off at the stadium on the thirteenth anniversary of Positive Action, killing four and injuring eighty-five. The Ministry of Interior explained that preliminary examination of the bomb fragments indicated that the bomb was of French origin. In the hunt for the culprits, one man was arrested at a rally at Bukom Square, Accra, in January 1963....

The attempt to get rid of Nkrumah next took the form of an assassination attempt in January 1964. One of his guards, Seth Nicholas Kwami Ametewe, shot at him with a rifle at Flagstaff House, where Nkrumah now lived and worked. Another guard was killed by the gunshot, but Nkrumah survived....Protesters poured out onto the streets to demonstrate in support of Nkrumah, calling for death for the plotters. Ametewe was sentenced to death for the murder of the guard.

Ametewe implicated S.D. Amaning, a Deputy Commissioner of Police as the instigator, claiming Amaning told him that people including Chief Justice Sir Arku Korsah, Dr. Danquah, Dr. Busia, Gbedemah, and even Krobo Edusei wished for Nkrumah's assassination. That probably accounts for the detention of Madjitey – the Commissioner of Police and his deputies, Amaning and

M.K. Awuku, as well as Dr. Danquah. Other officers were also sacked.

Assistant Commissioner of Police J.W.K. Harley was appointed acting Commissioner, and superintendents B.A. Yakubu and A.K. Biney, were appointed acting Deputy Commissioners. The substantive appointments were confirmed in March 1965, at the same time as A.K. Deku was also appointed a Deputy Commissioner. The detention was the end of Dr. Danquah's life as a free man; he died in jail of a heart attack about a year later, on 4 February 1965.

Nkrumah's end came on 24 February 1966, when he was overthrown by a coup d'etat while on his way to Hanoi on a peace mission on behalf of the Commonwealth to end the Vietnam war. His overthrow is reputed to have been aided by the US Central Intelligence Agency (CIA)."– (Obed Yao Asamoah, *The Political History of Ghana (1950 – 2013): The Experience of an Non-Conformist*, Bloomington, Indiana, USA: AuthorHouse, 2014, pp. 60 – 62, and 63).

Nkrumah survived seven assassination attempts. He was overthrown almost exactly nine years after he led Ghana to independence, the first black African country to emerge from colonial rule. He blazed the trail for the African independence movement and was determined to help liberate the rest of Africa.

He believed that the colonial rulers were not really interested in relinquishing power but wanted to reassert their control over their former colonies in an indirect way or by putting puppets in power whom they could manipulate at will. It was he who coined the term "neo-colonialism" to define this insidious phenomenon. The term became an integral part of the English vocabulary.

None of that won him accolades or genuine friendship among Western leaders and other powerful political and financial interests in the metropolitan powers. They were determined to remove him from office by any conceivable means – undermining his government; sabotaging Ghana's economy in order to turn the people against him and then blame him for it; and by simply killing him.

Akwasi Afrifa, 24 April 1936 - 26 June 1979

In his book, *Neo-Colonialism: The Last Stage of Imperialism*, Nkrumah exposed the insidious forces at work in African countries in pursuit of American imperialist goals and other Western interests.

Western embassies in Africa were hotbeds of intrigue. Covert activities by Western intelligence services were conducted from those diplomatic missions using diplomatic cover to undermine truly independent nationalist governments which refused to bend to Western wishes.

Nkrumah also bluntly stated that Africans must be vigilant against imperialist machinations and local elements working in collusion with external forces to undermine genuine leadership in African countries in order to enable Western powers to perpetuate their domination and exploitation of Africa through multinational corporations and other means.

The United States was determined to establish hegemonic control over Africa, using economic muscles and political power to impose a stranglehold on African countries not only to exploit the continent but to promote American geopolitical and strategic interests as well. And Nkrumah accused the CIA of fomenting trouble on the continent, including overthrowing governments the United States did not like.

After the book was published in 1965, the United States government sent a note of protest to Nkrumah and immediately cancelled a $35 million aid-programme to Ghana. A few months later, he was overthrown in a military coup.

His ouster was one of the most dramatic demonstrations of power projection capabilities by the United States on the African continent. And it was a warning to others: If you don't toe the line, America will get you. Might is right. That is the imperial dictum. As Prados states in his book, *Safe for Democracy: The Secret Wars of the CIA*:

"The CIA's role in Ghana seems to have flowed from both Washington and the field. A nationalist hero and first president of independent Ghana, Nkrumah had an uneasy relationship with the United States. Educated in missionary schools and in the segregationist America of the thirties and forties, he learned his Marxism there, influenced by the racial attitudes of the day. He was no Moscow puppet. Nkrumah called his program 'African Socialism'....

Ghana's economy went into deficit as prices for its cocoa plunged. Nkrumah attributed the hardship to the former colonial power, Great Britain, and to the United States. Washington blamed Nkrumah for anti-American agitation in Ghana. American aid for a dam on the Volta River and to develop new economic resources in aluminum hung in the balance.

Nkrumah attributed the January 1964 assassination attempt to the CIA. The Johnson administration stepped carefully around this thorny question, with U.S. Ambassador William P. Mahoney assuring LBJ that his country team – including CIA – was fully under control, and the CIA denying any role.

In February 1964 Nkrumah sent Johnson a letter asserting that there were 'two conflicting establishments' representing the United States, the diplomatic mission and the CIA, which 'seems to devote all its attention to fomenting ill-will, misunderstanding and even clandestine and subversive activities among our people, to the impairment of the good relations which exist between our two governments.'

Johnson conveyed reassurances on the CIA both in his response and through Ambassador Mahoney, who reportedly told Nkrumah that the five CIA officers in the station at Accra were under his strict supervision." – (John Prados, *Safe for Democracy: The Secret Wars of the CIA*, op. cit., pp. 328 – 329).

Denial by American officials of CIA involvement in covert and subversive activities in other countries is a standard response. Even Prados states that official documents don't show any direct connection between Washington and the coup in Ghana. Yet some CIA agents admitted CIA involvement in Nkrumah's ouster. And there is enough evidence, including circumstantial, to show that the coup was the work of the CIA working with the army and police officers who overthrew Nkrumah, although

Prados gives a slightly different version with regard to American involvement in the coup. He goes on to state:

"Washington's record was not entirely innocent. As early as February 6, 1964, Dean Rusk asked John McCone about suitable candidates to head a post-Nkrumah government, and they discussed the very general who was eventually to move against the Ghanaian (president). The two men speculated on the possibility of concocting a covert operation in concert with the British. When the State Department proposed an action program it had the explicit purpose of slowing Nkrumah's leftward political evolution. The proposal was to actively undermine him by threatening to halt aid to the Volta River project, recognizing opponents, and using psychological warfare and other means to diminish his support. President Johnson deliberated on this program at the exact moment Nkrumah sent his letter protesting CIA subversion.

LBJ went ahead with the Volta dam aid, but he may well have approved undermining Nkrumah. During a home visit in March 1965 Ambassador Mahoney met with (CIA) Director McCone and AF Division deputy chief John Waller. They specifically discussed a coup plot in Ghana hatched by police and military figures, including Gen. Joseph A. Ankrah, the same man McCone and Rusk had considered a year earlier.

Evidence indicates the Ghanaian military's plans were well-known to the CIA, which reported on them more than half a dozen times in 1965. As yet there is no evidence of direct CIA involvement from documents. What we do have is a series of confident predictions of a coup from the ambassador – who accurately foresaw that Nkrumah would be replaced by a military junta within a year – and NSC staffer Robert W. Komer. That summer Nkrumah detected the coup plot and cashiered Ankrah. The Ghanaian generals, their peripatetic plots more than a year old, were temporarily stymied." – (Ibid., p. 329).

They were now waiting for the best opportunity to carry out the coup. Colonel Akwasi A. Afrifa who led the coup stated in his book, *The Ghana Coup: 24th February 1966* (London: Frank Cass, 1966, 144 pages), that it would have been very difficult if not impossible to overthrow Nkrumah when he was still in Ghana. The best time to overthrow him was when he was out of the country. And that is exactly what the coup plotters did:

"William Mahoney left Accra for good in the summer of 1965, and for eight months there was no U.S. ambassador. (CIA) station chief Howard T. Bane had a much freer hand. Bane proposed the CIA sponsor a coup. The views of Africa Division chief Glen Fields are not known, but he had been amenable to the Congo, and his deputy John Waller had made his mark in the 1953 CIA coup in Iran.

The Special Group turned them down. Bane thought that shortsighted, and as a colleague later put it, he had 'no patience for management of which he was not a part.'

Howard Bane, another man who came to Africa from the DO Far East Division, had an affinity for the military and determination to go with it. A knuckle-dragger, in Korea he had run a net to rescue downed fliers. In India he had backstopped the Tibet project, insulating it from the jaundiced Harry Rositzke. He wet his teeth in Africa heading the CIA station in Kenya.

Not phased by the Special Group's rejection, the tobacco-chewing, cigar-smoking Bane took advantage of his instructions to keep a close watch on the Ghanaian military. With a complement variously reported at ten or up to three dozen case officers, Bane exploited his military contacts.

A few winks and nods from Bane betokened U.S. support to Ghanaian soldiers. With just a pair of brigades, both based in Accra, there were not that many to convince.

Bane had time to suggest that Langley send a few officers from the CIA Special Operations Division, who could not only concretize the impression of support but use the coup to purloin documents and code materials from the Chinese embassy in Accra, a unilateral operation under cover of the coup. Headquarters spurned him again.

But in mid-January 1966 Bane reported that a rash of coups elsewhere in Africa had reenthused Ghanaian officers, and on February 17 came concrete indications of a plot, Operation Cold Chop.

Twenty-four hours before the coup, Bane reported the military planned it for the time Nkrumah was out of the country. President Nkrumah left Ghana on February 22, the coup occurred on the 24th. General Ankrah returned to head the resulting junta....Langley credited Accra station with an assist. Howard Banes wound up as chief of operations for the AF Division.

In Tanzania, meanwhile, Che Guevara tarried for months after leaving the Congo. There he turned his diaries into a narrative, seeking to understand what had gone wrong. He stayed in Dar-es-Salaam until early 1966, when a top DGI official came to give Guevara the latest assessment of prospects for revolution in each Latin American country.

Guevara really wanted to fight in Argentina, but security services there had suppressed dissident networks. In Peru the CIA and the government had foreclosed that option. That left Bolivia as the major prospect.

Che's hope lay in what he called a *foco*, literally a focus or a lighthouse, in practice an exemplar activity that could lead the masses to rally to the revolution, much as Castro's small July 26th Movement had brought the end of Batista."
– (Ibid., pp. 329 – 331).

As in Ghana, the Americans had also accomplished their mission in the former Belgian Congo by getting rid of a leader they did not like. Together with the Belgians, they succeeded in getting rid of Patrice Lumumba whom they considered to be a threat to Western interests in Africa just like Nkrumah.

The British overseas intelligence service, MI6, also may have played a role in facilitating Lumumba's assassination. As Harry Stopes of London's Global University's history department stated in his article, "Did Britain's MI6 have Patrice Lumumba Murdered?," 13 May 2013:

"Towards the end of March (2013), (Bernard) Porter reviewed Calder Walton's book on the British security services, the Cold War, and the end of Empire. Porter mentioned in passing that Howard Smith, then an official in the British Foreign Office and later head of MI5, had advocated killing Patrice Lumumba as one of a number of possible 'solutions' to the problems he seemed to pose to Western governments and corporations....

Two weeks later, in the next issue of the *LRB* (*London Review of Books*), a letter from David Lea, a member of the British House of Lords, purported to shed more light on British involvement in Lumumba's death:

'I was having a cup of tea with Daphne Park – we were colleagues from opposite sides of the Lords – a few months before she died in March 2010. She had been consul and first secretary in Leopoldville, now Kinshasa, from 1959 to 1961, which in practice (this was subsequently acknowledged) meant head of MI6 there. I mentioned the uproar surrounding Lumumba's abduction and murder, and recalled the theory that MI6 might have had something to do with it. 'We did,' she replied, 'I organised it.''

....A few days after the letter appeared I was listening to BBC Radio 4 in the early morning and heard their security correspondent discussing Lea's letter. Did we do it? the presenter asked. The correspondent thought it was unlikely that MI6 played the decisive role but pointed out that Park was close to one of Lumumba's Congolese rivals." – (Harry Stopes, "Did Britain's MI6 have Patrice Lumumba Murdered?" See also Bernard Porter, "Quiet Sinners," his review of Calder Walton's book, *Empire of Secrets: British Intelligence, the Cold War and the Twilight of Empire*, in the *London Review of Books*, 21 March 2013; and Calder Walton, *Empire of Secrets: British Intelligence, the Cold War and the Twilight of Empire*, HarperPress, 2013).

And according to a report by Ben Quinn, "MI6 'Arranged Cold War Killing' of Congo Prime Minister," in *The Guardian*, London, 1 April 2013:

"Congo's first democratically elected prime minister was abducted and killed in a cold war operation run by British intelligence, according to remarks said to have been made by the woman who was leading the MI6 station in the central African country at the time.

A Labour peer has claimed that Baroness Park of Monmouth admitted to him a few months before she died in March 2010 that she arranged Patrice Lumumba's killing in 1961 because of fears he would ally the newly democratic country with the Soviet Union.

In a letter to the *London Review of Books*, Lord Lea said the admission was made while he was having a cup of tea with Daphne Park, who had been consul and first secretary from 1959 to 1961 in Leopoldville, as the capital of Belgian Congo was known before it was later renamed as Kinshasa following independence.

He wrote:

'I mentioned the uproar surrounding Lumumba's abduction and murder, and recalled the theory that MI6 might have had something to do with it. 'We did,' she replied, 'I organised it'.'

Park, who was known by some as the 'Queen of Spies' after four decades as one of Britain's top female intelligence agents, is believed to have been sent by MI6 to the Belgian Congo in 1959 under an official diplomatic guise as the Belgians were on the point of being ousted from the country.

'We went on to discuss her contention that Lumumba would have handed over the whole lot to the Russians: the high-value Katangese uranium deposits as well as the diamonds and other important minerals largely located in the secessionist eastern state of Katanga,' added Lea, who wrote his letter in response to a review of a book by Calder Walton about British intelligence activities during the twilight of the British empire.

Doubts about the claim have been raised by historians and former officials, including a former senior British intelligence official who knew Park and told the *Times*:

'It doesn't sound like the sort of remark Daphne Park would make. She was never indiscreet. Also MI6 never had a licence to kill.'

Mystery has continued to surround the death of Lumumba, who was shot on 17 January 1961, although Belgian troops were known to have been involved.

Park met Lumumba, the African leader who was to become the short-lived prime minister of an independent Congo. After his successor took power, she was arrested and beaten by his supporters.

She was able to get herself released and sought local UN intervention, securing the release of Britons and other foreigners, for which she was appointed OBE in 1960."

Also, Gordon Corera, a security correspondent of BBC News, stated the following in his report, "MI6 and the

Death of Patrice Lumumba," 2 April 2013:

"A member of the House of Lords, Lord Lea, has written to the *London Review of Books* saying that shortly before she died, fellow peer and former MI6 officer Daphne Park told him Britain had been involved in the death of Patrice Lumumba, the elected leader of the Congo, in 1961.

When he asked her whether MI6 might have had something to do with it, he recalls her saying:

'We did. I organised it.'

During long interviews I conducted with her for the BBC and for a book that in part covered MI6 and the crisis in the Congo, she never made a similar direct admission and she has denied that there was a 'licence to kill' for the British Secret Service.

But piecing together information suggests that while MI6 did not kill the politician directly, it is possible – but hard to prove definitively – that it could have had some kind of indirect role.

Daphne Park was the MI6 officer in the Congo at a crucial point in the country's history. She arrived just before the Congo received independence from Belgium in the middle of 1960.

'Elimination'

Congo's first elected prime minister was Patrice Lumumba who was immediately faced with a breakdown of order. There was an army revolt while secessionist groups from the mineral-rich province of Katanga made their move and Belgian paratroopers returned, supposedly to restore security.

Lumumba made a fateful step – he turned to the Soviet Union for help. This set off panic in London and

Washington, who feared the Soviets would get a foothold in Africa much as they had done in Cuba.

In the White House, President Eisenhower held a National Security Council meeting in the summer of 1960 in which at one point he turned to his CIA director and used the word 'eliminated' in terms of what he wanted done with Lumumba.

The CIA got to work. It came up with a series of plans – including snipers and poisoned toothpaste – to get rid of the Congolese leader. They were not carried out because the CIA man on the ground, Larry Devlin, said he was reluctant to see them through.

Murder was also on the mind of some in London. A Foreign Office official called Howard Smith wrote a memo outlining a number of options. 'The first is the simple one of removing him from the scene by killing him,' the civil servant (and later head of MI5) wrote of Lumumba, who was ousted from power but still considered a threat.

MI6 never had a formal 'licence to kill.' However, at various times killing has been put on the agenda – but normally at the behest of politicians rather than the spies.

Anthony Eden, prime minister at the time of Suez, had made it clear he wanted Nasser dead and more recently David Owen has said that as Foreign Secretary, he had a conversation with MI6 about killing Idi Amin in Uganda (neither of which came to anything).

But in January 1961, Lumumba was dead.

Did Britain and America actually kill him? Not directly. He went on the run, was captured and handed over by a new government to a secessionist group whom they knew would kill him.

The actual killing was done by fighters from the Congo along with Belgians – and with the almost certain connivance of the Belgian government who hated him even more than the American and the British.

Powerful enemies

The comments attributed to Daphne Park by Lord Lea are subtler than saying that Britain killed Lumumba.

Lord Lea claims Baroness Park told him that Britain had 'organised' the killing. This is more possible.

Among the senior politicians in the Congo who made the decision to hand Lumumba over to those who eventually did kill him were two men with close connections to Western intelligence.

One of them was close to Larry Devlin and the CIA but the other was close to Daphne Park. She had actually rescued him from danger by smuggling him to freedom in the back of her small Citroen car when Lumumba's people had guessed he was in contact with her.

Do these contacts and relationships mean MI6 could have been complicit in some way in the death of Lumumba? It is possible that they knew about it and turned a blind eye, allowed it to happen or even actively encouraged it – what we would now call 'complicity' – as well as the other possibility of having known nothing.

The killing would have almost certainly happened anyway because so many powerful people and countries wanted Lumumba dead.

Whitehall sources describe the claims of MI6 involvement as 'speculative.' But with Daphne Park dying in March 2010 and the MI6 files resolutely closed, the final answer on Britain's role may remain elusive."

After Lumumba was assassinated, his supporters including Cubans led by Che Guevara, used Tanzania as a rear base and as a conduit for the shipment of weapons to Lumumbist forces in Congo, a role that earned President Nyerere enemies in Washington who wished he had been overthrown as well.

Lumumba's downfall shares a number of similarities with Nkrumah's. Both were orchestrated by Western powers led by the United States. Both leaders were targeted by Western intelligence agencies led by the CIA. And both incurred the wrath of the United States and other Western powers because of their Pan-African militancy and the policies they pursued – including their determination to achieve genuine political and economic independence for Africa without the continent being dominated by world powers – which were considered to a threat to Western interests on the continent.

Patrice Lumumba in Leopoldville after his arrest
in December 1960.
(2 July 1925 – 17 January 1961)

There is no question that the United States played the biggest role in Nkrumah's ouster from power. Other Western countries also played a big role. The British, the French and West German governments, together with the United States, conspired to sabotage Ghana's economy in preparation for the coup.

They lowered the price of cocoa, Ghana's biggest foreign exchange earner, on the international market in order to squeeze Nkrumah. They also denied him much-needed economic assistance.

Their intelligence agencies also worked together to undermine him. Britain's MI6, not just the CIA, probably played a significant role in his ouster; so did other Western intelligence services, especially German and French. Nkrumah himself, in his book *Dark Days in Ghana*, named West Germany as one of the countries which played a role in overthrowing his government.

Declassified documents available in the United States since November 1999 clearly show that the American government played the biggest role in overthrowing Nkrumah.

The documents constitute an indispensable work, entitled *Covert Foreign Relations of the United States* from 3 January 1964 to late 1968, published by the Historian's Office of the US State Department. That was the period when Lyndon Johnson was president of the United States.

But even before the intelligence reports were partially declassified in 1999, testimony given to the US Senate Foreign Relations Committee under the chairmanship of Senator Frank Church of Idaho in 1975 showed that the CIA played a major role in overthrowing Nkrumah; although not much information was made public during that time in terms of details on exactly what the CIA did to undermine and overthrow the Ghanaian leader.

The hearings focused on the CIA's illegal activities which included assassination of foreign leaders, among them Patrice Lumumba.

There were other African leaders who were on the CIA's hit list. Julius Nyerere was another leader the CIA tried to overthrow in the mid-sixties. Nkrumah, in *Dark Days in Ghana*, discussed the CIA's involvement in his ouster and in a plot to overthrow Nyerere.

And in his book *Freedom and Socialism*, Nyerere also mentioned American involvement in a plot against his government. As he stated in 1966:

"We have twice quarrelled with the US Government; once when we believed it to be involved in a plot against us, and again when two of its officials misbehaved and were asked to leave Tanzania....

The disagreements certainly induced an uncooperative coldness between us, thus suspending and then greatly slowing down further aid discussions. A comparison of American aid to Tanzania and other African countries supports the contention that at any rate our total policies (including support of the African liberation movements) have led to a lower level of assistance than might otherwise have been granted." – (Julius K. Nyerere, *Freedom and Socialism: A Selection from Writings and Speeches 1965 – 1967*, Dar es Salaam, Tanzania: Oxford University Press, 1968, pp. 201, 202, and 203).

Although Nkrumah survived many assassination attempts, at least six, he was such a towering personality that one of the three solders who led the coup, Major Akwasi Amankwa Afrifa, in his book *The Ghana Coup*, conceded that had Nkrumah been in the country during that time, he and his co-conspirators would probably not have been able to overthrow him, obviously because Nkrumah would have been able to mobilise forces – in the army where he still had support among a significant number of junior and senior army officers as well as regular soldiers – to neutralise the coup.

The leader of the trio, Colonel Emmanuel Kwasi Kotoka, worked very closely with Afrifa right from the beginning, planning the coup, when they were together in Kumasi, in central Ghana, where Kotoka was the commander of the Second Infantry Brigade. Afrifa was an officer in that brigade.

The other officer who was one of the three leaders of the military coup, Colonel Albert Kwesi Ocran, was the commander of the First Infantry Brigade in the southern part of the country which includes the capital Accra. He later wrote a book about the coup, *A Myth Is Broken: An Account of the Ghana Coup d'Etat of 24th February 1966*, which was published in 1968. It was he who tipped the scales in favour of the soldiers who attacked Flagstaff House. As Joseph Amamoo states in his book, *Ghana: 50 Years of Independence*:

> "The invading forces encountered considerable resistance at Flagstaff House, where the Presidential Guard and other military detachments loyal to Nkrumah fought bravely.
> The intervention of General Albert Kwesi Ocran, then a brigadier and in command of the Southern Command (First Infantry Brigade), including Accra, tipped the balance in favour of the attackers. For as he was not privy to the coup, he took some last-minute strong convincing and persuading in the early hours of the coup on February 24, 1966, to get him to command his troops on the side of the invaders.
> Once Brigadier Ocran, a Fanti,...weighed in on the side of Col. Kotoka (an Ewe) and Major Afrifa (an Ashanti), the defenders of Flagstaff House, despite their bravery and military strategies, stood no chance at all. Outgunned, and out-maneuvered, they still fought courageously, but by evening...it was all over. All resistance had ceased completely, with many casualties among the defenders.
> But for the bold intervention of Ocran, the fighting would have gone on far longer and would have been far bloodier, although the outcome would have been little in doubt, especially as Nkrumah was thousands of miles away in China, with practically no contact with the few still loyal to him." – (Joseph Amamoo, *Ghana: 50 Years of Independence*, Bloomington, Indiana: Xlibris, 2010, p. 388).

It was a blessing for the coup makers. They knew that the best time to execute the coup was when Nkrumah was out of the country.

And that is exactly what they did when he was in Peking on his way to Hanoi on a peace mission to help end the Vietnam war; and no wonder with some encouragement from President Lyndon Johnson who wished him "good luck," knowing what was going to happen in Ghana when Nkrumah was not there. In fact, President Johnson sent him a message in the first week of February 1966 – when Nkrumah was preparing for the trip – to assure him of a safe landing in Hanoi. As June Milne, Nkrumah's former research and editorial assistant, stated in her article, "The Coup That Disrupted Africa's Forward March," in the *New African* :

"Contemplating the years between 1957, Ghana's independence, and 1972 when Nkrumah died, I have been re-reading some of my notebooks written during those years when I was Nkrumah's research and editorial assistant. I wrote daily accounts of our many meetings both before 1966, the year of the coup, and afterwards. The value I attach to the notebooks is because they were written at the time. Not from memory or hindsight.

A notebook entry made during the first week in February 1966 is significant because it was made only three weeks before the coup. It was at a time when Nkrumah was preparing to travel on the peace mission to Hanoi. I was with him in his office in the Osu Castle in Accra. He was checking the page proofs of his book, *Challenge of the Congo*. Occasionally he asked if I thought he had used the most appropriate word in a particular context. 'It is your language, not mine.'

We were suddenly interrupted by the appearance of Foreign Minister, Quaison Sackey, to report that he had just received an urgent message from the Ghanaian ambassador in Washington. The US president, Lyndon Johnson, wished to assure Nkrumah that America would stop the bombing of Hanoi to allow his aircraft to land safely. He could, therefore, travel to Vietnam with his peace proposals 'in perfect safety.'

Why were the Americans so anxious for Nkrumah to leave Ghana – especially when he had suggested peace talks could be held in Accra: For some months, Nkrumah had been working on a peace plan. But a coup to remove him from power was in the final stages of planning. For it to succeed, it was imperative that he was out of the country, and as far as possible to ensure he would be unable to make a quick return....

When news of the coup reached him, Nkrumah was in Peking (today's Beijing) en route to the Vietnamese capital, Hanoi, with plans to end the American war in Vietnam. He was too far away for a quick return to Ghana where he may have been able to end the military action.

Leaders of four African countries sent Nkrumah immediate messages of support and invitations. They were the presidents of Egypt (Gamal Abdel Nasser), Mali (Modibo Keita), Guinea (Sékou Touré), and Tanzania (Julius Nyerere). Nkrumah decided to accept Sékou Touré's invitation." – June Milne, "The Coup That Disrupted Africa's Forward March," the *New African*, London, 6 March, 2007).

This brings to mind what British Prime Minister Edward Heath said to Dr. Milton Obote and two other African leaders in January 1971.

At a Commonwealth meeting in Singapore, Nyerere, Kaunda and Obote told Edward Heath that their countries would withdraw from the Commonwealth if Britain proceeded with the sale of arms to the South African apartheid regime. In the ensuing debate, Heath is reported to have told the three leaders:

"I wonder how many of you will be allowed to return to your own countries from this conference?"

It was an ominous warning, confirmed shortly thereafter, when Obote learned in Nairobi, Kenya, on his way back to Uganda from the conference that he had been overthrown. And it directly implicated Britain in the coup. Britain's involvement in the coup was further confirmed only a few days later when the British government became the first to recognise Amin's military regime exactly one week after he seized power.

Milton Obote, 28 December 1925 – 10 October 2005

Obote never returned to Uganda after the Commonwealth conference. He was overthrown by Idi Amin. But it was the British – and the Israelis – who were behind Obote's downfall and simply used Idi Amin to get him out of power; so it was with Nkrumah in Ghana: the same trick, and the same approach, in this case masterminded by the CIA. Both leaders were out of their home countries when they were overthrown.

In the case of Obote, it was Britain's MI6 together with Mossad, Israel's intelligence service, which masterminded the coup against him. The CIA was also involved in Obote's ouster. In fact, one of Amin's close friends, when Amin was in power, was a CIA agent. As one of Amin's sons, Jaffar Amin, stated in an interview with the *Mail*, London, 13 January 2007:

"That year (1975) my father took us to Angola. It was a really nice day trip. My father was friends with a CIA agent who had new equipment from the US, including planes for our trips." – Jaffar Amin, in "Mad Ugandan Dictator's son reveals all about his 'Big Daddy'," the *Mail*, London, 13 January 2007).

Britain's and Israel's involvement in Obote's downfall was an open secret. As David Hebditch and Ken Connor state in their book, *How to Stage a Military Coup: From Planning to Execution*:

"Amin gained power in 1971 by overthrowing Milton Obote in a British-backed military coup....But it is the circumstances of his rise to power and the involvement of Britain's Secret Intelligence Service – MI6 – in sponsoring the coup that is of interest here....

Obote...introduced a one-party state. He ousted President Sir Edward 'King Freddie' Mutesa four years later and rewrote the constitution so he could take the job himself.

The British shrugged; such was the way of things in the new post-colonial Africa. Then Obote decided to nationalise business and industry, starting with about eighty UK-owned companies. The British stopped shrugging and decided that this Obote chap had gone too far – it was time for a *coup d'état*.

The man for the job was MI6 officer Beverly Gayer Barnard....Small, intelligent and bespectacled, Barnard had the job of cultivating a man who was almost entirely his opposite. Idi Amin Dada was a giant of a man in everything but intellect. His behaviour the first time the British put him in a position of authority should have been a warning sign.

Amin was a sergeant in the King's African Rifles during the 1950s and served in Kenya during the colonial power's bloody conflict with the Land Freedom Army, the 'Mau Mau.' While working as a guard at an internment camp, his favourite party trick was to grab a prisoner by the throat and lift him bodily from the ground, earning him the nickname, 'The Strangler.' For seven years he was heavyweight boxing champion of Uganda.

When Obote came to power, Amin was rapidly promoted through the ranks to general and made commander-in-chief of the armed forces.

His power base in the army was a large group of Sudanese mercenaries who had been recruited by the British. These soldiers were exclusively from the Christian and animist area of southern Sudan and were battle-hardened from the long and bloody war with the Muslim-led north of the country. Also owing allegiance were the Anya-Anya guerrillas, the military wing of the Nile Liberation Front from the Ugandan-Sudanese border region, home base to Amin's tribe, the Kakwa. This alliance was useful to MI6; the Sudanese fighters were loyal to Amin, not particularly to the state of Uganda, and certainly not to Obote.

Idi Amin was Beverly Barnard's first choice for coup

leader. He had Obote's trust and a considerable power-base. And, as military commander-in-chief, he had only one place to go – head of state. As the MI6 man reported to London, Amin was 'intensely loyal to Britain' although 'a little short on the grey matter.'

By the end of the 1960s, Barnard had set up a training camp over the Sudan border and his airline was delivering *matériel* to the five hundred irregulars being put through their paces there. The weapons and ammunition were being supplied by Anthony Divall, a British arms dealer and contract MI6 agent based in Hamburg. The UK spooks had also managed to solicit the support of Mossad, the Israeli intelligence service....

On 11 January 1971 President Obote was out of the country, having decided to attend the Commonwealth Heads of State conference in Singapore. This was a particularly unwise decision on his part; trouble had been brewing for some time and, only eighteen months earlier, he had survived an assassination attempt. At the conference, Obote made an impassioned speech condemning Britain's decision to renew arms sales to the apartheid regime in South Africa. In response, Prime Minister Edward Heath prodded his finger at Obote and said, 'I wonder how many of you will be allowed to return to your own countries from this conference'...(Heath did that in the presence of President Julius Nyerere of Tanzania and President Kenneth Kaunda of Zambia, both close friends, also both close friends of Obote)....

Indeed, Beverly Barnard's plan went smoothly. Amin's troops sealed off Kampala airport at Entebbe and tanks and infantry took to the streets of the capital. The presidential palace was seized and vehicle checkpoints set up on all major routes. And the plotters didn't forget to take over the radio station! A national broadcast announcing Idi Amin's self-elevation to head of state also accused government ministers and senior civil servants of widespread corruption; the army had acted in the belief that bloodshed would result from the president's policy of giving preference to his own tribal region.

....British High Commissioner Richard Slater rushed around to Amin's office. There, with his feet metaphorically on the general's desk, was the Israeli Defence Attaché Colonel Bar-Lev. (The two were old chums, Amin having facilitated the shipment of Israeli arms to the rebels in southern Sudan in return, no doubt, for a considerable commission.)

In a recently declassified cable to London, Slater stated: 'Amin is now firmly in control of all elements of [the] army which controls vital points in Uganda....the Israeli defence attaché discounts any possibility of moves against Amin'....

Amin showed his appreciation by making his first official overseas visit to Israel, where he alarmed Prime Minister Golda Meir by demanding enough munitions to keep her country's arms industry busy for a decade. Within months 'The Strangler' was having lunch with the Queen at Buckingham Palace. God only knows what they chatted about.

Not in the dark about developments in Uganda was a colourful Kenyan businessman-politician and World War II fighter called Bruce McKenzie. McKenzie had astutely backed jailed opposition leader Jomo Kenyatta during the build-up to independence and was later rewarded with the influential post of minister of agriculture. He was the ultimate wheeler-dealer....

When in the UK, McKenzie was a regular house-guest of Maurice Oldfield, Barnard's ultimate boss as 'M', the director-general of MI6. Indeed he had also been McKenzie's 'boss' since 1963 when the businessman had signed up as an agent of the Secret Intelligence Service.

Alarmed by the threat of Obote's policy of nationalising foreign businesses, McKenzie was a keen supporter of 'Amin for president' and those views were undoubtedly impressed on Oldfield and Prime Minister

Harold Wilson. When he lost his job as agriculture minister in 1970, he remained the most influential white man in East Africa." – (David Hebditch and Ken Connor, *How to Stage a Military Coup: From Planning to Execution*, New York: Skyhorse Publishing, 2009, pp.125 – 126, 127 – 129).

American officials shared the same position with their British counterparts on Obote and equally wanted him out of power. However, the biggest players who orchestrated Obote's downfall were the British and Israeli intelligence officers including Israeli military officers in Uganda. Still, Americans supported the coup and were aware of it from the beginning when it was being planned.

But it was in Ghana where the CIA's role in overthrowing an African government became so sinister, and so tragic for Africa, as it was earlier in the case of Congo under Lumumba. And Nkrumah's indictment against the CIA – which was also Africa's indictment – for its role in fomenting trouble and undermining African governments American leaders did not like, was not simply paranoia. It was grounded in reality and backed up by empirical evidence. The tentacles of the CIA reached far and wide.

When I was a student at Wayne State University in Detroit in the state of Michigan in the United States in the early and mid-seventies just a few years after Nkrumah was overthrown, I remember reading an article about the CIA's interest in recruiting African students in that state to work for the intelligence agency. The article was published in one of the country's leading newspapers, the *Detroit News*.

It said the CIA was active on university campuses recruiting foreign students, targeting those it considered to be potential leaders when they returned to their home countries. It also tried to identify those it felt were sympathetic towards the United States.

Ambassador Franklin Hall Williams, 22 October 1917 - 20 May 1990

The article named the University of Michigan and Michigan State University as the CIA's main recruiting grounds in the state of Michigan because of the large number of foreign students attending those schools. It concluded by stating: "The emphasis is on the emerging nations of Africa."

That was the kind of treachery Nkrumah warned against when he said the CIA and other Western intelligence agencies were always trying to find "quislings and traitors in our midst," as he stated in *Dark Days in Ghana,* to work for the enemies of Africa. And he became one of the first and biggest casualties of such machinations by the CIA when some of his fellow countrymen conspired against him and removed him from office.

Another "traitor" (we are "brothers in race, brothers in conflict," as Lumumba was once said) was Nkrumah's black classmate at Lincoln University, a predominantly black school in Pennsylvania in the United States, in the 1940s. His name was Franklin H. Williams. He was the American ambassador to Ghana when Nkrumah was overthrown. He was appointed by President Lyndon Johnson in 1965 and served as ambassador to Ghana until 1968 when he returned to the United States.

In fact, Ambassador Williams was happy when Nkrumah was overthrown. He tried everything he could to portray the soldiers who overthrew Nkrumah as respectable individuals who even refrained from using violence during the coup, contrary to overwhelming evidence which showed hundreds of people, including innocent civilians, were killed; also contrary to what eyewitnesses saw: violence, bloodshed, and bodies of the people who were killed by the rebellious soldiers.

Yet American leaders in Washington, who supported the coup, did not even have any respect for the Ghanaians whom they had helped to overthrow Nkrumah in spite of Ambassador William's effusive praise for them. They did not even care to help them when they asked for economic assistance but didn't mind giving them a few thousand tons of wheat or rice. That would be enough, they said. They saw them as mere puppets of the United States whom they could manipulate at will, unlike Nkrumah who refused to bend to their wishes. As Kevin K. Gaines, a professor of history and former director of the Center for Afro-American and African Studies at the University of Michigan-Ann Arbor, states in his book, *American Africans in Ghana: Black Expatriates and the Civil Rights Era*:

"In stark contrast to the accounts of Boone and other eyewitnesses, the version of the coup advanced by U.S. officials was echoed by the major Western news organizations, which portrayed the action as the humanitarian rescue of the Ghanaian people from Nkrumah's tyranny. In the coup's immediate aftermath, Ambassador Williams, the State Department, and Johnson administration aides were concerned with managing the worldwide perception of events in Ghana.

Williams's version of events from Ghana provides a fascinating contrast with the expatriates' accounts. Washington replied tellingly to Williams's reports of the situation and his relaying of the NLC's appeal for economic assistance.

The first move was the NLC's in channeling its request for assistance through the same international lending agencies – that is, the International Monetary Fund and the World Bank – whose conditions Nkrumah had refused to accept. Without naming his sources, Williams wrote a note to Johnson aide Bill Moyers celebrating the 'extremely fortunate' occurrence and noting that 'all the personalities involved are strong friends of ours.'

Also noteworthy to Williams was the lack of violence and bloodshed, save for the death of Major General Barwah, which Williams inaccurately suggested might have been a suicide. He praised the coup leaders for their restraint in allowing security officers three hours to surrender before attacking.

Whatever his methods of obtaining information, his

reports on the coup to State Department officials and colleagues in the foreign service were shaped by U.S. national security imperatives and accordingly sought to cast events in the most favorable light.

The note contained the first of Williams's several personal appeals to Moyers for economic assistance for the new regime:

'Bill, this is the kind of change people like you and I hope for. It must succeed – it can succeed – but we're going to have to be responsive to and vigorous in that response.'

But assistance of the magnitude Williams sought as well as an official recognition of the NLC would have to wait. Responding to the NLC's pressure for U.S. recognition too quickly might lend credence to charges that the U.S. masterminded the takeover. The State Department thus deemed it prudent to wait until other African states recognized the new regime. A White House memorandum agreed that caution was warranted yet acknowledged that 'privately, we think Nkrumah's demise is great.'

Ambassador Williams assured State of Ankrah's anticommunism and his total compliance with U.S. objectives.

Williams sent another exultant missive to Moyers about 'our local coup,' reiterating quid pro quo requests for support.

Williams would have been dismayed by the cynical response of the administration's national security team. Assessing the coup as a 'fortuitous windfall' and the ousted Nkrumah as having done 'more to undermine our interests than any other black African,' Johnson's national security affairs adviser described the NLC as 'almost pathetically pro-Western.' Only a little support would be required to keep the new government in the U.S. camp. A modest gift to the NLC...of a 'few thousand tons of surplus wheat or rice' would suffice.

Anticipating the State Department's reluctance to provide even minimal assistance, the aide insisted that lavish aid was unnecessary – 'indeed giving them a little only whets their appetites, and enables us to use the prospect of more as leverage.'" – (Kevin K. Gaines, *American Africans in Ghana: Black Expatriates and the Civil Rights Era*, Chapel Hill: University of North Carolina Press, 2006, pp. 238 – 239).

The CIA's plot to overthrow Nkrumah was executed from the embassy with the full knowledge and participation of the ambassador himself. As Nkrumah stated in his book, *Dark Days in Ghana*, it was impossible for Ambassador Williams not to have known what the CIA was doing at the embassy of which he was in charge. In fact, as the head of the American embassy in Ghana from which plots were hatched and executed to overthrow Nkrumah, it was his job to know what was going on.

In an article in a black American publication, *Jet* magazine, 20 August 1970 (pp. 20 – 22), Williams contended that he did not play any role in Nkrumah's downfall. The article was entitled, "Did Not Aid in Nkrumah's Ouster."

But evidence demonstrated otherwise. Also, a letter to Ambassador Williams written by CIA Director Richard Helms showed the ambassador knew about the coup – its planning and execution – more than he wanted to admit. The letter vindicated Nkrumah and others who say the coup was masterminded by the CIA and Ambassador Williams played a role in Nkrumah's ouster. As Gaines states:

"In an account of the coup from exile in Guinea, where Sékou Touré had given Nkrumah asylum, the deposed leader accused Williams and the CIA of complicity in the action....Williams strongly denied any involvement in the coup and enlisted an intermediary to convey his denial to Nkrumah.

Such suspicions of CIA involvement and Williams's complicity in the Ghana coup are supported by a sanitized letter the CIA Director Richard Helms wrote to Williams. Helms acknowledged Williams's letter praising the recent work of the station chief in Accra and informed Williams that the unnamed official (Howard T. Bane) had been rewarded with a promotion within the agency.

Williams's conduct after the coup did little to dispel such suspicions. The ambassador responded to a defense of Nkrumah by Elizabeth Drake published in the *Palo Alto Times* – her husband, St. Clair Drake, had recently been a visiting professor at Stanford. Elizabeth Drake noted the 'indecent haste' with which U.S. officials recognized the 'government' established by the military coup. That official recognition came just a week after the coup 'can only serve to deepen the widespread conviction among Africans and others, that the coup was accomplished with the active connivance of the U.S. and certain Western allies.'

For Drake, the lesson was that governments of small, underdeveloped countries were defenseless against the alliance of U.S. officialdom and military dictators.

Williams responded by claiming in a letter to the *Times* that Elizabeth Drake had failed to understand conditions in Ghana and the significance of diplomatic recognition. The NLC 'exercised complete control of the country and enjoyed the overwhelming support of the people.' Williams asserted that the people of Ghana did not share Drake's favorable assessment of Nkrumah's rule." – (Ibid, p. 239).

The coup was masterminded by the CIA. And the American embassy in Ghana was in touch with Washington when the coup was being planned. It is impossible for Ambassador Williams not to have known that. And as Marvin Wachman, a white American who was president of Lincoln University, when Nkrumah was overthrown and who knew Nkrumah, stated in his book, *The Education of a University President*:

"In February 1966, Nkrumah was on his way to Hanoi to visit North Vietnam's president, Ho Chi Minh, 'with proposals for ending the war in Vietnam.' When he stopped in Peking en route to Hanoi, he was greeted with the news that his regime had been overthrown.

In *Dark Days in Ghana*, a book he wrote while in exile in Conakry, Guinea, Nkrumah strongly implies that America's CIA masterminded the coup. He was particularly vituperative about the alleged role of Ambassador Franklin H. Williams in bribing Nkrumah's enemies to carry out his overthrow.

'It is particularly disgraceful that it should have been an Afro-American ambassador who sold himself out to the imperialists and allowed himself to be used in this way,' Nkrumah wrote. 'However, his treachery provides a sharp reminder of the insidious ways in which the enemies of Africa can operate. In the U.S.A. the 'Uncle Tom' figure is well-known. We have mercifully seen less of him in Africa. The activities of the C.I.A. no longer surprise us.'

Franklin Williams, a 1941 Lincoln University graduate, was so upset by this charge that he asked me to intercede for him with Nkrumah and explain that he had nothing at all to do with the coup. I did write to Nkrumah but did not hear from him." – (Marvin Wachman, *The Education of a University President*, Philadelphia, Pennsylvania, USA: Temple University Press, 2005, p. 82; Kwame Nkrumah, *Dark Days in Ghana*, New York: International Publishers, 1968, p. 49).

Kevin K. Gaines, in his book *American Africans in Ghana: Black Expatriates and the Civil Rights Era*, states that Nkrumah did respond to Wachman:

"The president of Nkrumah's alma mater, Lincoln University, Dr. Marvin Wachman, informed Nkrumah of Williams's assurance that he had not been a party to the Ghanaian coup.

In an otherwise cordial letter to Wachman, Nkrumah wrote, 'I have noted what you say about Franklin Williams' (Wachman to Nkrumah, July 21, 1969, Nkrumah to Wachman, August 10, 1969, in *Kwame Nkrumah: The Conakry Years, His Life and Letters*, comp. June Milne, London: PANAF, 1990, pp. 321, 325)." – (Kevin K. Gaines, *American Africans in Ghana: Black Expatriates and the Civil Rights Era*, Chapel Hill, North Carolina, USA: The University of North Carolina Press, 2006).

Franklin Williams's predecessor as ambassador to Ghana, William P. Mahoney, played a critical role – with the US State Department, the White House and the CIA – in drafting an eight-point "Proposed Action Program for Ghana" devoted to psychological warfare and other tactics to be used against Nkrumah to bring about his downfall. As the document stated:

"Intensive efforts should be made through psychological warfare and other means to diminish support for Nkrumah within Ghana and nurture the conviction among the Ghanaian people that their country's welfare and independence necessitate his removal."

The document was dated 11 February 1964, 13 days before Nkrumah was overthrown. Authorship of the document is credited to William C. Trimble, then director of the Office of West African Affairs at the State Department and his deputy director Leon G. Dorros, as well as William P. Mahoney.

It was addressed to G. Mennen Williams who was the assistant secretary of state for African affairs, a post he assumed in 1961 in the Kennedy administration after serving as governor of Michigan for 12 years; he decided not to run in 1960 for another term as governor.

Here is the full document:

"The course of action outlined below is based on the following assumptions:

(1) By his present actions, Nkrumah is daily rendering our position in Ghana more difficult. He sees us as an ideal scapegoat to cover his domestic shortcomings and a handy whipping boy to promote his extreme brand of Pan-Africanism. In contrast to his leftist advisors, it is doubtful, however, that he wishes us to leave. He probably desires to retain the Volta aid and also some connection with the West to give him a posture of neutrality. But his present conduct can only lead to circumstances under which our position could well become untenable.

(2) The U.S. should make a determined effort to remain in Ghana. Voluntary withdrawal of our representation would be interpreted both there and elsewhere in Africa as a defeat for the U.S. and a victory for the Communists. It also would encourage the Communists and leftist elements in other parts of Africa to adopt the same tactics they have been following in Ghana. The Soviet bloc desires us to leave Ghana and is actively engaged in promoting this end.

(3) Nkrumah is convinced that the U.S. is the principal obstacle to his program for African unity. He is also convinced that through the CIA we are seeking to engineer his downfall. He is living in a state of fear induced by the several assassination attempts and an overriding sense of insecurity, and consequently is increasingly irrational and irresponsible.

(4) Nkrumah's popularity has markedly declined in the past 18 months, especially among civil servants, police, businessmen, university students and the professions. Though he still enjoys a considerable following among the rural masses, the more politically-minded urban population has lost confidence in him.

(5) Time is not on our side. The Parliament, judiciary and police have been emasculated; a purge of the universities is now under way and one of the civil service imminent. Although moderate elements still exert a slight influence on Nkrumah, he increasingly depends for advice and counsel on the small group of leftists in his immediate entourage. Nkrumah is consciously and deliberately creating a police state based on national Marxist principles.

(6) Although Nkrumah's leftward progress cannot be checked or reversed, it could be slowed down by a well conceived and executed action program. Measures which we might take against Nkrumah would have to be carefully selected in order not to weaken pro-Western elements in Ghana or adversely affect our prestige and influence elsewhere on the continent.

(7) U.S. pressure, if appropriately applied, could induce a chain reaction eventually leading to Nkrumah's downfall. Chances of success would be greatly enhanced if the British could be induced to act in concert with us.

(8) Failure to act can only result in a further deterioration of the situation to the point where we may feel compelled to leave Ghana, thereby facilitating the chance of Soviet success.

B. Summary of Proposed Actions

(1) Postponement of Ambassador Mahoney's Return to Accra

Ambassador Ribeiro should be called to the Department and informed by Governor Williams that in view of the Ghanaian Government's expression of regret at the demonstrations before the American Embassy and the Foreign Minister's assurance that they would not reoccur, it had been decided that Ambassador Mahoney would return to Accra on February 14. Because of the subsequent expulsion of American professors at the University of Ghana and vicious attacks on an officer of our Embassy, we now intend to postpone the Ambassador's return. The same statement should also be made to Botsio by our Charge at Accra.

(2) Award of Medal of Freedom to Adger E. Player

Congressmen Oliver P. Bolton and Zablocki have proposed that the Medal of Freedom be awarded to Mr. Player for his action in preventing desecration of the American flag. The White House has asked for the Department's views on the proposal. Our response should indicate that a decoration is fully justified, and suggest that it be either the Medal of Freedom or the Legion of Merit. Mr. Player's valorous conduct has been widely reported in the American press, and the award would constitute tangible evidence of the country's gratitude and admiration. It would also underscore our contempt for the controlled Ghanaian press in seeking to besmirch Mr. Player's character.

(3) Representations to Nkrumah by Ambassador Mahoney

The Ambassador should see Nkrumah as soon as possible after his return to Accra and make clear to him our concern at the course of developments in Ghana and their seriously adverse implications for U.S.-Ghanaian relations. He should indicate that as Ghana has failed to carry out the understandings set forth in the 1961 exchange of correspondence between President Kennedy and Nkrumah, we may be forced to reexamine our commitments to Ghana. He should also express our shock that no action has been taken against the leaders of the demonstrations. The impact of the Ambassador's remarks would obviously be enhanced if he were in a position to state that he had seen the President just before leaving Washington and had discussed the Ghanaian situation with him. It is felt that the Ambassador should not bring a letter from the President to Nkrumah since it might (a) serve further to inflate Nkrumah's ego; (b) encourage him to initiate an exchange of correspondence with the President and (c) be quoted out of context by Nkrumah to serve his own purposes.

(4) Visit by Edgar Kaiser

Mr. Edgar Kaiser should be encouraged to seek an interview with Nkrumah in the near future at which he would stress the unfavorable reaction in the U.S. to recent events in Ghana and indicate that they are causing serious misgivings among the Directors of Kaiser Industries on the desirability of proceeding with the VALCO project.

(5) IBRD Review of Its Support of Volta

The recommendation should be made to the IBRD, preferably through the Secretary of the Treasury, that it send a team to Ghana to study the desirability of continuing its support of the Volta project in the light of Ghana's adverse financial situation.

(6) Slow-down in Payments on the Volta Dam Project

AID and the Eximbank should delay action on pending and future requests for draw downs of loan funds by the Volta Dam. (This course of action is possible only until around July 1, 1964 when the lake starts to form and further delays in construction might cause serious flooding and loss of life.) Because of the IBRD's direct involvement in the project, it should be informed in advance of any such action.

(7) Termination of NIH Facility

The Bureau of the Budget is anxious to close down the NIH research facility at Accra as part of its program to reduce the balance of payments deficit. Although useful, the facility has been unable to fully realize its potential as a source of data on tropical diseases because of the uncooperative attitude of the leftist Director of the Ghanaian Institute of Health. Although of marginal value, early announcement of our intention to terminate the facility would be interpreted in Ghana as an indication of our displeasure at recent developments there but should not alienate pro-Western groups. If feasible, the operation possibly on a reduced scale, in deference to Budget's B/P concerns, should be shifted to Sierra Leone thus making the point entirely clear to Nkrumah and at the same time achieving a favorable impact with moderate African leaders.

(8) Psychological Warfare

Intensive efforts should be made through psychological warfare and other means to diminish support for Nkrumah within Ghana and nurture the conviction among the Ghanaian people that their country's welfare and independence necessitate his removal. Themes which might be exploited include:

(a) The strong non-Ghanaian element among Nkrumah's closest advisors and their Communist backgrounds;

(b) Suppression of civil liberties as exemplified by the Preventive Detention Act, purge of the judiciary, etc.;

(c) Perversion of the trade union movement without regard to the interests of the working people;

(d) Announced intention to destroy civil service leadership;

(e) Parliament is no longer responsive to public opinion;

(f) Threat to academic freedom as evidenced by expulsion of eight professors, invasion of the campus by the mob, campaign to place political commissars in institutions of higher learning, removal of the respected headmaster of Achimoto, etc.;

(g) Decline in Ghana's international prestige and increasing alienation of sister African nations;

(h) Introduction of Soviet security agents among the President's household;

(i) Serious deterioration in Ghana's financial position resulting from Nkrumah's irresponsible policies;

(j) Creation of a police state;

(k) Likelihood that Nkrumah's policies will result in Soviet bloc domination of Ghana, thereby substituting one form of colonialism for another; and

(l) Increasingly precarious position of the ordinary Ghanaian citizen.

(9) Nkrumah an African Problem

We must bring home to other African leaders that Nkrumah is a problem which they must face up to in their own national interest." – (*Foreign Relations of The United States, 1964 – 1968, Volume XXIV, Africa, Document 237.* **Memorandum From the Director of the Office of West African Affairs (Trimble) to the Assistant**

Secretary of State for African Affairs (Williams). Source: Department of State, Central Files, POL 1 GHANA–US. Secret. Drafted by Trimble, Mahoney, and Deputy Director of the Office of West African Affairs Leon G. Dorros).

All that was an integral part of the revelations from the declassified documents released by the US State Department in 1999 which clearly show what the United States did to get rid of Nkrumah.

Franklin Williams was appointed ambassador to Ghana in 1965, obviously to oversee the execution of a coup against his former classmate and black "brother," Kwame Nkrumah. Nkrumah's ouster had been contemplated earlier. It was discussed by American officials and their allies, especially the British and the French.

In fact, the discussion to overthrow him started as far back as 6 February 1964. That was when US Secretary of State Dean Rusk and CIA Director John McCone met and chose Joseph A. Ankrah, a general in the Ghanaian army, as the best man who should replace Nkrumah after Nkrumah was overthrown.

The interest to overthrow Nkrumah was further fuelled by the publication of his book that was highly critical of the United States and other Western powers. The United States sent him a note of protest after his book, *Neo-Colonialism: The Last Stage of Imperialism*, was published in the same year, coincidentally or not, Williams was appointed ambassador to Ghana:

"In his book, *Neo-Colonialism: The Last Stage of Imperialism*, Ghana's first president, Dr. Kwame Nkrumah, addressed the subject in a pan-African context, warning of the danger the United States posed to Africa by trying to establish hegemonic control over the continent, using American economic muscles to impose a stranglehold on African countries in order to exploit the continent and promote American geopolitical and strategic interests. He also accused the CIA of fomenting trouble on the continent, including overthrowing governments the United States did not like.

After the book was first published in 1965, the United States government sent a note of protest to Nkrumah and immediately cancelled a $35 million aid-programme to Ghana. A few months later, Nkrumah was overthrown in February 1966 in a military coup masterminded by the CIA." – (Godfrey Mwakikagile, Pretoria, South Africa: New Africa Press, *Africa is in A Mess: What Went Wrong and What Should Be Done*, 2006, pp. 128 – 129. See also Kwame Nkrumah, *Neo-Colonialism: The Last Stage of Imperialism* (New York: International Publishers, 1965)).

Besides denying his involvement in the plot to overthrow Nkrumah, Franklin Williams even blamed Hershey's, the giant chocolate manufacturer, in a conversation with one African American scholar, Professor Nathan Hare, editor of the *Black Scholar*, according to what Hare said in one of his messages posted on an African discussion group, Mwananchi, in 2005.

Hare said Franklin Williams told him that it was Hershey's, not the United States government, who overthrew Nkrumah. And there were many other denials by Williams even before then. But facts do not bear him out.

The United States had been wary of Nkrumah from the time he became prime minister of Ghana when the country won independence from Britain on 6 March 1957. On 6 March 1960, he announced that Ghana would have a new constitution which would make the country a republic. He became president on 1 July the same year.

Attempts to undermine his government started in the early sixties, fuelled by his strong support of Lumumba in 1960 and his opposition to American intervention in Congo. From then on, American leaders started to watch him closely.

But it was not until 1964, even before the publication of his book *Neo-Colonialism: The Last Stage of Imperialism* which infuriated American officials and other Western leaders, that a concerted effort was launched to overthrow him. And to send a strong message to Nkrumah and his supporters as well as other African leaders who tried to emulate him or pursue truly independent policies, he was overthrown almost exactly one month after he inaugurated the Akosombo Dam which had been built with American help.

John A. McCone,

John A. McCone
4 January 1902 – 14 February 1991

The dam was officially opened on 26 January 1966. Nkrumah was overthrown on February 24th. The timing was not coincidental. It was a demonstration of American power at its worst in the Ghanaian context. It was also a warning to other African leaders who were fiercely independent-minded like Nkrumah. As the American declassified document cited earlier states:

"We must bring home to other African leaders that Nkrumah is a problem which they must face up to in their own national interest."

Dean Rusk, 9 February 1909 – 20 December 1994

Other American declassified documents also show that American officials started plotting against Nkrumah in February 1964, almost exactly two years before he was overthrown. US Secretary of State Dean Rusk and CIA Director John McCone met and felt that Major-General Joseph Arthur Ankrah would be a suitable choice to replace Nkrumah after the coup.

A series of events took place after that meeting including participation by Britain and France, together with the United States, in a plot to sabotage Ghana's economy in order to inflame passions among Ghanaians against Nkrumah. And many of them were alienated when life became harder because of the economic squeeze on the Ghanaian economy when the three Western powers implemented their nefarious scheme.

It was a scheme of economic strangulation of a country whose leader was a shining example of African independence and manhood in a world dominated by Western powers and who was determined to see Africa free politically and economically. He had to be destroyed, lest others try to emulate him.

Coco farmers earned less and less for their export crop and blamed Nkrumah and his government for that. As history has shown, economic mismanagement, and discontent among the masses, is one of the main reasons used by soldiers and others to justify military coups not in only Africa but in other countries as well. And this was a perfect setup against Nkrumah. It was only a matter of time before he would fall, given the big powers behind the plot against him.

Documents declassified by the US State Department show that on 6 February 1964, US Secretary of State Dean Rusk and CIA Director John McCone had a meeting to review what they described as "an anti-American agitation in Ghana" which they attributed to "Nkrumah's anti-American push." McCone suggested to Rusk that "the substantial aid programs, including the Volta Dam and the Aluminum Project [being financed by the United States] should be reviewed in view of Nkrumah's attitude."

As the conversation went on, Dean Rusk asked McCone if General Joseph Ankrah, who had recently retired as Nkrumah wanted him to, could take over after Nkrumah was overthrown. According to McCone's Memorandum, the CIA director said:

"We [have] no indication, observed the General [has]

no political ambition and [I think] that if it [is] desired to develop something, we might work with the British on a joint program."

Rusk then asked McCone to further "explore this prospect fully" and report to him. He also suggested that the subject should "be discussed with Home [British Premier Alec Douglas-Home] and [his Foreign Secretary] Butler" when they come to Washington. They had been scheduled for an official visit to the White House in about a week's time, and they did go to Washington.

Other officials attended the meeting, including the US State Department director of the West African desk, William C. Trimble who wrote the memo, "Proposed Action Program for Ghana" to the assistant secretary of state for African affairs, G. Mennen Williams (who besides having served as governor of the state of Michigan from 1949 – 1961, was also once the US ambassador to the Philippines from 1968 – 1969), which stated:

"Although Nkrumah's leftward progress cannot be checked or reversed, it could be slowed down by a well conceived and executed action program. Measures which we might take against Nkrumah would have to be carefully selected in order not to weaken pro-Western elements in Ghana or adversely affect our prestige and influence elsewhere on the continent.

US pressure, if appropriately applied, could induce a chain reaction, eventually leading to Nkrumah's downfall. Chances of success would be greatly enhanced if the British could be induced to act in concert with us.

Intensive efforts should be made through psychological warfare and other means to diminish support for Nkrumah within Ghana and nurture the conviction among the Ghanaian people that their country's welfare and independence necessitate his removal."

The British were not only induced to conspire with the Americans against Nkrumah; as the former colonial rulers of Ghana, they felt that they had an obligation to play an active role in his ouster.

According to declassified documents, a meeting of American and British officials – as well as intelligence officers – was held at the White House on 12 February 1964 to discuss Nkrumah's ouster. It was also attended by President Lyndon Johnson who chaired the meeting.

Others who attended the meeting included Secretary of State Dean Rusk; US under-secretary of state, Averill Harriman, who later served as roving ambassador to Nigeria under President Johnson; and special assistant to the president on national security affairs, McGeorge Bundy.

The British delegation to the meeting was led by Sir Alec Douglas-Home, the prime minister. He was accompanied by his foreign secretary, Richard Austen Butler, who served in that capacity from October 1963 to October 1964.

The under-secretary of state, Averill Harriman, said when the meeting started: "Nkrumah blames the United States for all his troubles, including the attempt at assassination." President Johnson responded: "His behavior has become intolerable."

Some of the American officials at the meeting wondered if it would not be a good idea to cut off financial assistance to Nkrumah which was critical to the successful completion of the Volta Dam project and which Nkrumah valued so much in his quest for industrialisation in Ghana; many industrial projects would depend on cheap electricity generated from the Volta River after the dam was completed. That was one of Nkrumah's most ambitious projects during his presidency.

In response to that, according to the minutes taken at the meeting:

"The [British] Prime Minister said he was worried about Ghana. Nkrumah has gone very close to being Communist. If the United States took away its aid to the Volta project, it was his opinion that Ghana would go right over to the Russians who would supply the money for the Volta dam."

The Americans and the British ruled against that option at the meeting but agreed to continue applying pressure on Nkrumah in different ways to weaken him, while being friendly towards him and pretending that they were on his side.

The British foreign secretary, Richard Butler, remarked at the meeting:

"One could not be sure how long Nkrumah would last."

But whatever doubts and suspicions some of them may have had at the meeting were soon dispelled, as a concerted effort to overthrow the Ghanaian president got underway.

Two weeks later on 26 February 1964, another strategy session was convened at the White House to discuss the same subject: how best to eliminate Nkrumah from power.

At the meeting was CIA Director McCone and his close friend Edgar Kaiser who was working with Nkrumah on the Volta River Project which led to the construction of the Akosombo Dam and creation of Lake Volta, the largest man-made lake in the world in terms of area.

The meeting was also attended by the American ambassador to Ghana, William P. Mahoney. He served as ambassador from 1962 – 1965.

According to records of the meeting extracted from declassified documents, McCone was quoted as saying:

"I asked Ambassador Mahoney if he felt that the CIA

was operating independently of his office [in Accra]. Mahoney answered absolutely and positively no."

It would, of course, have made no sense for the CIA to engage in a clandestine operation in pursuit of American interests and foreign policy without the full knowledge of the ambassador, including Mahoney's successor, Franklin Williams.

The ambassador was the head of the US diplomatic mission from which the operation against Nkrumah was being launched, hence the highest representative of the American government in Ghana where his government had targeted the Ghanaian president for elimination because he was perceived as a threat to American interests.

It was also, coincidentally or not, on the same day that Nkrumah wrote President Johnson to express his concern about covert activities against him and his government by CIA agents in and outside Ghana.

He was fully aware of the pressure that was being applied on him by Western powers in collusion with local elements and had this to say in his formal letter – partly reproduced – to the American president dated 26 February 1964, the same day the American and British officials were having another meeting at the White House in Washington, D.C., in a conspiracy against him:

"...I must express some concern about that which has come to my notice within recent times as a result of the activities of certain United States citizens in Ghana.

There appears to be two conflicting establishments representing the United States in our part of the world. There is the United States Embassy as a diplomatic institution doing formal diplomatic business with us; there is also the CIA organisation which functions presumably within or outside this recognised body.

This latter organisation, that is, the CIA, seems to devote all its attention to fomenting ill-will, misunderstanding and even clandestine and subversive activities among our people, to the impairment of the good relations which exist between our two Governments.

If my analysis of this situation is correct, and all the indications are that it is, then I could not, Mr. President, view this without some alarm. Neither will any other Government in a developing State, however weak its economic position, accept this situation without demur.

We of the Independent African States wish to be left alone to pursue policies and courses which we know to be in the best interests of our people, and at the same time conducive to the maintenance of good relations with other governments of the world."

President Johnson denied those charges by Nkrumah and attempted to allay his fears by reassuring him that the United States wanted to maintain good relations with Ghana on the basis of mutual respect; while it was at the same time busy, working round the clock, to undermine him.

After the February 26th meeting at the White House, Ambassador Mahoney returned to his post in Accra, Ghana, and went to see Nkrumah on 2 March 1964, coincidentally or not, just four days before Ghanaians were to celebrate their seventh independence anniversary on March 6th. After meeting with Nkrumah, he sent a message to President Johnson and other high-ranking American officials at the state department and at the White House stating:

"I said [to Nkrumah] that I am in full control of all US government activities in Ghana. I could assure him without hesitation that during my incumbency absolutely nothing has been done by any US agency, which could be construed in any way as being directed against him or his government. Nkrumah replied with words to the effect: 'I will take your word for it.'

I repeated that there had been no conceivable activity on our part to subvert or overthrow him. I pointed out how inconsistent our entire aid effort, aimed at assisting and strengthening his government is, with wild accusations in [the] Ghanaian press that the US [is] acting against him. I added that, speaking frankly, our main intelligence effort is to keep an eye on his Soviet and Chinese friends, whose activities are really large scale.

[A] beginning has been made in effort to dispel some of Nkrumah's misconstructions on [the] role of CIA, [but] *pressure should be kept up* (italics added by the author – Godfrey Mwakikagile)."

Nkrumah's vulnerability to CIA machinations was compounded by his dependence on American economic assistance especially involving the Volta River Project more than anything else.

When Dwight Eisenhower was president of the United States, Nkrumah asked him to use his personal influence to persuade Henry Kaiser to put together a consortium of aluminium companies to build an aluminium smelter in Ghana. Kaiser and the consortium were willing to build the aluminium smelter only if the price of electricity was extremely low.

Later the decision by Nkrumah – after much hesitation – to offer a low price for electricity was criticised as being exploitative. But the price had to be low enough to induce Kaiser, the aluminium producer, to build the smelter. Without such an inducement, the smelter would not have been built. Nkrumah had no choice but to agree to Kaiser's demand for cheap electricity.

It was President Eisenhower who authorised funding for the Volta River Project when Ghana's finance minister, Komla Gbedemah, met with him at the White House and asked for financial assistance to build the Akosombo Dam. He asked Vice President Richard Nixon to take Gbedemah to the State Department to help arrange financing for the project.

It was also when Gbedemah was on that trip to see American officials in Washington that he was denied service at a Howard Johnson's restaurant in the state of Delaware together with his African American secretary because the restaurant did not serve blacks, an incident which made headlines around the world. After being denied service, Gbedemah told the restaurant manager:

"The people here are of a lower social status than I am, but they can drink here and we can't. You can keep the orange juice and the change, but this is not the last you have heard of this."

He talked about the incident at a press conference in Washington, D.C., when he went to see Eisenhower and it became headline news.

The incident also may have facilitated approval of Gbedemah's request for American assistance to finance the Volta River Project to build the Akosombo Dam. The United States was concerned about its image abroad, especially among African countries which were emerging from colonial rule and asserting themselves on the international scene including gaining membership in the United Nations. It was during the Cold War and the United States was anxious to win friends in Africa – at the expense of the Soviet Union – in spite of its racist policies against its own black citizens who were descendants of African slaves.

Yet, while the United States was doing all this, making arrangements to finance construction of the Akosombo Dam Nkrumah which wanted so much, it was also busy, at the same time, undermining him and used the economic assistance it provided as a smokescreen to hide its real intentions towards him: which was to get rid of him.

A lot of this activity was directed from the American embassy in Ghana where the American ambassador played a critical role in fomenting trouble against Nkrumah. On 23 March 1964, Ambassador Mahoney sent another telegram to Washington, stating:

"I believe someone has to keep hammering him [Nkrumah]."

The assistant secretary of state for African affairs, G. Mennen Williams, followed the advice of Ambassador of Mahoney and on 9 April 1964 wrote a memo to the under-secretary of state, Averill Harriman, stating that the American government should continue to exert pressure on Nkrumah to maintain his relations with the United States on a tolerable basis:

"[The United States should] keep continuing pressure on [Nkrumah] to maintain his relations with the US on a tolerable basis... We shall consult with the British in the next few days to discuss what contribution they may be able to make in this area."

Almost by mid-March 1965, the plot against Nkrumah had reached critical stage. CIA Director John McCone held a meeting in his office on 11 March 1965 which was attended by Ambassador Mahoney and other high ranking officials to discuss what to do next.
The topic of discussion was "Coup d'etat Plot: Ghana." Also at the meeting was the deputy chief of the Africa division at the CIA whose name was not declassified when the intelligence documents were released to the public in 1999.
According to what was discussed at that meeting, Ambassador Mahoney told CIA Director McCone that pressure exerted on Nkrumah by Western powers was working. He went on to say there was dissatisfaction with his leadership among many people in Ghana because of the deteriorating economic situation as a result of various

measures taken by the United States, Britain, France and other Western countries to sabotage Ghana's economy and encourage his enemies to launch a coup.

But Mahoney was still not quite convinced that the coup that was being planned by Acting Police Commissioner John W.K. Harlley, General Ankrah who was chief of defence staff and his deputy Major-General Stephen J.A. Otu, would necessarily take place. However, he was sure that Nkrumah would be overthrown within a year. As he bluntly put it:

"One way or another Nkrumah [will] be out within a year."

And he was.

When, at the meeting at the White House before the coup, McCone asked Mahoney who would succeed Nkrumah, Mahoney said a military junta would probably take over. He also made it clear that a *coup d'état* was already "being planned by Acting Police Commissioner Harlley and Generals Otu and Ankrah."

Another person who attended the meeting was Robert W. Komer who had replaced George McBundy as President Johnson's adviser on national security. He was a veteran CIA officer and agreed with Mahoney's assessment of the situation in Ghana and said at the meeting:

"We may have a pro-Western coup in Ghana soon. Certain key military and police figures have been planning one for some time, and Ghana's deteriorating economic condition may provide the spark. The plotters are keeping us briefed, and State [Department] thinks we're more on the inside than the British.

While we're not directly involved, (I'm told) we and other Western countries (including France) have been helping to set up the situation by ignoring Nkrumah's pleas for economic aid. All in all, looks good."

In early January 1966, Ambassador Mahoney was recalled to Washington after he finished doing what he was supposed to do to prepare for the coup against Nkrumah. And President Johnson appointed Franklin Williams as the new American ambassador to Ghana just in time for the coup.

American officials felt that Nkrumah would trust him since he was his classmate at Lincoln University (the class of 1941), and was also a fellow black. Therefore he would not suspect him of being involved in any plot against him and would believe him if he told him that the CIA was not plotting to overthrow him. But Nkrumah knew better than that.

Within two months or so after Williams assumed his post as the American ambassador to Ghana, Nkrumah was overthrown. And he knew Williams was involved in the plot. His appointment as ambassador was perfect timing for him to oversee the execution of the coup against his former classmate and "fellow African" – American officials saw him as one, hence his appointment, in order for him to work with his own kind but against them!

Nkrumah never forgave Williams for what he did to him and to Africa as a whole. In his book *Dark Days in Ghana*, Nkrumah said Ambassador Williams' treachery provided a sharp reminder of the insidious ways in which the enemies of Africa can operate.

Williams said he knew nothing about the coup and was not involved in it. Nkrumah did not believe him. As he said to his research assistant, June Milne, who also became a publisher of some of Nkrumah's works:

"It is extremely unlikely that Williams did not know what was going on in the embassy with CIA officers operating from there."

When Dr. Marvin Wachman was about to end his tenure as president of Lincoln University, he wrote Nkrumah on 21 July 1969 – Nkrumah was then living in exile in Conakry, Guinea – stating:

"As I prepare to leave, I would like to write a word on behalf of Franklin H. Williams of the Class of 1941...

Mr Williams is a very bouncy and vigorous individual, and I have never seen him so crushed as he has been, concerning your feelings that he was involved in some way in the episodes in Ghana. He has assured me, personally, that he had no knowledge of the coup."

Assuming that he didn't, why was he so happy when Nkrumah was overthrown? Even he wanted Nkrumah ousted.

Ironically, Nkumah's assessment of CIA's involvement in his ouster and interference of external powers in African affairs also got support from an unlikely source, his political adversary Felix Houphouet Boigny, former president of the Ivory Coast, who said in an interview with a French magazine, *Jeune Afrique*, 4 February 1981:

"Destabilisation is not a new thing. Did you know why Idi Amin made his coup in 1972? It was not he who did it, but the British. He did not even know what he wanted himself.

It was the same in Ghana when the military overthrew Nkrumah. They [the Ghanaian coup makers] came to see me. I asked them why. They replied: 'All is not well any more.' 'Is that all?' [I asked them]. I also asked them what they were going to do; they did not know. People outside knew it for them."

Outsiders who were behind the *coup d'etat* did not even try to hide their feelings as they gleefully congratulated those who executed it and celebrated Nkrumah's downfall.

As President Johnson's special assistant on national security, Robert W. Komer, stated in his message to the president concerning the coup:

"The coup in Ghana is another example of a fortuitous windfall. Nkrumah was doing more to undermine our interests than any other black African. In reaction to his strongly pro-Communist leanings, the new military regime [in Accra] is almost pathetically pro-Western."

It shows how much respect they had for their puppets in Ghana. It was pathetic how subservient the coup makers were to the West even according to the assessment of their masters, as Komer put it, describing them as being "almost pathetically pro-Western."

Even their own intelligence officers, although years later, proudly talked about the role they played in overthrowing Nkrumah.

Howard Bane, the CIA station chief at the American embassy in Accra, Ghana, who masterminded and directed the entire operation – obviously with the full knowledge of the black American ambassador Franklin Williams – was awarded an Intelligence Star and got double promotion for the role he played in overthrowing Nkrumah.

He lived up to his reputation best exemplified, at least in the African context, by what he did and accomplished when he was the CIA station chief in Ghana. As Paul Lee stated in "Documents Expose US Role in Nkrumah Overthrow":

"Declassified National Security Council and Central Intelligence Agency documents provide compelling, new evidence of United States government involvement in the 1966 overthrow of Ghanaian President Kwame Nkrumah.

The coup d'état, organized by dissident army officers, toppled the Nkrumah government on Feb. 24, 1966 and was promptly hailed by Western governments, including the U.S.

The documents appear in a collection of diplomatic and intelligence memos, telegrams, and reports on Africa in *Foreign Relations of the United States*, the government's ongoing official history of American foreign policy.

Prepared by the State Department's Office of the Historian, the latest volumes reflect the overt diplomacy and covert actions of President Lyndon B. Johnson's administration from 1964-68. Though published in November 1999, what they reveal about U.S. complicity in the Ghana coup was only recently noted.

Allegations of American involvement in the *putsche* arose almost immediately because of the well-known hostility of the U.S. to Nkrumah's socialist orientation and pan-African activism.

Nkrumah, himself, implicated the U.S. in his overthrow, and warned other African nations about what he saw as an emerging pattern.

'An all-out offensive is being waged against the progressive, independent states,' he wrote in *Dark Days* in Ghana, his 1969 account of the Ghana coup. 'All that has been needed was a small force of disciplined men to seize the key points of the capital city and to arrest the existing political leadership.'

'It has been one of the tasks of the C.I.A. and other similar organisations,' he noted, 'to discover these potential quislings and traitors in our midst, and to encourage them, by bribery and the promise of political power, to destroy the constitutional government of their countries.'

A Spook's Story

While charges of U.S. involvement are not new, support for them was lacking until 1978, when anecdotal evidence was provided from an unlikely source – a former CIA case officer, John Stockwell, who reported first-hand testimony in his memoir, *In Search of Enemies: A CIA Story*.

'The inside story came to me,' Stockwell wrote, 'from an egotistical friend, who had been chief of the [CIA] station in Accra [Ghana] at the time.' (Stockwell was stationed one country away in the Ivory Coast.)

Subsequent investigations by *The New York Times* and *Covert Action Information Bulletin* identified the station chief as Howard T. Bane, who operated undercover as a political officer in the U.S. Embassy.

This is how the ouster of Nkrumah was handled as Stockwell related. The Accra station was encouraged by headquarters to maintain contact with dissidents of the Ghanaian army for the purpose of gathering intelligence on their activities. It was given a generous budget, and maintained intimate contact with the plotters as a coup was hatched. So close was the station's involvement that it was able to coordinate the recovery of some classified Soviet military equipment by the United States as the coup took place.

According to Stockwell, Banes' sense of initiative knew no bounds. The station even proposed to headquarters through back channels that a squad be on hand at the moment of the coup to storm the [Communist] Chinese embassy, kill everyone inside, steal their secret records, and blow up the building to cover the facts.

Though the proposal was quashed, inside the CIA headquarters the Accra station was given full, if unofficial credit for the eventual coup, in which eight Soviet advisors were killed. None of this was adequately reflected in the agency's records, Stockwell wrote.

Confirmation and Revelation

While the newly-released documents, written by a National Security Council staffer and unnamed CIA officers, confirm the essential outlines set forth by

Nkrumah and Stockwell, they also provide additional, and chilling, details about what the U.S. government knew about the plot, when, and what it was prepared to do and did do to assist it.

On March 11, 1965, almost a year before the coup, William P. Mahoney, the U.S. ambassador to Ghana, participated in a candid discussion in Washington, D.C., with CIA Director John A. McCone and the deputy chief of the CIA's Africa division, whose name has been withheld.

Significantly, the Africa division was part of the CIA's directorate of plans, or dirty tricks component, through which the government pursued its covert policies.

According to the record of their meeting (Document 251), topic one was the 'Coup d'etat Plot, Ghana.' While Mahoney was satisfied that popular opinion was running strongly against Nkrumah and the economy of the country was in a precarious state, he was not convinced that the coup d'etat, now being planned by Acting Police Commissioner Harlley and Generals Otu and Ankrah, would necessarily take place.

Nevertheless, he confidently – and accurately, as it turned out – predicted that one way or another Nkrumah would be out within a year. Revealing the depth of embassy knowledge of the plot, Mahoney referred to a recent report which mentioned that the top coup conspirators were scheduled to meet on 10 March at which time they would determine the timing of the coup.

However, he warned, because of a tendency to procrastinate, any specific date they set should be accepted with reservations. In a reversal of what some would assume were the traditional roles of an ambassador and the CIA director, McCone asked Mahoney who would most likely succeed Nkrumah in the event of a coup.

Mahoney again correctly forecast the future: Ambassador Mahoney stated that initially, at least, a military junta would take over.

Making it Happen

But Mahoney was not a prophet. Rather, he represented the commitment of the U.S. government, in coordination with other Western governments, to bring about Nkrumah's downfall.

Firstly, Mahoney recommended denying Ghana's forthcoming aid request in the interests of further weakening Nkrumah. He felt that there was little chance that either the Chinese Communists or the Soviets would in adequate measure come to Nkrumah's financial rescue and the British would continue to adopt a hard-nosed attitude toward providing further assistance to Ghana.

At the same time, it appears that Mahoney encouraged Nkrumah in the mistaken belief that both the U.S. and the U.K. would come to his financial rescue and proposed maintaining current U.S. aid levels and programs because they will endure and be remembered long after Nkrumah goes.

Secondly, Mahoney seems to have assumed the responsibility of increasing the pressure on Nkrumah and exploiting the probable results. This can be seen in his 50-minute meeting with Nkrumah three weeks later.

According to Mahoney's account of their April 2 discussion (Document 252), 'at one point Nkrumah, who had been holding face in hands, looked up and I saw he was crying. With difficulty he said I could not understand the ordeal he had been through during last month. Recalling that there had been seven attempts on his life.'

Mahoney did not attempt to discourage Nkrumah's fears, nor did he characterize them as unfounded in his report to his superiors.

'While Nkrumah apparently continues to have personal affection for me,' he noted, 'he seems as convinced as ever that the US is out to get him. From what he said about assassination attempts in March, it appears he still suspects

US involvement.'

Of course, the U.S. was out to get him. Moreover, Nkrumah was keenly aware of a recent African precedent that made the notion of a U.S.-organized or sanctioned assassination plot plausible – namely, the fate of the Congo and its first prime minister, his friend Patrice Lumumba.

Nkrumah believed that the destabilization of the Congolese government in 1960 and Lumumba's assassination in 1961 were the work of the 'Invisible Government of the U.S.,' as he wrote in *Neocolonialism: The Last Stage of Imperialism*, later in 1965.

When Lumumba's murder was announced, Nkrumah told students at the inauguration of an ideological institute that bore his name that this brutal murder should teach them the diabolical depths of degradation to which these twin-monsters of imperialism and colonialism can descend.

In his conclusion, Mahoney observed: 'Nkrumah gave me the impression of being a badly frightened man. His emotional resources seem be running out. As pressures increase, we may expect more hysterical outbursts, many directed against US.'

It was not necessary to add that he was helping to apply the pressure, nor that any hysterical outbursts by Nkrumah played into the West's projection of him as an unstable dictator, thus justifying his removal.

Smoking Gun

On May 27, 1965, Robert W. Komer, a National Security Council staffer, briefed his boss, McGeorge Bundy, President Johnson's special assistant for national security affairs, on the anti-Nkrumah campaign (Document 253).

Komer, who first joined the White House as a member of President Kennedy's NSC staff, had worked as a CIA analyst for 15 years. In 1967, Johnson tapped him to head his hearts-and-minds pacification program in Vietnam.

Komer's report establishes that the effort was not only interagency, sanctioned by the White House and supervised by the State Department and CIA, but also intergovernmental, being supported by America's Western allies.

'FYI,' he advised, 'we may have a pro-Western coup in Ghana soon. Certain key military and police figures have been planning one for some time, and Ghana's deteriorating economic condition may provide the spark.'

'The plotters are keeping us briefed,' he noted, 'and the State Department thinks we're more on the inside than the British. While we're not directly involved (I'm told), we and other Western countries (including France) have been helping to set up the situation by ignoring Nkrumah's pleas for economic aid. All in all, it looks good.'

Komer's reference to not being told if the U.S. was directly involved in the coup plot is revealing and quite likely a wry nod to his CIA past.

Among the most deeply ingrained aspects of intelligence tradecraft and culture is plausible deniability, the habit of mind and practice designed to insulate the U.S., and particularly the president, from responsibility for particularly sensitive covert operations.

Komer would have known that orders such as the overthrow of Nkrumah would have been communicated in a deliberately vague, opaque, allusive, and indirect fashion, as Thomas Powers noted in *The Man Who Kept the Secrets: Richard Helms and the CIA.*

It would be unreasonable to argue that the U.S. was not directly involved when it created or exacerbated the conditions that favored a coup, and did so for the express purpose of bringing one about.

Truth and Consequences

As it turned out, the coup did not occur for another nine months. After it did, Komer, now acting special assistant for national security affairs, wrote a congratulatory assessment to the President on March 12, 1966 (Document 260). His assessment of Nkrumah and his successors was telling.

'The coup in Ghana,' he crowed, 'is another example of a fortuitous windfall. Nkrumah was doing more to undermine our interests than any other black African. In reaction to his strongly pro-Communist leanings, the new military regime is almost pathetically pro-Western.'

In this, Komer and Nkrumah were in agreement. 'Where the more subtle methods of economic pressure and political subversion have failed to achieve the desired result,' Nkrumah wrote from exile in Guinea three years later, 'there has been resort to violence in order to promote a change of regime and prepare the way for the establishment of a puppet government.'"

The mastermind behind the coup, Howard T. Bane, was glorified again when he died in July 2007. As John B. Roberts II, who worked in the White House when Ronald Reagan was president, stated in his article, "Original CIA Spymaster," in *The Washington Times*, 2 August 2007:

"In our YouTube, media-saturated, 15-minutes-of-fame Warholian world, it may seem incomprehensible that there are actually people who keep their greatest achievements secret. They shun publicity, book and movie deals, and the unrelenting self-promotion that characterizes our era. They are spies, and not just any kind of spies, but the cadre of intelligence officers whose creativity, daring and discretion make them the CIA's greatest generation.

They are an unlikely amalgamation of Ivy Leaguers, OSS veterans and country boys, who came together to form an elite organization. They served the CIA from its beginning through the gutting of the clandestine services under CIA Director Stansfield Turner.

Unlike today, when intelligence officers are recruited over the Internet and even through television ads, their recruitment itself was a clandestine affair. Secrecy was the foundation of their organizational culture. It was born of loyalty to one another, a sense of honor to the agents they recruited whose lives and safety depended on them, and to the cause they served.

Like World War II veterans, these spymasters are fast leaving us Howard T. Bane, whom I was privileged to know over three decades, is one who will be laid to rest this week.

Howard's 39-year career exemplifies the best of the CIA. He held the Distinguished Intelligence Medal, the CIA's highest award, and spent more than 20 years in overseas posts. Twice he participated in rebuilding the CIA's capabilities, first in the 1980s as a Reagan administration transition team member and a member of the Vice President's Task Force on Terrorism, and then again after September 11, when he returned to the CIA as a 're-employed annuitant.' Despite a cancer diagnosis, Howard worked until the end, calling the CIA his support group.

Early in his career, Howard showed an astonishing ability to pitch and recruit agents. In one three-year posting, he recruited 33 quality agents.

He likened it to seduction, and had a rare talent for spotting junior politicians on the rise, insiders in foreign intelligence agencies and mavericks with unique access to hard targets.

He took up flying gliders to get close enough to pitch one particularly productive agent. When a coup in Africa overturned a pro-Soviet government (Nkrumah's government), the Soviet ambassador had heart palpitations. Knowing that the diplomat had no access to an EKG, Howard took the U.S. Embassy's machine and went to the Soviet's heavily guarded residential compound, where he administered the test — and pitched the diplomat to spy for the United States. Such exploits earned him the nickname 'Give-it-a-Go-Bane,' a paraphrase of the cables from headquarters OK'ing his more unorthodox agent recruitment proposals.

After years in the Third World, Howard became station chief in The Hague just in time for the Japanese Red Army terrorist takeover of the French Embassy Howard kept his teams going in round-the-clock shifts and worked in tandem with the Dutch for the duration of the hostage crisis. It earned him a promotion to chief of the CIA's first-ever Office on Terrorism.

Howard also handled risky covert actions. In one Cold War operation, the agency netted 1 million AK-47s stockpiled in Africa and flew them to Laos for use in the covert war there.

In 1979, he ran the CIA's end of Desert One, the Iranian hostage rescue attempt. The military failure at Desert One is well known, but the CIA's exploits remain untold. Although the CIA's clandestine capacity had been badly damaged by the late 1970s, Howard found one CIA asset, a Tito partisan retired in Italy, who returned to Iran under deep cover to prepare for the raid. Given current relations with Iran it is inappropriate to say more except that had there been no helicopter collisions at Desert One, the affair would have had a surprise ending.

In the early 1990s, Howard was among the first to identify militant Islam as a direct challenge to U.S. interests. He monitored events in the Middle East and Iraq very closely and was keenly aware of the shortfalls of U.S. intelligence. He deplored the CIA's cutbacks in stations, posts and personnel. The shortcomings he identified were serious enough that in the summer of 2002 I wrote to my former Reagan-era associate, then-Chief of Staff Andrew Card, to urge him to discount intelligence purporting that Iraq had weapons of mass destruction.

After September 11, Howard and other 're-employed annuitants' kept vital functions at CIA going so that the agency could rapidly staff up overseas stations with experienced younger officers.

The CIA literally could not have expanded to cover the breadth of terrain required to combat terrorism without men and women like Howard willing to continue their service in their golden years. Among the things they have tried to pass on to the thousands of new intelligence officers brought into service since September 11 are the risk-taking, creative techniques and spirit that characterized the CIA's 'Silent Generation.'

Howard understood that there were no guarantees that a revitalized CIA would be his legacy. He hoped for it, but also recognized the bureaucratic and cultural obstacles. That isn't what motivated his return to service. He did it because it was the right and honorable thing to do, without fanfare or acclaim, just as he and his generation have done from the start."

He also changed the history of Ghana forever because of the role he played in overthrowing Nkrumah. Without his involvement in the coup, Nkrumah could have lasted longer in power and the history of Ghana would have been different. As John Stockwell stated in an interview with CCTV Africa, "Faces of Africa, Kwame Nkrumah: A Story of Vision and Tragedy," December 2014:

"Howard Bane, who was the CIA station chief in Accra, engineered the overthrow of Kwame Nkrumah. Now, obviously, you can look at it different ways. A Ghanaian might say I thought we did it. Inside the CIA, though, it was quite clear, Howard Bane got a double promotion and Intelligence Star for having overthrown Kwame Nkrumah in Ghana. The magic of it, what made it so exciting to the CIA, was that Howard Bane had had enough imagination, and drive, to run the operation, without ever documenting what he was doing, and to sweep along his bosses in such a way – they knew what he was doing, tacitly they approved, but there wasn't one shred of paper that he generated, that would nail the CIA hierarchy as being responsible."

Four African leaders – Sékou Touré of Guinea, Nyerere of Tanzania, Modibo Keita of Mali, and Gamal Abdel Nasser of Egypt – immediately offer Nkrumah asylum. He eventually decided to go to Guinea.

Richard Helms, 30 October 1913 – 22 October 2002

Also, the four leaders, together with Nkrumah himself and Ben Bella of Algeria, worked closely together and constituted what was known as "The Group of Six" within the Organisation of African Unity (OAU). In an interview in 1995, Ahmed Ben Bella told Jorge Castañeda, the author of *Companero: The Life and Death of Che Guevara*, that the six leaders worked together secretly on a number of issues, excluding other leaders. One of those issues was the Congo crisis:

> "Six African leaders, more than any others on the African continent, made the most determined attempt to help the Congolese nationalist forces in their war against the puppet government in Leopoldville and its Western sponsors. They were Julius Nyerere of Tanzania, Kwame Nkrumah of Ghana, Gamal Abdel Nasser of Egypt, Ben Bella of Algeria, Sékou Touré of Guinea, and Modibo Keita of Mali.
> They even had a group of their own within the Organisation of African Unity (OAU) known as 'The Group of Six,' and secretly worked together as Ben Bella said in an interview years later.... They were determined to liberate Congo. But as Ben Bella said in an interview in Geneva, Switzerland, on November 4, 1995: 'We arrived in the Congo too late.'" – (Godfrey Mwakikagile, *Nyerere and Africa: End of an Era*, Pretoria: New Africa Press, 2010, pp. 160 – 161. See also, Ahmed Bella, quoted by Jorge G. Castañeda, *Companero: The Life and Death of Che Guevara* (New York: Alfred A. Knopf, 1997), p. 276).

The coup against Nkrumah is also remembered in another respect. It galvanised some military officers into action to try and reinstate Nkrumah. The first casualty in one of those attempts, Lieutenant-General Emmanuel Kwasi Kotoka who was also the person who announced on the radio that Nkrumah had been overthrown and the armed forces had taken over the government, was even mocked by Nkrumah after he was killed on 17 April 1967 in an abortive counter-coup code-named Operation Guitar Boy. Nkrumah wrote in *Dark Days in Ghana* stating that even *juju* could not protect Kotoka:

"Kotoka subsequently boasted of his killing of... [Nkrumah loyalist Major-General Barwah, Army Chief of Staff and Deputy Chief of Defence Staff] but said because he was protected by a 'juju' he was able to catch the bullets which Barwah fired in his defence and to throw them back at him. When the counter-coup of April 1967 took place Kotoka's 'magic' could not save him. Unlike Barwah he surrendered without protest or struggle to those who had captured him at his headquarters. His 'juju' did not prevent him being shot in his turn." – (Kwame Nkrumah, *Dark Days in Ghana*, quoted by Harcourt Fuller, *Building the Ghanaian State: Kwame Nkrumah's Symbolic Nationalism*, op. cit., p. 165).

The officers who launched the counter-coup – Lieutenant Samuel Arthur and Lieutenant Moses Yeboah were tried by a six-man military tribunal and sentenced to death by firing squad, while Second-Lieutenant Osei-Poku received a 30-year prison sentence – are also remembered for their patriotism as army officers who refused to betray their government, and for their bravery in battle when they almost succeeded in overthrowing the NLC military junta.

Even Nkrumah himself, in his book *Dark Days in Ghana*, praised Lieutenant Arthur and his colleagues for trying to overthrow the NLC and for sacrificing their lives in the hope that the former president would return to Ghana and be reinstated.

Their executions are also remembered as a testament to their patriotism and the ideals they died for, although there is some disagreement on the motives of the coup attempt and whether the young soldiers really wanted to return Nkrumah to power.

Arthur and Yeboah were executed on 26 May 1967 before a crowd of about 20,000 outside the nation's capital Accra. As Kabudi Wanga Wanzala states in his book, *Ghanaman*:

"Operation Guitar Boy was the code name the rebel soldiers had given their insurrection. Ghanaians thought the soldiers were probably inspired to name their plot to assassinate members of the National Liberation Council after 'Guitar Boy and Mammy Water,' the popular highlife tune by Nigerian musician Sir Victor Uwaifo and his Melody Maestroes that had been blasting the airwaves ever since last Christmas.

Organized by a 120-man army reconnaissance squadron based based in Ho in the Volta Region, Operation Guitar Boy was commandeered by a Lieutenant Samuel Arthur.

The rebel soldiers began their coup attempt as early as five o'clock in the morning, and they engaged in heavy fighting against the loyal forces of the NLC. Equipped with bazookas, machine guns, and rifles, they were able to overpower three strategic sites: Christianborg Castle, the new seat of government; Flagstaff House, the new headquarters of the Ghana Armed Forces; and the Ghana Broadcasting Corporation.

At six o'clock, the architects of the countercoup proudly announced that the NLC government had been overthrown and Lieutenant General Emmanuel K. Kotoka, the General Officer Commanding the Ghana Armed Forces, had been captured and killed. His bullet-riddled body was later found by the roadside near the Accra Airport, a few miles away from Flagstaff house where his office was situated. Kotoka's batman, Sergeant Osei Grunshie, and two other soldiers, Captain C.Y. Borkloe and Captain A.K. Avevor, were also killed when the soldiers captured Flagstaff House.

Lieutenant Arthur and his friends staged the countercoup because they felt that the NLC had betrayed the aims of the February 24 revolution by amassing wealth. They were also totally dissatisfied with the current status of the Ghana army. In the past year, there had been so many rapid promotions in the army; and as a result, there was a large number of senior officers many of whom were very young. This situation was preventing the promotions of other young deserving soldiers.

Unfortunately, Operation Guitar Boy was short-lived. A few minutes after the rebelling soldiers' broadcast, the coup was foiled, and all the ringleaders were captured. Lieutenant Samuel Arthur was was accused of killing Captain Avevor, Lieutenant Moses Yeboah was accused of killing Kotoka, and Second Lieutenant E. Osei Poku was accused of the attempted murder of General Ankrah, the chairman of the NLC.

Fifty-one-year-old General (Joseph Arthur) Ankrah was at Christianborg Castle when the fighting broke out, but it was rumored that he escaped from Lieutenant Osei Poku by jumping out of his bedroom window, scaling the high barbed-wire walls of the castle, and swimming the frigid waters of the Atlantic Ocean to a nearby village along the coast.

Incidentally, other members of the council were not attacked. The only NLC member who was not in Accra at the time of the counter coup was colonel A.A. Afrifa. He was on a visit to Tamale in the Northern Region of Ghana....

On April 28, 1967, the trial for the coup plotters who had been arrested began. It didn't last long. Arthur, Yeboah, and Poku were all found guilty of subversion. Arthur and Yeboah were to be executed in public while Poku was given thirty years in prison....The NLC gave the order for the executions to take place.

Angry soldiers grieving the loss of General Kotoka, Sergeant Osei Grunshie, Captain C.Y. Borkloe, and Captain A.K. Avevor did not waste any time setting up a firing range at a beach a few miles away fro Accra. Thousands of Ghanaians, men, women, and children lined up on the beach to witness the execution. It was a first in the nation's history, and people were both excited and curious about the gruesome event....Samuel Arthur looked at his executioners defiantly. He wasn't afraid to die." – (Kabudi Wanga Wanzala, *Ghanaman*, Bloomington, Indiana: Xlibris, 2012, pp. 432 – 433, 434).

Although there is no guarantee Nkrumah would have returned to power had the counter-coup succeeded, there was high probability he could have because the army officers who overthrew him expected resistance – to the first coup – to come from some soldiers who were based at Ho in the Volta Region, from the very same place where those who attempted to overthrow the NLC were based. Therefore it is very much possible the attempted counter-coup launched by Lieutenant Arthur and his colleagues was intended to reinstate Nkrumah, although no counter-offensive was launched from Ho to resist the first coup as Kotoka and Afrifa expected.

The ouster of Nkrumah was one of the most tragic events in the history of post-colonial Africa.

Nkrumah was the strongest proponent of immediate continental unification, a stand which put him in a class almost by himself.

He was also, together with leaders such as Nyerere, Sékou Touré, Modibo Keita, Obote and Kaunda one of the strongest supporters of African unity and of the African liberation movements and an uncompromising opponent of interference in African affairs by world powers and other external forces. And that made him an enemy of the West.

He became prime target for the CIA and other Western intelligence services including Britain's MI6. As he himself stated in *Dark Days in Ghana*:

"In Ghana, the embassies of the United States, Britain, and West Germany were all implicated in the plot to overthrow my government.

It is alleged that U.S. Ambassador Franklin Williams, offered the traitors 13 million dollars to carry out a *coup d'état*. Afrifa, Harlley and Kotoka were to get a large share if they would assassinate me at Accra airport as I prepared to leave for Hanoi.

I understand Afrifa said: 'I think I will fail,' and declined the offer. So apparently did the others." – (Kwame Nkrumah, *Dark Days in Ghana*, London: Panaf Books, 1968, p. 49. See also *Black World/Negro Digest*, Chicago, Johnson Publishing Company, May 1969, pp. 71 – 72).

An astute observer of the international scene, Nkrumah knew that the former colonial powers which had ruled Africa, together with the leading Western power, the Untied States, were determined to dominate Africa in order to continue to exploit the continent. He was vindicated by history.

The American government never stopped its subversive activities in Africa. And that includes recruiting African students studying in the United States to be its agents when they return home.

The CIA's interest in Africa and in African students is nothing new; it goes back to the fifties.

In 1954, the United States government established the African-American Institute, based in New York City, to promote American interests in Africa. The institute was funded by the CIA and published an influential magazine *Africa Report*. Coincidentally or not, publication of the magazine ended in 1989-1990, during the same time when the Soviet Union and other communist regimes collapsed in Eastern Europe.

The African-American Institute also had a scholarship programme, funded by the CIA, as a way of buying influence in Africa, especially with African governments. The CIA, hence the American government, hoped that after the students returned to Africa, they would help to advance or serve American interests on the continent, especially if they worked in the government as many of them were expected to.

American interest in Africa included plans to invade Nigeria. In August 1975, a secret military plan for the invasion of oil-producing countries, including Nigeria which is one of the world's largest producers, was sent to Congress for approval in case a second oil embargo – after the 1973 one during the Arab-Israel conflict – was imposed by the oil-exporting countries, thus threatening vital Western interests.

Nigeria did not participate in the 1973 – 1974 embargo imposed by the Organisation of Petroleum Exporting Countries (OPEC), of which it is a member, and entered a period of unprecedented economic growth during which this giant African nation had one of the highest per capita incomes in the world. It ranked 33rd during the oil boom of the seventies.

However, the American government did not want to take any chances and feared that the militant new Nigerian military ruler, Brigadier-General Murtala Muhammed, would join a second oil boycott against the United States and other Western countries, "crippling" their economies.

Fears in Washington of a possible oil embargo by Nigeria increased when the Nigerian leader rejected a proposed visit to Nigeria by the US Secretary of State Henry Kissinger, which would have been the first visit by an American secretary of state to black Africa's most powerful country and its largest in terms of population.

American officials also expressed deep concern about Nigeria's growing influence and the country's support for the liberation movements and independence struggle on the continent. They suggested that the United States can contain or neutralise Nigeria's rise to power only through sabotage.

In fact, on 2 February 1976, a secret despatch from the American embassy in Lagos, Nigeria, warned that Nigeria enjoyed a "very healthy current account balance as a result of booming oil sales," and advised that the country was moving towards having a modern, well-equipped army.

It was Donald Easum, former American ambassador to Nigeria at the time of Murtala Muhammed's assassination and later head of the African-American Institute, who recommended ways to contain Nigeria's growing military strength; a recommendation which was taken seriously by the CIA and top American government officials and other leaders including senators and congressmen.

American interest in Nigeria – including plans for clandestine operations in this major African country – has frightening parallels to what happened in Congo which became the bleeding heart of Africa because of American intervention since the sixties with the support of other Western powers in order to control and dominate the country and the rest of Africa. And it amounts to nothing less than attempts at recolonisation of Africa, best demonstrated in Congo, renamed Zaire, during Mobutu's reign.

The largest CIA station in Africa was in Kinshasa, capital of Zaire, when the country was ruled by Mobutu. And it was from Kinshasa that the CIA launched its missions to destabilise the MPLA government in Angola and support anti-government factions during the Angolan civil war which lasted for almost 30 years since seventies.

Therefore, fears of recolonisation of Africa are not paranoia or a figment of the imagination but reality grounded in history and validated by contemporary experience. One contemporary aspect of this is the deep penetration of Africa by Western business interests in this era of globalisation at the expense of the indigenous people.

Little is done to meet their needs or redress their grievances, tragically demonstrated by the callousness of the oil companies operating in the Niger Delta in Nigeria where members of the local ethnic groups have been subjected to all kinds of abuse including environmental pollution, thus denying them basic human rights, including food and shelter.

Their water, fish, and land have been polluted, destroying their means of livelihood without getting compensation from the Western oil companies or from the federal government itself. Their aspirations as a people have been stifled right in their homeland without the slightest concern for their future and well-being.

Yet all this is taking place in a country which is supposed to be free and independent, and under the leadership of Africans who are supposed to care about the welfare of their own people. All they care about is themselves, as they work to serve the interests of their Western masters who never really left when we won independence in the sixties. As Nyerere said, they went out through the front door and returned through the back door. That is what neo-colonialism is all about. And it is a reality in Africa today as much as it has been since independence.

Nyerere also warned of the danger of recolonisation as far back as the sixties. As he stated in August 1960, even before he led Tanganyika to independence the following year, at a conference in the capital of Tanganyika, Dar es Salaam:

"The phase through which we are emerging successfully (from colonial rule) is the phase of the first scramble for Africa – and Africa's reaction to it. We are now entering a new phase. It is the phase of the second scramble for Africa....

So I believe that the second scramble has begun in real earnest. And it is going to be a much more dangerous scramble than the first one....

The phrase 'the second scramble for Africa' may sound far-fetched, in the context of the Africa of the 1960's....But anybody who thinks this is far-fetched has been completely blind to what is happening on the African continent. Take, for example, the Congo: There were obvious weaknesses in the Congo situation, but those weaknesses were deliberately used in a scramble for the control of the Congo." – (Julius Nyerere, "Nationalism and Pan-Africanism," excerpts from a speech delivered to the Second Pan-African Seminar, World Assembly of Youth (WAY), reprinted from WAY *Forum*, No. 40, September 1960, in Paul E. Sigmund, Jr., editor, *The Ideologies of the Developing Nations*, New York: Frederick A. Praeger, 1963, pp. 205, 209, and 208).

Throughout his presidency, Nyerere continued to warn about the danger of neo-colonialism and did so even after he stepped down. As he stated in a speech in Atlanta, Georgia, in the United States in 1998 not long before he died, multinational corporations were playing a leading role in the recolonisation of Africa. And they did not want civil wars and other conflicts to end in African countries because it was easier for them to exploit the continent if there were no strong governments; with the rebels playing a critical role in looting the continent and selling the resources to foreigners at very low prices.

And there is a very simple explanation for that. Where there is no law and order, it is very easy to steal. Only the strongest survive. And it is multinational corporations and other foreign interests which benefit the most, while the people, the poor masses of Africa, get nothing.

Nyerere's warning is an enduring reality and will remain valid as long as Africa continues to be dominated and exploited by foreigners:

"On May 7, 1998, Mwalimu Nyerere spoke with eloquence and prescience about Africa's recent past and its immediate future during the first National Summit on Africa Southeastern Regional Summit in Atlanta.

He warned of a second scramble for Africa, not unlike the one that partitioned Africa at the Berlin conference in 1884 (November 1884 – February 1885) in the interest of

European political domination and free trade. He suggested that this time the scramble was led by multinational corporations aligned with rebel leaders, whose goal is to plunder the mineral resources of Africa with the result of introducing new political instability and even civil wars in several regions on the continent. This was the case in Liberia and Sierra Leone and it still prevails in Angola and the Democratic Republic of the Congo." – (Julius Nyerere, cited by Herschelle S. Challenor, chairman of the board of directors, National Summit on Africa, in a memorial tribute to Mwalimu Julius Nyerere, Washington, D.C., 18 February, 2000. See The National Summit on Africa).

Nkrumah also foresaw that, as he clearly explained in some of his speeches and writings including his books, *I Speak of Freedom: A Statement of African Ideology*, published in 1961; *Africa Must Unite*, published in 1963; *Neo-Colonialism: The Last State of Imperialism*, 1965; *Challenge of the Congo*, 1967; *Voice from Conakry*, 1967; and *Dark Days in Ghana*, published in 1968 when he was living in exile in Conakry, Guinea, where he was invited by his ideological compatriot, President Ahmed Sékou Touré, to be co-president soon after he was overthrown.

But it was his book, *Neo-Colonialism: The Last Stage of Imperialism*, which exposed American imperialist designs in Africa including ruthless exploitation of the continent's resources at the expense of Africans, that angered the Americans. The book, published in October 1965 just before the OAU summit held in Accra at the end of the same month, was intended be given to his fellow leaders for them to read it during that time.

It amounted to signing a death warrant for himself the same way Patrice Lumumba did in his independence speech in the presence of the Belgian king, Baudouin I, in Leopoldville, on 30 June 1960, when he denounced the Belgian colonial rulers for ruthlessly exploiting the people of Congo and the country's resources under a system that amounted to slavery.

G. Mennen Williams, 23 Feb 1911 – 2 Feb 1988

Nkrumah's book encouraged American leaders to get rid of him even faster. He was already on their elimination list. He probably knew the book would infuriate the Americans. But he also knew he had to tell the truth.

What he probably did not know was that it would play a major role in his downfall. His policies had already infuriated the West, especially the United States, the seat of global capitalism and the world's financial centre, whose policies Nkrumah strongly disagreed with. As Professor Kevin Gaines states in his book, *American Africans in Ghana: Black Expatriates and the Civil Rights Era*:

"In September (1965), the Ghanaian government rejected the recommendation of a World Bank mission to cease trading with socialist countries and adopt stringent fiscal reforms. The government's refusal to accede to the bank's terms, as much as any of Ghana's difficulties, may well have sealed Nkrumah's fate.

In October, Nkrumah published *Neo-Colonialism: The Last Stage of Imperialism*, in time for distribution at the

OAU summit in Accra. Forty years later, it may be difficult to imagine that the publication of a book could roil officials in the corridors of metropolitan power. Such, however, was the impact of Nkrumah's gloss on Lenin's *Imperialism: The Highest State of Capitalism*, in which the Ghanaian leader sought to convince reluctant African states of the necessity for continental unity. Its detailed exposé of the West's financial stranglehold on African economies sparked outrage among U.S. officials, confirming their worst suspicions regarding Nkrumah's leftist leanings.

For those who had for some time contemplated Nkrumah's ouster, the book's appearance represented the last straw after many months of articles and editorials in the Ghanaian press lambasting American imperialism, neocolonialism, and CIA subversion. Well before the book's appearance, the Ghanaian press had previewed the volume's thesis of persistent American and Western corporate control over the resources and economies of small, underdeveloped African nations after they achieved political independence.

The book was said to have resulted from Nkrumah's collaborations with several expatriate ghostwriters, including Shirley Graham Du Bois, Dorothy Padmore, and Hodee Edwards, a white American woman linked by marriage to the African American expatriates. The government had engaged Edwards to help build the intellectual case for scientific rather than African socialism.

Nkrumah had previously disclaimed responsibility when Ghanaian press attacks on the United States elicited protests from Ambassador William Mahoney. Journalists were free to write as they pleased, Nkrumah shrugged. He studiously kept aloof from the press's more radical utterances.

The highly favorable terms enjoyed by the U.S.-based Kaiser Corporation for the Volta River project and Valco aluminum smelter notwithstanding, now that Nkrumah had signed his name to the condemnation of neocolonial Western financial interests, U.S. officials responded angrily. In Washington, Assistant Secretary of State G. Mennen Williams gave Ambassador (Miguel Augustus) Ribiero a tongue-lashing, threatening that Nkrumah's book would be the cause of any negative consequences that might ensue. Soon thereafter, Ghana's request to the United States for $100 million worth of emergency surplus food aid was turned down. Nkrumah's book merely gave State Department officials and the Johnson administration, who were already expecting a pro-Western coup against Nkrumah in July (165), a pretext to deny any material assistance that might prolong Nkrumah's regime." – (Kevin K. Gaines, *American Africans in Ghana*, op. cit., pp. 225 – 226).

The United States was already working against Nkrumah even before his book was published. But while it is true that what he wrote in the book infuriated the Americans and was one of the main reasons American leaders decided to overthrow him, Ghanaian soldiers who executed the coup could not have said they ousted him because they were offended by what he wrote in the book; it was the Americans who were, although they still would have overthrown him, or would have tried to, even if he had not written *Neo-Colonialism: The Last Stage of Imperialism*. And Ghanaian soldiers would still have used "dictatorial rule" and "mass discontent" against Nkrumah as the main reasons they decided to depose him.

Nkrumah's ardent call for armed intervention by African countries to oust the white minority regime in Rhodesia – under Prime Minister Ian Smith – which unilaterally declared independence on 11 November 1965 at the expense of the black majority was also given, by the soldiers, as one of the main reasons they decided to overthrow him.

It was only a pretext. Plans were already underway – by the United States and Nkrumah's opponents in Ghana including the soldiers who carried out the coup in 1966 – to overthrow him even before the white minority rulers of Rhodesia declared independence in November 1965.

President John F. Kennedy with Ghanaian ambassador Miguel Augustus Ribiero, 25 April 1965

The coup against Nkrumah was expected to take place in July 1965, about four months before Rhodesia's Unilateral Declaration of Independence (UDI); it been in the planning for a long time. But the soldiers did use Nkrumah's decision to prepare his army for military intervention in Rhodesia as an exercise for the impending coup which took place in February 1966 only about three months after Rhodesia's white minority rulers declared independence. They used the military exercises as a cover, in preparation for the coup, while pretending they were getting ready to go to Rhodesia as Nkrumah wanted them to. As Kevin Gaines also states:

"The furor over Nkrumah's book (*Neo-Colonialism: The Last Stage of Imperialism*) coincided with the crisis on the African continent sparked by the announcement by Ian Smith, the prime minister of Rhodesia, of his country's unilateral declaration of independence (UDI) from Britain.

...Many African governments strongly protested the UDI and criticized Britain for refusing to take more forceful measures against Smith's regime. The ambassador (to the UN) of the moderate Ivory Coast urged African military intervention in Rhodesia, citing the recent alliance of Belgians, Americans, and the British for the so-called humanitarian rescue of white hostages in the Congo.....

Nkrumah joined other African governments in demanding military action against the Salisbury regime but appeared willing to back up his statements with action. He requested authorization from Parliament to form a militia and planned to begin recruitment, warning the population that sacrifices would be necessary.

Nkrumah's threats of military intervention provided an additional grievance to those army officers already plotting a coup against him. Indeed, training maneuvers in preparation for a possible intervention in Rhodesia provided the coup leaders with the pretext for marching their troops to Accra." – (K. Gaines, ibid., pp. 226 – 227).

Besides Nkrumah's determination to send Ghanaian troops to Rhodesia, the soldiers also remembered the Congo crisis in 1960 when Nkrumah sent Ghanaian troops – as a part of a United Nations peace-keeping mission – to help Prime Minister Lumumba who was embroiled in conflict with his enemies who were determined to eliminate him. More than 40 Ghanaian solders were killed in Congo during that time.

Colonel Akwasi Afrifa remembered with bitterness the Ghanaian soldiers who died in Congo and blamed Nkrumah for their deaths; he and his colleagues were determined to prevent that from happening again in the case of Rhodesia. They were not going to Rhodesia. Therefore, they had to overthrow Nkrumah.

Ghana's intervention in Congo was one of the reasons the soldiers, including Afrifa, said they overthrew Nkrumah – who was also Lumumba's friend. The two leaders even secretly signed an agreement in August 1960 to unite their countries under one government.

American leaders knew that Nkrumah's involvement in Congo was risky for him; it would help to mobilise his enemies in the army to stop him from pursuing his "wild" Pan-African ambitions, trying to send them to fight in wars they had "nothing to do with," mainly liberations wars, in countries far away from Ghana.

He also had enemies in a number of African countries whose leaders did not like his Pan-African militancy including his quest for continental unity under one government. Some of them also accused him of sponsoring their opponents to overthrow them in pursuit of his ambition to unite the continent under his leadership.

Therefore, he had a lot of enemies, within and without. Even some of his colleagues in the government suspected there was a plot to overthrow him and advised him not to leave the country during that critical period. Had he stayed in Accra, instead of trying to go to Hanoi, the coup may not have taken place; at least not when it did.

An attempt to overthrow him in his presence, in Accra, could have enabled him to mobilise support among the soldiers who were loyal to him. Some of them are the ones who tried to reinstate him when they launched a counter-coup in which Emmanuel Kotoka was killed at the national airport. That showed he had support among some elements in the army. But he made a fatal decision to leave Ghana to go to Hanoi, as his enemies including American officials rejoiced at his departure and impending downfall:

"As U.S. officials had decided that Nkrumah's support

for Congolese rebels and intelligence operations against rival African governments made him expendable, Nkrumah sought to conciliate Washington, refraining from criticism of America's involvement in Vietnam.

In late January, Ambassador Mahoney returned for the dedication of the Volta hydroelectric dam (it was officially opened by Nkrumah on 22 January 1966). Mahoney, who had departed the previous summer, was replaced by Franklin Williams, an African American civil rights attorney and former Peace Corps official. Williams was an acquaintance of Nkrumah's from their days as classmates at Lincoln University. At the Volta dedication, Williams and Mahoney watched as Nkrumah praised the United States for upholding its share of the responsibility for the development of Africa.

With the failure of attempts to smooth over tensions with the United States, Batsa advised Nkrumah not to leave for Hanoi (Kofi Batsa was the editor of the *Spark*, the organ of the ruling Convention People's Party). Against the advice of several aides, on February 21, 1966, Nkrumah boarded a jet bound for Beijing and then Hanoi while guards, aides, ministers, and diplomats at the airport reportedly speculated on the likelihood and timing of the coup. Three days later, Nkrumah arrived in Beijing, where Chou En Lai informed Nkrumah that his government had been overthrown by mutinous members of the army and police forces.

Nkrumah's absence had provided his enemies the chance to strike." – (K. Gaines, ibid., pp. 227 – 228).

The coup was well-planned and well-coordinated. The coup makers seized the radio station but after stiff resistance by the soldiers there. However, the resistance did not last very long.

The radio station is usually the first target enabling coup makers to go on the air to announce they have overthrown the government. That has been the pattern in

African countries on a continent where about 100 military coups have taken place since independence in the sixties.

The soldiers also captured the Ghana national airport, another key facility. Telecommunications installations were also seized.

Although the coup had the support of a number of army officers, there were those who were against it even when it was going on. They included the head of the army, Major General Charles Barwah, who was killed during the military operations to seize power. He resisted and that cost him his life.

Nkrumah's guards at his official resistance, Flagstaff House, also resisted the coup and fought hard against the soldiers who were trying to overthrow the government. But in general, coordination of the operation by the coup makers was successful from the beginning:

"Early on the morning of February 23, a convoy of six hundred troops in thirty-five vehicles traveled south from Tamale. After 150 miles they were met by two officers from Kumasi, Major Akwasi Afrifa and Colonel Kotoka. Afrifa, who had contemplated plots against Nkrumah after returning from the Congo in 1962 and again in November 1964, took command, and the convoy continued the remaining 250 miles to the coast. Kotoka traveled ahead to Accra to notify General A.K. Ocran and Police Commissioner John Harlley that the coup could proceed as planned for 4:00 A.M. the next day.

That night, the police began arresting Nkrumah's ministers, members of Parliament, and any CPP officials it could find. By dawn of February 24, Major Afrifa's column had reached Accra. Detachments of troops easily gained control of the radio station, airport, and cable office.

The commander of the Ghanaian army, Major General Charles Barwah, was killed when he resisted the coup. The president's guard in Flagstaff House put up a fierce though brief resistance.

The coup leaders installed General Joseph Ankrah, whom Nkrumah had dismissed in June 1965, at the head of the National Liberation Council. Ankrah informed the nation of the coup, citing Nkrumah's autocratic rule and corruption, the squandering of Ghana's reserves into massive external debts by ruinous policies, the 'adventurism' of a communist-leaning foreign policy, and political interference in the army and police. At 6:00 A.M., Ankrah announced over Ghanaian radio that 'the myth of Kwame Nkrumah is broken.'" – (Ibid., p. 228).

The new military rulers were so hostile to everything Nkrumah had done and stood for that they even expelled the African freedom fighters who had been welcomed by Nkrumah and found safe haven in Ghana under his leadership. As Kevin Gaines states:

"Freedom fighters from throughout the African continent who were receiving training at the African Affairs Center under the guidance of T. Ras Makonnen and Chinese advisers were deported, reportedly deposited by several planeloads in Dar es Salaam." – ((Ibid, p. 234).

One of the people who provided a written eyewitness account of what took place during the coup was Preston King, an African American living in Accra. It was a very bloody coup, contrary to what the new military rulers and American officials claimed, that it was bloodless; a claim also made by Robert Smith who once served as the American ambassador to Ghana – he also served in Nigeria – and was a veteran of African affairs at the US State Department. As he stated:

"They had had enough and Nkrumah was overthrown in a coup. They did this in relatively bloodless fashion.
While Nkrumah was in the air flying to Red China, he

was met on the ground in Peking by his Chinese host and it fell to them to inform him that he was no longer Head of State in the Republic of Ghana. So that was a fascinating time in a fascinating country....

Nkrumah dropped the straw that broke the camel's back, so to speak, in that he published a new book called *Neo-Colonialism (The Last State of Imperialism)*...which was simply outrageous. It accused the United States of every sin imaginable to man. We were blamed for everything in the world.

The book was so bad that I remember the then Assistant Secretary, G. Mennen Williams, called me up and gave me that book and said, 'Bob, I know this is bad. I don't know how bad. I want you to take it home tonight and read it. You're not going to get any sleep and I apologize for that, but on my desk, by eight o'clock tomorrow morning, I've got to have a written summary of this because I have called the Ghanaian ambassador in at ten o'clock tomorrow morning. We're going to protest this book.'

There had already been advance publicity so we knew it was bad, but we hadn't had our hands on a copy. And it was everything we feared it would be. It was awful.

And the next morning – of course, he had me in on this meeting as the note taker – a lovely, old man, Michael Ribiero, was the Ghanaian ambassador. Hated Nkrumah privately, but was a good soldier trying to put the best face on this, a career officer in their foreign service and very respected here and in Ghana.

Governor Williams, of course, was a relatively mild-mannered man. I had never heard Soapy Williams raise his voice until that conversation. Neither have I ever heard an ambassador get a tongue lashing like Ribiero got from Assistant Secretary Williams that morning. He, unfortunately, tried a couple times to interrupt the governor when he was making a point. He had my notes in front of him. And at one point, when Ribiero interrupted him, said, 'Just a minute, Mr. Ambassador, don't interrupt me. I'm not through.' And he continued to go on.

He was raising his voice. He was shaking his finger in the ambassador's face. And it was a very painful, hour-long interview. To put it mildly, he protested vigorously the contents and publication of this book.

I think the publication of that book might also have contributed in a material way to his overthrow shortly thereafter. The Ghanaian people, as I say, did not share Nkrumah's views on many things. The Ghanaians have always had a warm relationship with the United States. Nkrumah simply, as the British say, went round the bend and they got a belly full of it and booted him out of office....

It was tragic for us to sit back and see Nkrumah running this country into the ground the way he did, and it was happening right before our eyes. When I went there in 1965, there were still a number of hotels in downtown Accra that served excellent meals. I remember having lunch on the patio of one of those hotels. By the time I went back years later as ambassador, none of them could do that. There was nothing to be had. There was nothing to eat, et cetera. And almost all of it was attributed to Nkrumah's madness. I don't mean that literally." – (Ambassador Robert P. Smith, interviewed by Charles Stuart Kennedy, 28 February 1989, *The Association for Diplomatic Studies and Training, Foreign Affairs Oral History Project*, pp. 13 – 14).

Ambassador Smith was one of the American officials who were glad Nkrumah was overthrown in a coup he claimed was "relatively bloodless."

Hundreds of people were killed in the coup. As Gaines states concerning the eyewitness account by King:

"Before dawn on February 24, Preston King was jolted by an explosion, followed by the crackling of rifle and small-arms fire. He awakened his wife, Hazel, and they set out from their residence near the university (University of Ghana at Legon, about 7 miles northeast of Accra) to investigate. They drove their Volkswagen Beetle through darkness toward the highway leading to Accra, where the firing seemed to originate. The sound of gunfire as they approached Flagstaff House convinced them that a coup was on.

They stopped behind some empty army transport trucks, hearing persistent submachine gun and rifle fire. Mustering the nerve to venture closer to the shooting, the Kings were met by a young soldier, who warned of 'trouble ahead.'

The Kings wisely retreated and decided to visit Ana Livia Cordero, who lived nearby. It was still dark, about five o'clock in the morning. The gunfire crackled on, and a fire illuminated the gated entrance of Flagstaff House....

Careful to avoid soldiers posted at checkpoints, Preston King decided to return to Flagstaff House to assess the situation there. By afternoon, the shooting had subsided, with no guards visible along the road from the south. Independence Avenue was littered with the wreckage of smashed vehicles and army trucks.

The entrance to Flagstaff was blocked by two vehicles, a small sedan and a large sand-dumping truck. The front of the car was riddled with bullets, the windshield gone. A door hung open, with a bloodied shoe sitting outside it. The bodies of a man, a woman, and a child remained in the car, civilians caught in the crossfire. The truck's only sign of damage was a single bullet hole in the windshield.

The southern-facing wall of Flagstaff House was pockmarked by bullet holes, with several gaping holes evidently made by grenade explosions. As King recalled, 'Suddenly, there was a tremendous explosion behind me,' at the barracks for security personnel across the road. King hit the ground.

He heard doors slamming and then the ominous sound

of 'evenly spaced and deliberate rifle shots.' Near the gate sat a riddled Ghana Airways bus. It had been raked by machine gun fire while traveling past Flagstaff House toward the airport that morning. One of the flight hostesses inside had been killed, and many of the rest had been wounded. King learned that several university workers had died in the same way.

Inside the main gate, in front of Flagstaff House, two army trucks were smoldering, hit by mortar shells. Other trucks and vehicles had been damaged in the fighting. The main gate still stood, though surrounded by signs of carnage. Abandoned rifles, submachine guns, helmets, and shoes were strewn about. Blood patches dotted the road like the painterly handiwork of death itself, the grisly scene further adorned by broken glass and a lingering haze of smoke. A solitary, overlooked corpse of a soldier lay in a trench. No one was in sight." – (Ibid., pp. 228 – 229, 230).

There was violence even on the campus of the University of Ghana, Legon, where students who were members of Nkrumah's ruling Convention People's Party (CPP) were attacked by other students. Even some faculty members were targeted by the soldiers. One of them was the renowned Ghanaian philosopher, Dr. Willie E. Abraham, the author of *The Mind of Africa*, who was also Nkrumah's friend and court philosopher. As Gaines states:

"As King decided to rejoin his wife, a truckload of soldiers brandishing weapons raced by. The sound of gunfire resumed, this time from deeper within Flagstaff House. As King passed the car and the truck, a little boy appeared, whispering that a dead man was inside the truck. Peering in, King saw a young man, doubled over in his seat, a bullet hole in his temple. 'I climbed on the running board to make sure he was dead. The boy who had seen him now was repeating in a muted voice, may he rest in peace.'

Any further curiosity dampened by the sight of the dead man, King headed back to Cordero's house, where he found Hazel. Preston and Hazel King returned home to Legon, where students lost no time in persecuting the new regime's enemies. Students mobbed a Chinese student and rounded up student members of the CPP for similar beatings, ransacking their rooms for good measure. The once-mighty Willie Abraham, vice chancellor pro tem of the university and Nkrumah's court philosopher, was arrested and detained.

The university hastily pledged its support to the new regime without consulting the faculty. 'Everyone is assuring the new regime of everyone's support,' King observed dryly. Such declarations of unanimity struck him as being just as dubious as those only recently staged by the ousted regime.

In subsequent days, King gathered information about what had transpired. Only a fragment of the army had taken part in the coup. No more than seven hundred troops stationed five hundred miles north of Accra had been involved.

The troops, under the command of Major Afrifa and Colonel Kotoka, were incited by rumors that Nkrumah intended to to have them fight in Rhodesia and Vietnam and that the Russians were taking over Ghana.

The troops were divided into three groups. One seized control of the airport and then headed for the Accra garrison. Other detachment of troops took control of the castle at Osu – formerly Christianborg Castle – and the Broadcasting House before moving on to the siege at Flagstaff House. The soldiers then demolished the quarters of security officers, looting the residences, beating and raping the residents, and shooting those who resisted.

The initial attack on Flagstaff House cost the rebel troops twenty men killed and many more wounded.

The coup leaders expected forces loyal to Nkrumah to

arrive from Ho and Sekondi-Takoradi to resist, but these troops never came.

A separate attack on a government munitions facility lasted for two days, with seventeen attackers and twelve defenders killed.

Based on his investigations, King estimated the number of dead at least two hundred, basing that figure on a coroner's estimate. King regarded the initial reports of a bloodless coup as 'part of the old style of lying mercilessly.'

The government had forbidden morgue workers and pathologists to divulge casualty figures in an effort to safeguard the legitimacy of its action. In any event, the toll was high, with many people killed inside Flagstaff House. Others, mostly security personnel, were killed in the flats nearby while sleeping. Many civilians, including stewards and other workers, had been caught in the crossfire.

While King's estimate was more conservative than those of other expatriates and later Nkrumah's, it contradicted Ghanaian and U.S. press reports of a bloodless coup. That characterization was, in fact, the official American version of events, encouraged by Ambassador (Franklin) Williams and the State Department in anticipation of the allegations of slaughter by the nation's political adversaries." – (Ibid., pp. 230 – 231).

The extent to which American officials and the American press went to defend the coup, claiming it was bloodless, shows how much they supported the new military rulers in spite of the large number of people – including innocent civilians – they killed just to seize power. It also shows how much they hated Nkrumah; and how they did everything they could to help the soldiers burnish their image and justify the coup as they continued to demonise Nkrumah.

The new military rulers even questioned Nkrumah's citizenship and parentage, spreading rumours to tarnish his image and cast doubts on his commitment to the wellbeing of Ghana and Ghanaians.

Even the freedom fighters who had fled from persecution in their home countries which were still under white minority rule and sought refuge in Ghana were demonised by the new military rulers. It was if the new rulers were saying the liberation struggle itself against colonial regimes on the continent was unjustified. For a country that had been in the forefront of the struggle to liberate the African continent, and which had provided sanctuary to those who fled from oppression under white minority rule, it was a complete reversal of policy. Nkrumah may have had his own faults, but supporting the freedom fighters to help them liberate their countries was not one of them. Also, the new rulers themselves did some of the same bad things they accused Nkrumah of doing:

"The Preventive Detention Act, often cited as evidence of Nkrumah's dictatorial methods, proved as useful to the NLC (National Liberation Council) as it been to the previous government. The council freed twelve hundred prisoners imprisoned by Nkrumah, clearing the jails for as many members of Parliament, high-ranking ministers, security men, advisers, and journalists as could be arrested. The CPP was banned outright. According to King and contrary to press reports, none of the mass demonstrations hailing the coup and its leaders was spontaneous. As before the coup, they were staged, this time by the NLC.

King correctly predicted that the military regime would terminate the Nkrumah government's costly prestige, propaganda, and anticolonial liberation projects. Freedom fighters from other parts of the continent were expelled. Frank Robertson (an African American living in Ghana) took on himself the responsibility and cost of arranging the safe passage to Tanzania of more than a dozen freedom fighters." – (Ibid., p. 231).

When the Organisation of African Unity (OAU) was founded in Addis Ababa, Ethiopia, in May 1963, by the African heads of state and government, Tanzania was chosen to be the headquarters of all the African liberation movements under the auspices of the OAU Liberation Committee based in Dar es Salaam under the stewardship of President Julius Nyerere. Therefore, it was the right place for the African freedom fighters to go after they were expelled from Ghana by the country's new military rulers.

They also were sent to a country where Nkrumah was held in very high esteem. After Nkrumah was overthrown, Tanzania under the leadership of Nyerere refused to recognise Ghana's successive governments including the civilian government of Prime Minister Kofi Busia which, like the NLC, was virulently anti-Nkrumaist. President Kenneth Kaunda of Zambia also refused to recognise the leaders who assumed power after Nkrumah was overthrown and publicly said even in the seventies that the Ghana's legitimate president was still Dr. Kwame Nkrumah.

I remember when Ghana's minister of foreign affairs, Victor Owusu who served under Busia, came to Tanzania in 1969 to explain his government's position on Nkrumah and obviously to seek recognition for his government. His visit was covered by Tanzania's main newspaper, the *Daily News*. But he was snubbed by the government and only met with a junior officer from the ministry of foreign affairs.

Even after Busia was overthrown in January 1972, Tanzania still refused to recognise Ghana's new military government of Colonel Ignatius Acheampong. And when Ghana's permanent representative to the United Nations rose to address the UN General Assembly, the Tanzanian delegation walked out.

Kofi Busia, 11 July 1913 - 28 August 1978

Tanzania also honoured Nkrumah in June 1974 when the Sixth Pan-African Congress was held in Dar es Salaam in a hall named after him during that time. It was the first such conference to be held on Africa soil. The last one before that, which is also the most well-known, was held in Manchester, England, in 1945.

President Nyerere, who was the main speaker at the Sixth Pan-African Congress, opened the conference in Nkrumah Hall on the campus of the University of Dar es Salaam. It is the largest conference hall on the campus and the most prestigious. All major conferences at the university, including international gatherings, are held in Nkrumah Hall; it is also one of the most prestigious and one of the largest conference halls in the entire country.

There is also Nkrumah Teacher Training College in Tanzania and Kwame Nkrumah University in Zambia.

Attempts to tarnish or erase Nkrumah's legacy have failed. The National Liberation Council made the first attempt to do so. It launched a vicious campaign to smear his name within hours after he was overthrown.

Ignatius Acheampong
23 September 1931 - 16 June 1979

The coup which ended the political career of one of Africa's most prominent and most influential leaders of international stature who is also acknowledged as the father of Pan-Africanism also produced some of the most memorable eyewitness accounts of what happened on the day Nkrumah was overthrown:

"(Preston) King wrote his eyewitness account of the Ghana coup within a week of the events...and mailed copies to family and friends in the States.

King's boldness and curiosity produced an account that both supplements and contradicts aspects of official Ghanaian and U.S. versions of the coup....

For anyone living near Flagstaff House, the terror of the fighting, looting, harassment, and threatened detention by troops made for a harrowing experience....Those expatriates closely aligned with Nkrumah, such as Geoffrey Bing (a British and Ghana's attorney-general under Nkrumah), and H.M. Basner, were detained and faced mistreatment at the hands of troops....

Another expatriate, Sylvia Boone, wrote an informative and insightful account of the coup while in Ghana three months after the event...and...likened the coup to the day of Kennedy's assassination, a moment eternally suspended in memory.

Amid speculation as to which minister would replace Nkrumah, Boone traveled with a friend to the Trans Volta region. There, market and harvest celebrations continued without interruption or even awareness of the violence in the capital....

For a couple of days, Boone recalled, a shocked silence prevailed in Accra as people waited to see what would happen....Mobility was restricted by checkpoints, and police were harassing the public with frequent searches. Hundreds of people were being arrested. Accra was abuzz with stories of escapes and near escapes and of soldiers' menace and capriciousness. An unnamed African American woman's house had been robbed by soldiers, who also threatened to rape her. In the end, they decided to spare her...

The NLC raided the offices of Flagstaff House, destroying many of Nkrumah's government records, and bonfires of books, pamphlets and records associated with the CPP and its expatriate supporters were a common sight....E. Franklin Frazier's library, donated to Ghana in an act of Pan-African idealism, was reportedly destroyed in the rampage....

Accusations of his personal corruption were exaggerated. Their propagandistic intent was to undermine the source of Nkrumah's popularity among Africans and African descended peoples in the West: Nkrumah's use of Ghana's resources for its diplomatic and foreign policy objectives of anticolonialism, material and military aid to nationalist parties, and continental unity.

The widespread violence, rapes, beatings, vandalism, looting, and detentions that had occurred in the aftermath of the coup suggested that Ambassador (Franklin) Williams's claim, to a colleague at the United Nations, that the coup was carried out in a 'sensitive, civilized fashion' was at best premature.

....The ultimate purpose ...of the coup...was never to liberate...the people of Ghana.....

After the coup, few African American expatriates remained in Africa. Although Tanzania under the leadership of Julius Nyerere replaced Ghana as the leading exponent of African liberation and continental unity, only Bill Sutherland (an African American) among the Ghanaian expatriates emigrated there.

....Dispersed by the coup, most of the African American expatriates returned to the United States...." – (Ibid., pp. 231 – 232, 239 – 240, 244).

Although the soldiers had grievances against Nkrumah, that was not the main reason they overthrew him. The CIA exploited whatever differences Nkrumah's opponents had with him in order to overthrow him. However, the soldiers highlighted their grievances with Nkrumah, including his decision to send Ghanaian troops to Congo in 1960 and his decision to send them to Rhodesia next, as a major reason for the coup.

Also, grievances against Nkrumah among many people in Ghana in general were cited by American leaders as the reason for his downfall. But that was not the reason the CIA masterminded his ouster. Had Nkrumah's "despotic" rule been the primary reason the American government authorised the CIA to engineer his downfall, the same American government should have done the same thing to other African leaders who were also dictators. Instead, the United States left them alone and even protected those who served American interests; for example, Mobutu and Jomo Kenyatta. In fact, Mobutu and Kenyatta were some of the African leaders who were on the CIA payroll.

The suffering of Africans under dictatorship and the economic hardship they endure under their governments have never the concern of American leaders. Nkrumah was more authoritarian than dictatorial; so were most African leaders of that era besides outright dictators such as Dr.

Hastings Kamuzu Banda of Malawi and Joseph Mobutu – later renamed Mobutu Sese Seko – of Zaire.

Therefore, it is simply not true that the United States government wanted Nkrumah out of power because it was concerned about the wellbeing of the people of Ghana who were, supposedly, suffering under Nkrumah's brutal dictatorship and bad economic policies.

If the plight of Africans really bothered them, and if it was on their policy agenda or if it was one of their priorities, they would have intervened in South Africa and would have exerted enormous pressure on the apartheid regime to force it to abandon its racist policies when black people and other non-whites were suffering racial oppression at the hands of the white minority rulers. Or they would have overthrown Mobutu. Instead, they protected him as much as they did the apartheid regime in South Africa. But Nkrumah had to go. Why?

He had to go because he was a threat to American interests in Africa, not just in Ghana. His close ties to Eastern-bloc countries, especially the Soviet Union, as well as the People's Republic of China which was not a member of the Eastern bloc led by the Soviets but was communist nonetheless, were not viewed favourably by the Americans and other Westerners who saw Africa as their own sphere of influence. They saw Nkrumah as providing an opening for communists to "penetrate" and "dominate" Africa.

His socialist policies threatened American economic interests in Africa. The United States feared others on the continent would follow his example.

Also, his strong support for the liberation movements against the white minority regimes in Africa and his call for continental unification equally angered the United States. The white minority rulers were allies of the United States and other Western powers who supported them as much as the United States did. Ending white minority rule in the countries of southern Africa was perceived by the

United States and other Western powers as a threat to their geopolitical and strategic interests on the continent; so was Nkrumah's advocacy of continental unity.

They also saw the white minorities in Africa as an integral part of Western civilisation on the "dark" continent and as their natural allies because they were their kith and kin.

Also, the United States and her allies did not want to see a strong, united Africa because, once united, it would be able to protect its interests and challenge Western powers in the international arena. No African leader represented that threat more than Nkrumah did. As Nyerere stated in his speech in Accra, Ghana, on 6 March 1997 on the 40th anniversary of Ghana's independence:

""'Nkrumah was the great crusader of African unity. He wanted the Accra Summit of 1965 to establish a union government for the whole of independent Africa. But we failed....We did not even discuss a mechanism for pursuing the objective of a politically united Africa. We had a Liberation Committee already. We should have at least had a Unity Committee or undertaken to establish one. We did not. And after Kwame Nkrumah was removed from the African scene, nobody took up the challenge again."

Nkrumah was an embodiment of the African personality in a way most African leaders were not. He lived African and died African. He made Ghanaians proud of who and what they were. He also made other Africans proud of who and what they were. His ouster by the United States only enhanced his stature among his fellow Africans across the continent and elsewhere. He was one of the most influential Africans who ever lived.

In a BBC survey in December 1999, Nkrumah stood out among all African leaders because of his influence and contributions to the struggle for African liberation and unity. As he stated on the day when the flag of the new nation of Ghana went up at midnight, on independence day, 6 March 1957:

"We are going to see that we create our own African personality and identity. We again rededicate ourselves in the struggle to emancipate other countries in Africa, for, our independence is meaningless unless it is linked up with the total liberation of the African continent."

His message resonated across the continent for decades, and it still does today. According to BBC World Service, 14 September 2000:

"Last December, BBC listeners in Africa voted Kwame Nkrumah, the first head of an independent Ghana, their 'Man of the Millennium.'"

This is not to overlook the great opposition he faced and the jubilation that greeted his downfall, especially in the capital Accra and in other urban centres where the people were most affected by economic hardship because of high living expenses and scarcity of goods when the economy declined. Many urban residents were also some of the most strident critics of Nkrumah's one-party rule which stifled dissent. And they exploded with joy when he was overthrown. As Jerry Rawlings, who was an admirer of Nkrumah but not an Nkrumaist and who himself became president of Ghana, stated in an interview with CCTV Africa, "Faces of Africa, Kwame Nkrumah: A Story of Vision and Tragedy," December 2014, on what he witnessed on the day Nkrumah was overthrown:

"I have never seen such an explosion of joy."

It is true there was great dissatisfaction with his rule for various reasons. But what is overlooked by many people is the American involvement in the coup and the role the

CIA played in masterminding his ouster.

What is critical to understand is that even if Nkrumah did not face strong opposition to his rule, which the CIA exploited to overthrow him, the United States still would have plotted against him in order to get rid of him because the policies he pursued threatened American interests in Africa.

Nkrumah was the most prominent African leader who was ousted in a military coup in the sixties. Nyerere and Sékou Touré survived coup attempts. The United States and other Western powers were disappointed that the two leaders had not been removed from office in military coups which came to characterise transfer of power across the continent during that turbulent decade.

Even years before the coup that ousted Nkrumah from office, it was clear he was not trusted by the Americans. They were very concerned about his ideological orientation which they felt threatened the interests of the United States in Africa, especially at a time when socialism had a great appeal among most of the leaders of the newly independent states across the continent as the best way to achieve rapid economic development through central planning; with a few exceptions such as the Ivory Coast, Malawi, and Kenya.

But even in Kenya, there was an acknowledgment of the virtues of the traditional way of life and its egalitarian values similar to those of socialism among a few leaders such as Tom Mboya who was the minister of economic planning and development under President Jomo Kenyatta. But it was Nkrumah who set the pace and who became one of the strongest proponents of socialism in Africa besides Nyerere. As Professor Ali Mazrui states in his book, *Towards a Pax Africana: A Study of Ideology and Ambition*:

"A former Labour Party Colonial Secretary, Arthur Creech Jones, once remarked that he did not consider it the duty of that office to impose socialism on the colonies.¹ In the case of Africa it has now turned out that such an imposition was not necessary.

No ideology commands respect so widely in Africa as the ideology of 'socialism' – though, as in Europe, it is socialism of different shades.

In Guinea and Mali a Marxist framework of reasoning is evident. In Ghana Leninism was wedded to notions of traditional collectivism. In Tanzania the concept of *Ujamaa*, derived from the sense of community of tribal life, is being radicalized into an assertion of modern socialism. In Kenya there is a dilemma between establishing socialism and Africanizing the capitalism which already exists. In Nigeria, Senegal and Uganda some kind of allegiance is being paid to the ideal of social justice in situations with a multi-party background.

There are places, of course, where no school of socialism is propagated at all. But outside the Ivory Coast there is little defiant rejection of the idea of 'socialism' in former colonial Africa.²" – (Ali A. Mazrui, *Towards a Pax Africana: A Study of Ideology and Ambition*, London: Weidenfield & Nicolson, 1967, p. 97. See also, cited by A.A. Mazrui, A. Creech Jones, "The Labour Party and Colonial Policy," in *New Fabian Colonial Essays*, London: Hogarth, 1959, pp. 21 – 23; William H. Friedland and Carl G. Rosberg, Jr., eds., *African Socialism*, Palo Alto, California: Stanford University Press, 1964; Kenneth W. Grundy, "Marxism-Leninism: The Mali Approach," *International Journal*, Vol. XVII, No. 3, Summer 1962; L. Gray Cowan, "Guinea," in Gwendolen M. Carter, ed., *African One-Party States*, Ithaca, New York: Cornell University Press, 1962; Kenneth W. Grundy, "Nkrumah's Theory of Underdevelopment: An Analysis of Recurrent Themes," *World Politics*, Vol. XV, No. 3, April 1963; Kenya Government Paper, *African Socialism and its Application to Planning in Kenya*, 1965; *Africa Report*, Special issue on African Socialism, VIII, May 1963).

Central planning was a common strategy which almost all African countries shared in their quest for economic development; an aspiration even President John F. Kennedy seemed to share with African leaders who were anxious to transform and develop their economies by mobilising resources under central command instead of leaving the invisible hand of the free market to do most of the work as is the case in capitalist countries. As Paul E. Sigmund states in *The Ideologies of the Developing Nations*:

"Economists of a wide variety of political and economic beliefs accept the need for a rationalized development through expert planning. When the Kennedy Administration reorganized the U.S. foreign-aid program in the Agency for International Development (AID) in 1961, it indicated that greater U.S. assistance would be forthcoming to those countries presenting an integrated program or plan of economic development. It recognized that in countries where per capita income is under $100 a year – and this applies to areas containing 50 per cent of the world's population – the transition from traditional and subsistence economies to an expanding and developing dynamic economic system must be made by government planning, whether it is described as socialism or not." – (Paul E. Sigmund, Jr., ed., *The Ideologies of the Developing Nations*, New York: Frederick A. Praeger, 1963, p. 18).

Socialism seemed to have even more legitimacy in the Africa context as an ideological alternative to capitalism because of the strong kinship ties in traditional societies across the continent which have evolved from the extended family, nurturing virtues of cooperation, communal living and the imperative need to help each other.

Nyerere became the strongest and most articulate exponent of African socialism, which he called *ujamaa* in Kiswahili, meaning familyhood. Proponents of scientific socialism dismissed it as being "unscientific" because it was not derived from the tenets of Marxism-Leninism, which Nkrumah espoused as did a few other African leaders including Sékou Touré, and Modibo Keita of Mali, all of whom were also Nyerere's ideological compatriots, especially as ardent Pan-Africanists committed to African liberation and unity.

Yet, in spite of all the criticism, African socialism or ujamaa *was* socialism, nonetheless. As Nyerere, who was not a doctrinaire socialist like those who espoused Marxist dogma, stated in his book, *Freedom and Socialism*:

"There is no theology of socialism. There is, however, an apparent tendency among certain socialists to try and establish a new religion – a religion of socialism itself. This is usually called 'scientific socialism' and the works of Marx and Lenin are regarded as the holy writ in the light of which all other thoughts and actions have to be judged....Its proponents are often most anxious to decry religion as the 'opium of the people,' and they present their beliefs as 'science.' Yet they talk and act in the same manner as the most rigid of theologians....

Marx was a great thinker....But he was not God....It is no part of the job of a socialist (today) to worry about whether not his actions or proposals are in accordance with what Marx or Lenin wrote, and it is a waste of time and energy to spend hours – if not months and years – trying to prove that what you have decided is objectively necessary is really in accordance with their teachings. The task of a socialist is to think out for himself the best way of achieving desired ends under the conditions which exist now....

We in Africa...are in danger of being bemused by this new theology, and therefore of trying to solve our problems according to what the priests of Marxism say is what Marx said or meant....Africa's conditions are very different from those of the Europe in which Marx and Lenin wrote and worked. To talk as if these thinkers provided all the answers to our problems, or as if Marx invented socialism, is to reject both the humanity of Africa and the universality of socialism. Marx did contribute a great deal to socialist thought. But socialism did not begin with him, nor can it end in constant reinterpretation of his writings....

Despite the existence of a few feudalistic communities, traditional Tanzanian society had many socialist characteristics. The people did not call themselves socialists, and they were not socialists by deliberate design. But all the people were workers, there was no living off the sweat of others. There was no very great difference in the amount of goods available to the different members of the society. All these are socialist characteristics. Despite the low level of material progress, traditional African society was in practice organized on a basis which was in accordance with socialist principles.

These conditions still prevail over large areas of Tanzania – and indeed in many other parts of Africa. Even in our urban areas, the social expectation of sharing what you have with your kinsfolk is still very strong – and causes great problems for individuals! These things have nothing to do with Marx; the people have never heard of him. Yet they provide a basis on which modern socialism can be built. To reject this base is to accept the idea that Africa has nothing to contribute to the march of mankind; it is to argue that the only way progress can be achieved in Africa is if we reject our own past and impose on ourselves the doctrines of some other society.

Nor would it be very scientific to reject Africa's past when trying to build socialism in Africa. For, scientific socialism means finding out all the facts in a particular situation, regardless of whether you like them or not, or whether they fit in with preconceived ideas. It means analysing these facts, and then working out solutions to the problems you are concerned with in the light of these facts, and of the objectives you are trying to achieve. This is what Marx did in Europe in the middle of the nineteenth century; if he had lived in Sukumaland, Masailand, or Ruvuma, he would have written a different book than *Das Kapital*, but he could have been just as scientific and just as socialist....

A scientist works to discover the truth. He does not claim to know it, nor is he seeking to discover truth as revealed – which is the job of the theologian. A scientist works on the basis of the knowledge which has been accumulated empirically, and which is held to be true until new experience demonstrates otherwise, or demonstrates a superior truth which takes precedence in particular situations.

A really scientific socialist would therefore start his analysis of the problems of a particular society from the standpoint of that society....(and) could do all this with or without a knowledge and understanding of Marx and Lenin – or for that matter Saint-Simon, Owen or Laski....If he tries to use any of these...philosophies as a gospel according to which he must work out solutions he will go wrong. There is no substitute for his own hard work and hard thinking." – (Julius K. Nyerere, *Freedom and Socialism: A Selection from Writings and Speeches 1965 – 1967*, Dar es Salaam: Oxford University Press, 1968, pp. 14, 15, 16, and 17).

Nyerere's version of socialism, *ujamaa*, not just the scientific socialism of leaders such as Nkrumah and Sékou Touré, was also anathema to the West. Whatever version it was, or whatever name or names the people in different African countries called it (in Zambia, it was called 'humanism' and in Tanzania, 'ujamaa') as long as it was socialism, it was perceived to be a threat to Western interests in Africa because it was a credible counter-thesis, and counter-force, to capitalism espoused by the West.

13 April 1922 – 14 October 1999

In fact, most African countries which pursued socialism did not have very good relations with the United States and other Western countries. They were perceived to be "friends of our enemies": the Soviet Union and other socialist countries in Eastern Europe as well as socialist

East Germany and the People's Republic of China.

If the leaders of those countries were swept out of power in military coups like Nkrumah was, it would have been very good news for the United States and other Western countries.

American leaders, CIA agents and State Department officials including ambassadors who dealt with Africa were also arrogant and racist, clearly demonstrated by their attitude towards Nkrumah, Nyerere and Sékou Touré, leaders they did not like because of the ideological and political differences they had with them.

Their condescending attitude towards these leaders and Africans in general, and the disparaging remarks they made about them, obviously played a major role in the formulation of American policy towards Africa.

Americans did not consider Africans to be their equal intellectually and in terms of sophistication; an assessment that can not be reconciled with reality in the case of highly intellectual and knowledgeable leaders such as Nyerere and Nkrumah and can be nothing other than a product of racial arrogance on their part and other Westerners who had very low regard for Africans in general.

They also believed African leaders were misleading their people in almost every conceivable way – spanning the economic and socio-political spectrum.

Besides President Lyndon Johnson who was in office when Nkrumah was overthrown, his predecessor, John F. Kennedy, was also suspicious of Nkrumah as someone who was taking Africa in the wrong direction.

Compounding the problem for Nkrumah was the fact that most African leaders did not like him. They were concerned about his subversive activities in their countries where – they believed – he wanted to institute governments sympathetic to his cause and which would support him in his quest for continental leadership. He supported dissidents from a number of countries across the continent. Nkrumah's critics felt that he was megalomaniac and wanted to rule Africa.

American leaders exploited all those fears to their advantage which seemed to justify their own assessment of Nkrumah as someone who could not be trusted. Other prominent African leaders – Sékou Touré and Nyerere – fared no better in the perception of Americans. As Professor Larry Grubbs of Georgia State University states in his book, *Secular Missionaries: Americans and African Development in the 1960s*:

"If Africans lacked emotional stability and maturity, their passionate attachment to novel concepts and ideologies, or political causes such as the liberation of Southern Africa from colonialism and apartheid, need not be seriously engaged at an intellectual level. One scholar noted that 'the emergence of African states has not been universally received with respect for the integrity of Africans,' as Westerners at times dismiss African nationalism 'as little more than grotesque comedy.'[51]

U.S. Intelligence analysts considered Pan-Africanism 'a mystical concept, glorifying racial kinship and the African personality and culture' whose 'chief target is 'neocolonialism'"[52]....

When asked by President Kennedy if Nkrumah was a 'Marxist,' Ambassador William Mahoney declared Ghana's leader 'a badly confused and immature person who is not quite sure of what he wants except that he wants to lead all of Africa.'[54]

African critics, too, questioned Nkrumah's sanity, often to flatter Americans. Senghor told Kennedy that the Ghanaian leader 'required the attentions of a psychiatrist' to cure him of his stupendous dreams of leading Africa and his absence of principles.[55]

As for Guinea's nationalist leader, Sékou Touré, American observers repeatedly belittled his economic decisions, and a Central Intelligence Agency report insisted he lacked 'any grasp of the economy and how it functions, even less of development and how it is achieved.'

While his long rule over Guinea certainly failed to produce great economic growth, Touré did devote three books of over 1,000 pages to discussion of socialism and development." – (Larry Grubbs, *Secular Missionaries: Americans and African Development in the 1960s*, Amherst, Massachusetts: University of Massachusetts Press, 2009, pp. 155, and 156).

Grubbs goes on state:

"The main American concerns seemed to have less to do with the credentials of the African leaders than the ideology they espoused or specific policy disagreements.[56] U.S. Officials believed it would be difficult to speak with Touré about details of the aid he had received from the Communist Bloc not only because of his secretiveness but also because, as a White House aide put it, 'apparently Touré himself is totally ignorant about foreign assistance to Guinea, whether it be Bloc or non-Bloc – he simply does not and will not understand it.'[57]

Attwood's successor in Conakry reported 'Touré's unhappiness over the US aid program in Guinea,' though he claimed 'that the issue is being resolved' and that 'the major problem...is educating Touré' on how U.S. aid works.[58]

Julius Nyerere, according to an American diplomat in Tanganyika, though a good political leader, had proven a 'poor administrator' who 'has no head for complex economic development programs.'[59] By the mid-1960s the CIA regarded him as 'enigmatic.'

At a time when Tanzania courted Communist China's support for the construction of a railroad that would permit Zambia to transport goods without going through white-ruled Rhodesia, Nyerere became increasingly less identified with the West. CIA analysts sneered at his 'newly-found mission as the prime mover in the 'liberation' of southern Africa,' as well as his efforts to help Congolese rebels gain access to 'Communist arms' in their struggle against the American-backed regime.

The United States provided a small $6 million annual aid program, and 'the Peace Corps largely staffs Tanganyikan secondary schools,' yet Nyerere complained the volunteers spread anti-government propaganda.

Speculating that he now believed the Americans would not help him fight colonialism and apartheid, 'and that Communist China represents the wave of the future,' CIA analysts predicted that, under his 'weak and ineffectual leadership,' radicals and Communists would grow increasingly influential. Rather than stop there and chalk up Nyerere's views and behavior to a political or ideological conflict, the CIA report groped for ways to neutralize his intransigence.....

When Nyerere responded to the U.S. airlift in the Congo by writing to President Johnson, the U.S. Ambassador called the letter a product of 'emotionalism, suspicions, and fear,' rather than the understandable concerned reaction of an African nationalist. Unable to understand him as anything other than a typically emotional African, the United States came to hold the view that 'under the mercurial and fiercely independent leadership of Nyerere, Tanzania is the bastion of radicalism in East Africa'[61]....

Americans' only real regret about the wave of African coups was that Sékou Touré and Julius Nyerere were not among its victims....

A State Department review of CIA activities noted that, in the Congo, the agency had covertly helped Adoula and Tshombe 'to buy the support of political and military leaders.'" – (Ibid., pp. 156, and 157).

Nyerere himself knew that the United States tried to undermine him in the sixties. As he stated in June 1966:

"We have twice quarrelled with the US Government; once when we believed it to be involved in a plot against us, and again when two of its officials misbehaved and were asked to leave Tanzania." – (Julius Nyerere, "Principles and Development," in Julius K. Nyerere, *Freedom and Socialism: A Selection from Writings and Speeches 1965 - 1967*, Oxford University Press, Dar es Salaam, Tanzania, 1968, pp. 202 – 203).

The U.S. State Department even wanted the American government to provide arms to some people in Tanzania who wanted to overthrow Nyerere. The Secretary of State during that time was Dean Rusk who was first appointed by President John F. Kennedy and who continued to serve in the same capacity under Lyndon Johnson. As John Prados states in his book, *Safe for Democracy: The Secret Wars of the CIA*:

"The Special Group (at the CIA) reportedly considered a State Department proposal to supply arms to certain groups in Tanzania, where secret-war wizards saw President Julius Nyerere as a problem, in the summer of 1964....Like Nyerere, Washington viewed Ghana's leader Kwame Nkrumah as a troublemaker." – (John Prados, *Safe for Democracy: The Secret Wars of the CIA*, Ivan R. Dee, Publisher, Chicago, Illinois, USA, 2006, p. 328).

The assessment of African leaders by the CIA, American ambassadors and other American leaders was not realistic. And it was clearly biased, a product of preconceived notions and expectations by Americans of what African leaders should be. In many cases, they grossly underestimated them; for example, Nyerere's commitment to African liberation. As Professor Piero Gleijeses of Johns Hopkins University states in his book, *Conflicting Missions: Havana, Washington, and Africa,*

"Of all the African leaders who proclaimed their support for the liberation struggle in Africa – Nkrumah, Nasser, Ben Bella, Sékou Touré – he (Nyerere) was the most committed. And by the second half of 1964, spurred by events in Zaire and the obvious failure of peaceful attempts to end white rule in southern Africa, this commitment, and his a disappointment with the Western powers, was increasingly evident.

By the time Che arrived (in 1965), Dar es Salaam had become the Mecca of African liberation movements....Dar es Salaam 'has become a haven for exiles from the rest of Africa,' the CIA lamented in September 1964. 'It is full of frustrated revolutionaries, plotting the overthrow of African governments, both black and white'....

In September 1964, Frelimo, the movement against Portuguese rule in Mozambique, had launched the opening salvo of its guerrilla war from bases in southern Tanzania, its only rear guard.

Following Stanleyville, Nyerere had thrown his full support to the Simbas, and Tanzania had become their main rear guard and the major conduit of Soviet and Chinese weapons for them.

It was also the seat of the Liberation Committee of the OAU. The head offices of Frelimo and a host of other movements struggling against the white regimes in South Africa, Namibia, and Rhodesia were in Dar es Salaam.

The Cuban embassy there was, the CIA reported accurately in March 1965, 'the largest Cuban diplomatic station in sub-Saharan Africa.' The ambassador, Captain Pablo Ribalta, was a close friend of Che Guevara.

In early 1964 Ribalta had been the commander of the Libertad air force base near Havana. 'One day,' he told me, 'Che arrived and said, 'Listen, Fidel wants to send you to Tanzania.' He told me I had to establish good relations with the liberation movements there. So they sent me to the Foreign Ministry to learn about Africa, and especially about Tanzania.'

Ribalta arrived in Tanzania on February 25, 1964, with four trusted aides from Libertad...." – (Piero Gleijeses, *Conflicting Missions: Havana, Washington, and Africa, 1959 – 1976*, Chapel Hill, North Carolina: The University of North Carolina Press, 2002, pp. 84 and 85).

Ahmed Sékou Touré, 9 January 1922 – 26 March 1984

Sometimes even when American diplomats and CIA

agents are right on the spot when they make assessments of African leaders and conditions prevailing in a given country, they are dead wrong in their assessments and reports although they have ample time and enough resources, and access to sources they can use to verify and support their conclusions.

One typical example involved Tanzania's First Lady, Salma Kikwete, the wife of President Jakaya Kikwete (2005 – 2015). Shabyna Stillman, a senior diplomat at the American embassy in Dar es Salaam, Tanzania, wrote in a confidential cable to Washington on Thursday, 5 May 2005, stating that Salma Kikwete was a cousin of the late Rwandan president, Juvenal Habyarimana, without verifying the information although there were numerous people in Dar es Salaam she could have contacted to verify that.

The diplomat was dead wrong. Salma Kikwete came from Lindi in southern Tanzania, not from Rwanda, and she was not a Hutu. She was a member of an ethnic group, Ndengereko, indigenous to that southern part of Tanzania. As Stillman stated:

"For years, observers of the Great Lakes conflicts have considered Kikwete to be virulently pro-Hutu. Rumors that he was facilitating arms transfers to Burundian Hutu rebels (when he was minister of foreign affairs) persisted, but have never been substantiated. Kikwete's marriage to a cousin of former Rwandan President Juvénal Habyarimana may have fueled these rumors." – (Shabyna Stillman in CONFIDENTIAL SECTION 01 OF 02 DAR ES SALAAM 000888 SIPDIS DEPARTMENT FOR AF/E E.O. 12958: 5/5/15 TAGS: PGOV TZ. SUBJECT: It's Kikwete: the CCM Party Chooses a Presidential Candidate. The cable was released by Wikilleaks.org/cable/2005/05/05DARESSALAAM888.html).

The report that Salma Kikwete was a cousin of the late Rwanda president, Habyarimana, was probably a product of propaganda by the Rwandan government under President Paul Kagame which was at war with Hutu extremists and which perceived Kikwete, rightly or wrongly, to be pro-Hutu when he was Tanzania's minister of foreign affairs and probably thought he would continue to be that way when elected president.

The cable by the American embassy was an update of the political situation in Tanzania during the selection of the presidential candidate for the ruling Chama Cha Mapinduzi (CCM) which, in Kiswahili, means the Party of the Revolution or the Revolutionary Party.

There are many people in Tanzania including leaders who could have provided the American diplomat with the right information about the true identity of Mrs. Kikwete.

Just as the Americans were wrong about Salma Kikwete being a cousin of Habyarimana, they were equally wrong in their assessment of a number of African leaders in the sixties. They grossly underrated them and made disparaging remarks about them which did not correspond to reality; for example, doubting or questioning the leadership qualities of Nkrumah, Nyerere, and Sékou Touré.

They even doubted Nyerere was a strong nationalist leader. Yet his stature as an ardent nationalist and Pan-Africanist has been vindicated by history; so has Nkrumah's and Sékou Touré's.

Like Nkrumah and Sékou Touré, Nyerere was also underestimated as a leader capable of understanding complex issues of development.

Simply because these leaders pursued policies Americans did not like and sought solutions – to African problems – which did not reflect American thinking does not mean they did not understand the nature of underdevelopment and what needed to be done; nor does it mean they did not understand complex issues of global significance including Cold War rivalry which had direct impact on the African continent itself, tragically demonstrated by the Congo crisis in the bleeding heart of Africa.

They may not have been trained economists, and they may not have had a full grasp of abstract economic concepts, but they understood the nature of underdevelopment and the problems their countries faced in the quest for development. As Professor Gerry Helleiner of the University of Toronto stated in "The Legacies of Julius Nyerere: An Economist's Reflections":

"I spent some of the best years of my life working in Dar es Salaam in the late 1960s when Mwalimu Julius Nyerere was its inspiring young President.

In later years, I worked for shorter periods in Tanzania – under each of its Presidents – and had many occasions to reflect on the longer-term role that Nyerere played in his own country. Internationally, too, I have frequently had the honour and privilege of working in Mwalimu's ambit, most notably through the South Commission and the South Centre.

I believe I may be the only economist to speak at this conference. (In fact, it is quite possible that I am the only economist in attendance.) Much of the economics profession has taken rather a dim view of the legacy of Julius Nyerere. (I won't dignify with quotation or repetition some of the things I have heard said about him in the World Bank.)

It is precisely *because* I am an economist – and Mwalimu so evidently was not – that I want to put my profound admiration of his record and his legacy on the record.

It is undoubtedly in the field of economics that Julius Nyerere has received his worst press, and in which his legacy has been seen as most negative. The heading for his obituary in the (London) *Financial Times* read 'Man of integrity whose policies hurt his country.' That in *The Economist*, while generally friendly, concluded: 'He was a magnificent teacher: articulate, questioning, stimulating, caring. He should never have been given charge of an economy.'

Personally, I see his legacy in the realm of economic and development policy rather differently.

Mwalimu's grasp of the traditional tenets of economic theory was probably weak and so was that of his closest advisors and speechwriters (although there were those within government of whom this could certainly not be said).

Most of the criticism coming from economists relates to his 'socialist' policies. But his government's most damaging economic policy errors, in my view, had little to do with socialism *per se*. They came relatively late in his Presidency and were on the relatively non-ideological issue of exchange rate policy; they were errors shared by many other low-income countries in the early 1980s.

As for his "socialism", some elements can be faulted as far more serious in their negative economic consequences than others. Nationalizations and restrictions on competition (including price controls) in the trading, industrial, agricultural and financial sectors were far beyond governmental management capacities and proved costly. Widespread (and even forced) 'villagization' in the rural sector was not only economically costly but also deeply unpopular.

The 'basic industry' policy – to the extent that it was part of Nyerere's 'socialism' – was also mistaken in that it was premature and inappropriate for so economically small a country; it too proved costly.

All of these 'socialist' policies could be foreseen (and were) as likely to slow overall economic growth and development both immediately and over the longer run. (My personal anxieties in this regard, circa 1969-70, may be found in an article in the *Journal of Development*

Studies, Vol. 8, no. 1, January, 1972.) Arguably, none seemed likely, of themselves, however, to create the degree of economic collapse that occurred in the early 1980s. Nor, in my view, did they. Severe macroeconomic shocks – oil prices, weather, and war against Amin – and their serious domestic mismanagement were required for that.

In the early 1980s, as the UK White Paper on international development put it in its commentary on African experience, the 'worldwide international climate ... left little margin for policy errors' (*Eliminating World Poverty: A Challenge for the 21st Century, White Paper on International Development*, November 1997, p. 9).

In Tanzania, there undoubtedly were such policy errors. Again, my view is that Tanzania's economic dislocations in the early 1980s were only partially attributable to its efforts to restructure the economy towards socialism. Far more serious were the errors in macroeconomic policy in the face of severe shocks (as well as, of course, the shocks themselves).

It is important for critical economists (and others) to recall that there were other elements in Nyerere's socialist programme – increased equity in the distribution of income; an attempt at a direct assault on bottom-end poverty (including provision of primary education and clean water); a 'leadership code' for politicians and civil servants; major reform of the educational syllabus; and (at least rhetorical) emphasis on self-reliance and reduced aid dependence.

These elements of Nyerere's 'socialist' programme excited widespread admiration and support (ultimately too much support of an unhelpful kind) from many academics and policymakers in the capitalist West, particularly in the Nordic countries and the Presidency of the World Bank. So compelling was this side of his socialist aspirations and practice that, for some time, admirers were prepared to give Tanzania the benefit of the doubt on the less propitious elements of its 'socialist' development policy and its economic sustainability.

Sadly, as Tanzania's resource constraints tightened and macroeconomic policies faltered in the late 1970s and early 1980s most of these supporters lost confidence in the overall Nyerere socialist vision. Their withdrawal of financial support then worsened what had already become a crisis situation.

The first serious external pressures upon the Government of Tanzania to reform its economic policies were related primarily to its macroeconomic management policies, *not* to its socialism, and they came, of course, from the IMF. According to the IMF tenets of the times, what Tanzania most required in the late 1970s and early 1980s was across-the-board governmental austerity and severe currency devaluation.

It was the effort at imposition of such IMF conditionality that prompted Nyerere's famous public outburst (in 1981): 'Who elected the IMF to be the Finance Ministry for every country in the world?' (or words to that effect).

There followed an almost total breakdown in Tanzania-IMF relations. Julius Nyerere may be said to have fired the first African salvo in the great debate over the role of the IMF in Africa. (By a quirk of chance, it was at about the same time, 1980 that the annual meetings of the IMF were to be chaired by Amir Jamal, Tanzania's then Minister of Finance. I remember his recounting his surprise when, upon his arrival in Washington for the meetings, IMF staff presented him with a draft of his introductory remarks. He thanked them for their thoughtfulness he delighted in recalling, but told them he had brought his own speech.)

At this point (1980-81), Nyerere and Tanzania were still sufficiently respected that the then-President of the World Bank, Robert McNamara, initiated a mediation effort to seek an accommodation between the IMF and the Tanzanians. This was to be attempted through the provision of technical assistance for the preparation, in Tanzania, of an alternative to the IMF's stabilization and structural adjustment plan; the Government of Tanzania was given a voice (and indeed veto power) over the composition of the three-person team which was given the ultimate responsibility for the task.

With both expatriate and local staff working together in Dar es Salaam for a year, an alternative structural adjustment programme was tortuously constructed. Anticipating later African debates, it called for much greater emphasis upon supply-side expansion than demand-side restraint; much greater care over the distributional effects of required macroeconomic adjustment (with conscious effort to maintain equity of sacrifice); and a more gradual programme for the implementation of reforms.

The effort failed, however, when neither the Government of Tanzania nor the IMF found the programme satisfactory. (This is probably the appropriate point to recount another anecdote, one of my favourite Mwalimu stories.

Upon personally welcoming the agreed three-person team to Tanzania as it embarked on its task, the President followed his initial niceties to the group, each of whom he knew, with the prescient introductory substantive comment: 'You know, gentlemen, I asked for money, not advice!' A more succinct statement of the problem of conditionality has probably never been made.)

A major 'sticking point' in the failure to agree on what was, for its time, a highly innovative programme (as well as a potentially important model for IMF-member country dispute resolution), though not the only one, was the Government's (mistaken) reluctance sufficiently to devalue its currency. I am personally convinced that, like so many laymen, Mwalimu did not understand the role of the exchange rate; some (not all) of his advisors gave him very bad advice.

As the Government went ahead on its own more and more donors (including now the World Bank) lost faith in Tanzanian macroeconomic management, the economy spiralled further downward, corruption grew, and all-around confidence in the entire Nyerere vision was lost.

The advent of Reagan-Thatcher influences on economic policy throughout the world and in the Bretton Woods institutions (McNamara left the World Bank in 1981) furthered darkened external views of the Tanzanian situation.

The necessary policy turnaround – now in much more dire economic circumstances, and with both much more external policy leverage and, significantly, a degree of non-governmental (mainly university) technical influence – finally began in 1986, *after* Nyerere's departure.

When the turnaround came, except for exchange rate action, which, by its nature, had to come more swiftly (in effect, it began with the 'own funds' import programme in 1984), it came fairly *gradually* and slowly. By the mid-1990s, the economy had significantly recovered and donors had returned. Remarkably, political stability had been a constant.

By this time, however, Tanzania was in trouble over other issues. Corruption had reached the highest levels of the Government and party (attracting public criticism from, among others, the now-retired Mwalimu, who now also supported competitive elections in a multi-party system); the central economic policymaking machinery was demoralized and in disarray; and, partly in consequence, aid donors were almost totally 'driving' such development efforts as were under way (outside the private sector).

Economic growth was taking place but there was a notable absence of any public 'vision,' such as had characterized the Nyerere years, as to where the country was going and why. Economic policy was seen as dictated by the international financial institutions and the aid donors. (For an account, see the Helleiner Report, *Report of the Group of Independent Advisers on Development Cooperation Issues Between Tanzania and Its Aid Donors*, Gerald K. Helleiner, Tony Killick, Nguyuru Lipumba, Benno J. Ndulu and Knud Erik Svendsen, Royal Danish Ministry of Foreign Affairs, June 1995.)

The Government of Benjamin Mkapa, newly elected in 1995, set out with the encouragement of some of the major aid donors, to restore ownership of its own development programmes, fight corruption, and recreate a sense of vision of the country's direction.

While much remains to be done, to a remarkable degree, it seems to me, it has been succeeding. It reached an important agreement, in principle, with the aid donor community on appropriate aid relationships – and, again, while much remains to be done, there can be no doubt that ownership of economic policy and programmes is returning to Tanzania.

The Government has prepared its own policy framework paper (PFP) and its own long-term vision statement (both with non-governmental inputs), led its own public expenditure review (PER) and the new Tanzania Assistance Strategy (TAS), and will now develop its own Poverty Reduction Strategy Paper (PRSP). Increasing (though still too small) proportions of aid expenditure are flowing through (or at least reported in) the national budget as the central economic administration strengthens.

Tanzanian-led sectoral strategies and policies are being developed and implemented in health, roads and education. Prime emphasis throughout these efforts is to address the principal problems of poverty and to do so under Tanzanian, not donor, leadership. (More details on all this can be found in a paper prepared for the May 1999 meeting of the Consultative Group for Tanzania: Gerry Helleiner, "Changing Aid Relationships in Tanzania, December 1997 through March 1999", Dar es Salaam, mimeo, 1999.)

One senior (and informed) World Bank official has remarked (to me privately) that, despite all the favourable press on Uganda, Tanzania is actually about four years or more ahead of it in terms of truly nationally-owned (and thus sustainable) economic policy for overall development. Tanzania may seem to move more slowly, he noted (and I agree), but it does so on a firmer and more stable base.

This base was established, I would argue, in the time of Julius Nyerere – a politically unified country; shared values as to equity in income distribution and political participation; and determination to develop and implement one's own policies and programmes.

Because Tanzania now has in place all of the key elements for sustained development – macroeconomic stability; broadly sensible incentive structures; broad political participation and stability; growing national self-confidence, ownership and capacity – I believe it is likely that, barring calamities of weather or the terms of trade, Tanzania will soon be everyone's favourite African 'success story' (and model).

It is now 'conventional wisdom' in Washington (even in the IMF, at least in terms of its rhetoric) and in donor capitals that poverty needs to be addressed as a matter of highest priority; that political stability and good governance (notably reduced corruption) are prerequisites for development; and that national ownership of programmes is critical to their success.

It has taken them a long time to reach these positions. But Julius Nyerere was espousing them and trying to build practice upon them 30 years ago. His slogan of 'socialism and self-reliance,' if transmitted today as 'equity, honesty and ownership,' would win universal assent. He was decades ahead of his time in these matters.

Today's key Tanzanian policymakers – both politicians and technocrats – grew up and were educated in the

Nyerere years. They have undoubtedly learned from earlier economic and other policy mistakes. (Mwalimu was himself a learner and pragmatist, who often changed policy positions when the evidence as to the failure of previous approaches seemed clear.)

I believe that the respect, which Mwalimu enjoyed in his own country right up until his death indicates that they also retained much that Mwalimu had taught. They now can build 'humane governance' on the political and value base he constructed. (The apt concept of 'humane governance' has recently been developed to encompass sound and equitable economic *and* political governance, including responsive and participatory institutions, respect for human rights, and special provision for the most needy and most vulnerable. See *Human Development in South Asia, 1999*, Mahbub ul Haq, The Human Development Centre and Oxford University Press, Pakistan, 1999.)

Whatever his other mistakes in the realm of economics, in one area of economic policy Mwalimu was dead right – and, again, ahead of his time.

Both in his anguished cry about the IMF in 1981 and in his subsequent work in the South Commission and the South Centre, he steadily maintained the need for fairer international (or global) systems of economic governance, particularly in the financial sphere.

It is important to underline his consistent emphasis upon *equity* in global economic governance arrangements because there is every sign that current reform efforts in the international financial arena are overly focussed upon efficiency considerations and the avoidance or minimization of the effects of systemic crises.

This focus has resulted in some effort to incorporate some of the interests and concerns of the newly emerging countries and the largest of the poor countries and this certainly constitutes important progress in global economic and financial governance; but it leaves out the poorest and weakest. The latter are unrepresented – either in the new Financial Stability Forum or in the even newer Group of Twenty (G20), chaired by the Canadian Finance Minister. (The G20 has also contrived to exclude all of the so-called "like-minded" countries, who might be expected to take a deeper interest in the problems of the poorest countries and peoples, as they have done in the past on debt relief and other issues.)

Nyerere's activities in the international/global sphere included efforts to bolster analysis, both economic and political, to inform those who speak for the developing countries, especially the poorest among them, in international negotiations and organizations. The developing countries are still woefully weakly equipped to deal with the batteries of well-funded economists, lawyers and lobbyists who defend Northern interests in international discussions and the media.

He was among those who saw, far ahead of others, that there is ultimately no substitute for one's own technical, professional and institutional strength. Today it is known as 'capacity building,' and it has entered 'conventional wisdom' as to what is to be done not only in Africa but throughout the developing world.

Yes, Julius Nyerere made some economic policy mistakes. In this he was certainly not alone. He also left a country capable of learning from its experience with a minimum of political ruckus, a country now moving forward economically on a firm political and value base. That is a significant legacy.

At the international level the fruits of his efforts are probably more distant. I expect, however, that one day they too will come." – (Gerry Helleiner, "The Legacies of Julius Nyerere: An Economist's Reflections," University of Toronto, 2000. See also Gerry Helleiner in Godfrey Mwakikagile, *Tanzania under Mwalimu Nyerere: Reflections on an African Statesman*, Pretoria: New Africa Press, 2006, pp. 199 – 207).

As Nyerere was grappling with economic problems, he also faced another major problem, probably the biggest threat to his government since independence.

In October 1969, a coup attempt masterminded by Tanzania's former minister of foreign affairs, Oscar Kambona, who also had been one of Nyerere's closest colleagues, was foiled by the nation's intelligence service:

"In spite of his immense popularity, President Nyerere was not immune from subversion. He became a target of a number of attempts, from within and without, to oust him from power. There were also many attempts to destabilize and weaken his government which his enemies and detractors hoped would eventually lead to his downfall.

He was fiercely independent, a stance that rankled Western powers as he went on to forge links with Eastern-bloc countries including the People's Republic of China and the Soviet Union, but especially with China, while maintaining ties with the West in pursuit of his policy of non-alignment. And his strong support for the African liberation movements was not endorsed by Western powers which wanted to perpetuate white minority rule in Africa for hegemonic control of the continent by the West.

So, Western powers wanted him out. Apartheid South Africa and other white minority regimes on the continent including Rhodesia and the Portuguese colonial governments – hence their mother country Portugal – also wanted him out. They did everything they could, including infiltrating and bombing Tanzania, to destabilise his government. One of the attempts to undermine his government involved the United States in the mid-sixties."
– (Godfrey Mwakikagile, *Nyerere and Africa: End of an Era*, op. cit., p. 361).

Dr. Kwame Nkrumah, in his book *Dark Days in Ghana*, also wrote about attempts by the CIA and the American government to undermine and overthrow

Nyerere. He wrote the book not long after he himself was ousted from power by the CIA.

After Nkrumah was overthrown, the military rulers prepared the country for a transition to civilian rule, partly to legitimise and justify their usurpation of power as a genuine attempt to restore democracy in Ghana.

The person who won the election was Nkrumah's long-time opponent and strong Western ally, Dr. Kofi Busia, a former sociology professor. Not long after Nkrumah was overthrown on 24 February 1966, Busia returned to Ghana within a month (in March) and became chairman of the National Advisory Committee of the military ruling National Liberation Council (NLC) which Nkrumah, in his book *Dark Days in Ghana*, dismissed as the Notorious Liars Council.

And it should always be remembered that it was a bloody coup, contrary to what some reports said. As John Mahama, the president of Ghana since 2012, who has recounted some horrifying scenes during the coup when he was a young boy, states in his book, *My First Coup D'etat: Memories from the Lost Decades of Africa*:

"It happened on February 24, 1966. I was seven years old, a class 2 pupil in the primary division of Achimota, an elite boarding school in Accra, Ghana's capital. That day there was a lot of commotion; teachers rushed about in a noticeably scattered fashion and huddled in corners whispering. It did not take long for the news to spread, first through the upper school's student body, then down to the younger pupils....

At Achimota we heard that all the ministers of state had been arrested. This particular tidbit of information gave me pause because my father was a minister of state....

As coup d'etats go, that first one which took place in Ghana was swift and unexpected. It is sometimes incorrectly referred to in texts as a bloodless coup, yet it was anything but. The night after the coup while my eldest brother, Peter, was being taken to his mother's house, the taxi in which he was riding was made to stop at the Flagstaff House (the president's official residence and office).

Once there, the military officer posted at the entrance ordered Peter and the other children in the taxi to close their eyes while he interrogated the driver. They did as they were told, but not before Peter had caught a glimpse of the courtyard in front of the Flagstaff House, which, he later told me, was filled with rows and rows of dead bodies. It is an image that Peter, who was only ten years old at the time, has never been able to forget." – (John Dramani Mahama, *My First Coup D'etat: Memories from the Lost Decades of Africa*, London: Bloomsbury Publishing, 2012, pp. 7, 9, 15).

Other sources also provide high numbers of casualties during the coup. As Professor Roger Gocking states in his book, *The History of Ghana*:

"The coup had been far from bloodless, as its defenders asserted. According to Nkrumah, around 1,600 people had been killed in the fighting and 'in the looting and robbery that followed.'" – (Roger S. Gocking, *The History of Ghana*, Westport, Connecticut, USA: Greenwood Press, 2005, p. 139).

The United States, which played the biggest role in overthrowing Nkrumah, continued to be actively involved in Ghanaian affairs after Dr. Busia became the country's new civilian leader (with the title of prime minister under the new constitution) and even provided security for him; further validating the accusation against the United States that she was behind Nkrumah's ouster. As Fred Hadsel, who was the American ambassador to Ghana (1971 – 1974) when Busia was in power (1969 – 1972), said in an interview years later:

"The next phase of my career started with my transfer (from Somalia) to Ghana as Ambassador from 1971 to 1974....

Ghana was (a) very different country from Somalia. In the first place, the Ghanaians had had decades of experience with Europe. It had an educational infrastructure that was extensive; they were by nature one of the most generous, hospitable, relaxed group of people in all of Africa. They had a sense of humor, they had a complex religious pattern of Catholics and Anglicans and other Protestants. They burst with vitality.

However, they had gone through the shock of Nkrumah's deposition in the Spring of 1966. They had reestablished in due course a parliamentary government under the very able scholar rather than politician, Busia. He was Prime Minister at the time of our arrival, but he too was overthrown by a coup six months later. My friends noted jokingly that every place I was sent had a coup. They questioned where else I might be sent.

The military coup had some interest. The leader of the coup was the leader of a regiment which had been trained by our CIA to be the special unit available to the Busia government to prevent a possible coup. So when the coup started, Busia pushed the button, but there was no answer because the coup leader was the officer in charge of protecting the government against such actions.

He was a man who had gone through Fort Leavenworth's Staff and Command College without leaving a trace. No one could find a record, good, bad or indifferent.

His name was Acheampong, a man of adequate intelligence, modest education whose eventual downfall, long after I left, was due to the avarice of his wife. In fact, he and his wife were the first Ghanaians to be killed as a result of the first counter-coup in the modern history of Ghana. Up to that point, coups had been bloodless." –

(Ambassador Fred L. Hadsel, interviewed by Edward W. Mulcahy, 17 October 1989, *The Association of Diplomatic Studies and Training, Foreign Affairs Oral History Project,* p. 14).

American involvement in Nkrumah's ouster was even acknowledged, although indirectly, by the American ambassador to Ghana, Robert Smith, who assumed his post ten years after Nkrumah was overthrown. What he said in an interview years later amounted to circumstantial evidence which implicated the United States as a major player in Nkrumah's downfall:

"Q: You were, again, dealing with Ghana at a difficult time. Could you explain what our relations were in 1965 and 1966, how you saw it from the desk?
Smith: Before coming back (to Washington) and taking over the desk (Ghana desk at the State department) I drove overland from Enugu, west to Lagos, and then all the way across the west coast into Accra for a week's visit there with the embassy staff in Ghana. I'd been there before but only briefly. We had a very fine staff there, one of whom, a junior political officer on the staff then, is now our ambassador in Moscow, Jack Matlock. That was where I first met Jack.

Kwame Nkrumah was still in power in 1965. And to say that he was difficult for the embassy and the United States Government would be the understatement of the year. He seemed to be, at times, almost losing his mind. Ghana had been left--Ghana was the first to come to independence--in really excellent shape by the British--myths to the contrary notwithstanding. They had a very favorable balance of payments. They had millions and millions in foreign reserves, hard currency. And Nkrumah simply ran the country into the ground by his tortured anti-Western, Socialistic, anti-capitalist attitudes.

The strange thing about that initial visit to Ghana was, even though I was being briefed on the idiosyncrasies of Nkrumah, at the same time individual Ghanaians, even senior civil servants, to say nothing of the man on the street, couldn't have been nicer or more blatantly pro-American to the extent of their saying at times that, 'You mustn't pay too much about what Osaygefo says.'

Osaygefo was a name he was called by the Ghanaian people. Ghanaians, perhaps second only to the Ibos, from whom I had just come, are among the most likeable, pleasant, nice people in all of Africa. They are simply an enormously likeable, warm, generous, outgoing people. I can't find enough adjectives to use with respect to the Ghanaians.

It was tragic for us to sit back and see Nkrumah running this country into the ground the way he did, and it was happening right before our eyes. When I went there in 1965, there were still a number of hotels in downtown Accra that served excellent meals. I remember having lunch on the patio of one of those hotels. By the time I went back years later as ambassador, none of them could do that. There was nothing to be had. There was nothing to eat, et cetera. And almost all of it was attributed to Nkrumah's madness. I don't mean that literally.

Q: Was there concern that there might be a mental problem there?

Smith: I don't think seriously, no.

Q: This was an attitude?

Smith: An attitude, yes. It was fascinating to deal with it. He was concentrating on the urban areas. And this is an age-old story in Africa where African leaders tend to concentrate on keeping their urban populations happy at the expense of their rural populations. And Nkrumah did this with respect to his cocoa farmers, cocoa being the largest source of foreign exchange. And as a result, they couldn't get people to man cocoa farms and the country just spun out of control.

So much so that, while I was on the Ghana desk nine or ten months later, they had had enough and Nkrumah was overthrown in a coup. They did this in relatively bloodless fashion. While Nkrumah was in the air flying to Red China, he was met on the ground in Peking by his Chinese host and it fell to them to inform him that he was no longer Head of State in the Republic of Ghana. So that was a fascinating time in a fascinating country.

Q: Was our feeling one of passivity towards Nkrumah? I'm talking about the time that you were dealing with it. Were we trying to say enough is enough because the man was attacking us, at least verbally, all the time.

Smith: He certainly was. We tried for years to get along with Nkrumah. We would turn the other cheek at times and do everything we could to assuage his anger. Nothing worked with him, however. And, again, while I was on the Desk, I think Nkrumah dropped the straw that broke the camel's back, so to speak, in that he published a new book called *Neo-Colonialism*. I've forgotten the subtitle (*The Last Stage of Imperialism* – added by Godfrey Mwakikagile), which was simply outrageous. It accused the United States of every sin imaginable to man. We were blamed for everything in the world.....

I also remember, the morning of the coup, I got the call about 2 a.m. here at the house and went into the Department and immediately set up a little task force in the Operations Center. Later in the same morning, about 8 or 8:30, Secretary Rusk wandered down the hall and came in and said, 'I've seen the early reports, but I just want to hear it firsthand. What's going on in Ghana?' When I related how Nkrumah had landed in Peking and had been informed by his Chinese hosts of what had happened in Ghana, Dean Rusk broke into an ear-splitting grin. I've never seen him look so happy.

Q: Enough was enough, I guess.

Smith: Enough was enough, yes.

Q: Again, this is an unclassified interview, and I

know there's been accusations. I think, actually, while you were in Ghana they came out to the fore again that the CIA had been involved. Did you have any feel towards that while you were there?

Smith: Yes. We had been accused of that all along. There was nothing to it. I mean, it was obvious that we were not among his legions of supporters, but neither were we involved because there was no reason to be involved. The Ghanaian military were quite capable of dealing with this on their own, as they did. Unfortunately, the government that followed was, in its own way, almost as bad as Nkrumah's. We had high hopes for it, but it didn't materialize.

In just a few years that civilian, truly democratic government, elected in a free election, was itself overthrown by the military because they hadn't been able to correct the economic imbalances and so forth, and there was corruption, which just seemed to be endemic. So Ghana then went on without any direct involvement on my part until I later went back as ambassador years later." – (Ambassador Robert P. Smith, interviewed by Charles Stuart Kennedy, 28 February 1989, *The Association for Diplomatic Studies and Training, Foreign Affairs Oral History Project*, pp. 12 – 15).

Nkrumah's ouster was a momentous event not only in the history of Ghana but of Africa as a whole. Ghana never regained the stature she once had as a beacon of hope for African liberation and continental unification when Nkrumah was in power. And Africa lost a leader of immense stature who was the embodiment of Pan-Africanism and true expression of the African personality. He put Africa first, prompting one of his critics and admirers, Kenyan Professor Ali Mazrui, to say the following about him: "He was a great African but not a great Ghanaian."

The establishment of military rule in Ghana after

Nkrumah was overthrown marked the beginning of a new era for the country which would last for almost 30 years.

After Nkrumah was overthrown, the new rulers pursued policies which were unabashedly pro-Western. They did so partly out of gratitude to the Western powers, especially the United States, who sponsored and supported the coup against Nkrumah, but mainly because they themselves were pro-Western and did not like the Russians and the Chinese whom he had embraced as his allies in his quest for Ghana's radical transformation into a socialist state.

They also reversed Ghana's position on African liberation and continental unification which Nkrumah pursued vigorously during his presidency. In fact, one of the reasons the soldiers who overthrew Nkrumah gave to explain why they ousted him was that he was getting ready to send them to Rhodesia to fight the white minority rulers who had unilaterally declared independence, totally ignoring the black African majority in that country as if they did not even exist.

In his book, *The Ghana Coup*, Akwasi Afrifa expressed strong anti-Pan-Africanist sentiments in his denunciation of Nkrumah who was committed to African liberation, including his desire to send troops to Rhodesia to fight in a war which, Afrifa claimed, Ghanaian soldiers had nothing to do with. They had already served in Congo during the Congo crisis, which was also a mistake according to Afrifa and his colleagues, and were in no mood for another war; which partly explained why they overthrew Nkrumah.

Afrifa and his colleagues had a totally different interpretation of the role of the Ghanaian army. The army was only for the defence of Ghana. But according to Nkrumah, it was also a liberation army which should be ready to go to any part of Africa to help liberate Africans still under white minority rule if there was a need to do so; a sentiment shared by other African leaders such as Nyerere who stated in interview with the American

Broadcasting Company (ABC) in 1977 that he would do so when he was asked if he would commit troops to help liberate South Africa from the apartheid regime: "Yes, I will commit troops. We would rather hang together than hang separately."

Soon after Tanganyika won independence in December 1961 under his leadership, he opened the doors to the freedom fighters from the countries of southern Africa, promised them material and financial support, allowed them to establish guerrilla training camps, and made it clear, like Nkrumah, that no part of Africa was free until every inch of African soil was free from foreign domination.

Tanzanian soldiers fought in Mozambique, supporting FRELIMO; they fought in Zimbabwe alongside ZANU forces, and they fought in Angola on the side of the MPLA. The Tanzanian army was an African liberation army, not just a national army to defend Tanzania; a position also articulated by Nkrumah with regard to the Ghanaian army.

Ghanaian soldiers who overthrew him stated exactly the opposite, also in deeds, when they expelled the freedom fighters from the countries of southern Africa who had been given sanctuary in Ghana by Nkrumah. Their narrow nationalism was reflected in the statement by Afrifa in his book when he implied that Ghanaian soldiers had nothing to do with what was going on in Rhodesia since going to fight in that country to help liberate fellow Africans was something they had nothing to do with, as if fellow Africans suffering under racial oppression were nothing to them.

After Nkrumah was deposed, Ghana lost her position as a leader in the quest for African unity and liberation the country was known for when he was in power. Freedom fighters in the countries which were still under white minority rule no longer saw Ghana as a beacon of hope and source of inspiration and support in their struggle for liberation. The shining black star no longer shone beyond its borders; and it never did again after Nkrumah was gone.

It is difficult to reconcile Professor Mazrui's assessment of Nkrumah with Nkrumah's achievements in the domestic arena when he says Nkrumah "was not a great Ghanaian." Mazrui contends that Nkrumah pursued his Pan-African goals of continental liberation and unification at the expense of Ghana. He ignored Ghana; he was also a dictator.

Nkrumah would not have been able to build what he built, and in so a short a time during his presidency of less than six years, if he pursued his Pan-African ambitions at the expense of his country.

It was Nkrumah who led Ghana to independence. It was also Nkrumah who laid the foundation for modern-day Ghana.

Ghana's rapid industrialisation and modernisation was started by Nkrumah. Almost all the institutions which have sustained Ghana and on which the country has continued to build and sustain its economy and increase its educational opportunities and development in other areas of national life were built by Nkrumah.

Without the infrastructure Nkrumah built, Ghana would not be where it is today. Here are a few examples of what he built:

Schools including technical schools in different parts of the country; Cape Coast university, Kwame Nkrumah University of Science and Technology, Ghana Medical School, Ghana Law School, and other institutions as well as provision of free education; factories; modern houses and flats in Accra, Tema and elsewhere; modern roads including the Tema-Accra Motorway, the only one during that time and which was intended to be part of a highway system Nkrumah wanted to build to link all the major towns and cities in Ghana; the modern Tema Harbour, the Akosombo Dam – which led to the creation of Lake Volta

– to provide electricity without which development and industrialisation is impossible.

To say a leader who built all that was not a great Ghanaian is to ignore such achievements which still stand today as a monument to his legacy.

Even the people who overthrew him and successive governments in one way or another invoked his name and achievements to burnish their image and sustain themselves in power. And not long after he was overthrown, many people in Ghana continued to acknowledge him as a national hero in spite of the mistakes he made. Even his critics acknowledged that and could not destroy his legacy and achievements. As Professor Harcourt Fuller states:

"The death of Nkrumah in 1972 ushered in a renewed public fervor for all things Nkrumah. Since then, contemporaneous and successive governments – both military and civilian – have sought to appropriate or capitalize on Nkrumah's posthumous resurgence and popularity for their own purposes or at least to manage the renewed interest of Ghanaians and foreigners alike in the legacy of Kwame Nkrumah.

Acheampong was also symbolically and substantively sympathetic to Nkrumah, but only because of the outpouring of popular, pro-Nkrumah sentiments in Ghana and elsewhere. His 'party' – the NRC (National Redemption Council) – included the word 'Redemption' – the English-language verbiage of the Twi-language root word that was given as a title to Nkrumah – *Osagyefo* (meaning Redeemer).

The NRC had sent a small delegation to observe Nkrumah's funerary festivities in Conakry, and shortly thereafter succumbed to Sékou Touré's prodding to allow his remains to be flown to Ghana from Guinea for final burial in July 1972 in Nkroful. As with his first state burial in Guinea, Nkrumah received a second – but not final –

state funeral in his native Ghana that reflected the Acheampong government's reluctant acknowledgment of his legacy and continuing appeal even in death:

'In Ghana, General Acheampong headed a long queue of people who filed past the coffin at the lying-in-state at State House. He and other members of the NRC were also present at a memorial service held in Accra. Flags flew at half mast until 6 p.m. on Sunday, 9 July. On that day, the coffin was taken to Nkroful. There it was placed in tomb on the site of the dwelling in which Nkrumah was born...that arrangement suited the Acheampong government, as well as successive regimes which felt threatened by a revival of Nkrumaism.'

....Even the police force, elements of which took part in the 1966 coup, now sought to exonerate itself from what had increasingly become a blot on Ghana's history. In June 1975, the commissioner of police, J.E. Tibiru, wrote to the director of the Ghana Museums and Monuments Board, notifying him that 'The statue of ex-President Kwame Nkrumah which was removed after the coup in 1966 and placed at the Central Barracks is still lying there, in the open'....Through public media outlets such as the Ghana Broadcasting Corporation (GBC), they pressured the government to completely restore the statue....Public pressure on the GMMB (Ghana Museums and Monuments Board) had paid off, and Nkrumah's legacy had been symbolically rewritten through his re-erected statue." – (Harcourt Fuller, *Building the Ghanaian Nation-State: Kwame Nkrumah's Symbolic Nationalism*, op. cit., pp. 168, 169, 172, 173).

If there had been any attempts by the people who overthrew Nkrumah – and others who did not like him – to have him consigned to oblivion, they achieved exactly the opposite. As Professor Fuller goes on to explain

Nkrumah's legacy and redemption in and outside Ghana:

"In almost five decades since the coup, his historical legacy has gone through a process of rejection, reevaluation, reconstruction, and redemption within and outside of Ghana.

Since the late 1970s in particular, successive administrations have sought to symbolically capitalize on the increasing nostalgia with which Ghanaians and other Africans view Nkrumah and the other cohorts of first-generation African independence leaders, after the dust had settled on that period in the continent's history. This reassessment of Ghana's self-professed *Founding Father* has continued worldwide up to the present era, reaching its zenith during Ghana's Golden Jubilee of Independence in 2007, as well as during the year-long commemoration of his birth centenary in 2009 – 2010....Nkrumah has been largely absolved by the *longue durée* of history.

A new atmosphere of reverence for Nkrumah began to become evident only a few years after the physical and symbolic return of his remains to African and then Ghanaian soil after his death (at a hospital in Bucharest, Rumania) in 1972. The first evidence of Ghana's rekindling relationship with Nkrumah was the restoration and display of Nkrumah's statues at the National Museum in the late 1970s, which could only have been possible because the political environment had changed significantly in favor of Nkrumah's legacy. The cautious endorsement of the legacy of Nkrumah in the early 1970s would be continued from the 1980s and into the new millennium by different Ghanaian governments.

The administration of Flight Lieutenant Jerry John Rawlings...completed the third and final burial of Kwame Nkrumah. On July 1, 1992 – during the 32nd anniversary of Republic Day begun by Nkrumah on July 1, 1960 – Nkrumah's remains were reinterred at a mausoleum specially built for him at the Memorial Park. The latter was the old colonial Polo Ground where Nkrumah proclaimed Ghana's independence from Britain on March 6, 1967....

There were numerous notables present at Nkrumah's reinterment, which reflected Nkrumah's support for and appeal to African nationalists and Pan-Africanists worldwide. They included the widow of Malcolm X (Betty Shabazz), Julia Wright, daughter of the African American scholar Richard Wright, the Namibian president and nationalist leader of the South West African People's Organization (SWAPO) Sam Nujoma, and then African National Congress (ANC) chairman Oliver Tambo. (June) Milne (Nkrumah's research assistant and publisher who was also at the ceremony) asserts that, although it was Rawlings government – the National Democratic Congress (NDC) – and Rawlings himself who organized and presided over the final reinterment of Nkrumah, Rawlings

'Had never claimed to be a Nkrumaist....Among some of those listening there was speculation as to whether it was opportunism, from strength, or from weakness that the NDC regime had decided to respond to Nkrumaist pressures from Ghanaians and from PanAfricanists to accord Nkrumah the long overdue recognition of his greatness.

Perhaps a clue may lie in the failure to arrange for the funeral procession to pass through the streets of Accra before entering the Memorial Park, which was closed to all but authorized groups and invited guests. Such a procession would have allowed the thousands of Ghanaians who had gathered in the capital to demonstrate their deep affection and nostalgia for Osagyefo. Perhaps it was thought Nkrumaism could be finally buried with the man.'" – (Ibid., pp. 175 – 177).

Rawlings himself has been quoted to have said he admires Nkrumah but he is not Nkrumaist. According to an article published on GhanaWeb on 9 June 2004, "I admire Nkrumah, but I'm not an Nkrumaist – JJ":

"THE FORMER President, Flt. Lt. Jerry John Rawlings, has dismissed assertions by the Managing Editor of the *Crusading Guide*, Mr. Kweku Baako, Jnr. that he hates the first President, Dr. Kwame Nkrumah.

Mr. Victor Smith, Special Aide to the ex-President, had quoted Mr. Rawlings as saying he did not hate Nkrumah but admired him for the good things he had done for the nation. However, he said Mr. Rawlings was not an Nkrumaist and it was therefore totally wrong and out of context for somebody to say a thing of that sort.

Speaking to *The Chronicle* in Accra on behalf of Mr. Rawlings in reaction to remarks attributed to Mr. Baako about the ex-president's alleged aversion to Nkrumah, the special aide said the assertions by Mr. Baako were malicious and a calculated attempt to malign the former president.

Mr. Smith, who said the ex-President did not share the ideologies of Dr. Nkrumah, asked: 'If the old man hated Nkrumah, how would he choose people like Prof. Evans Atta Mills, Mr. Harry Sawyer and others to work with him, knowing their political lineage as CPP members? If Rawlings hated Nkrumah, how would he recommend that money be spent to transport his body to Accra and to erect a monument in his memory?'....Mr. Baako was reported to have stated that the former President had developed hatred for the first President to the extent that wherever they (Baako and Rawlings) went, the ex-President had demanded the removal of Dr. Nkrumah's picture." – (Ghanaweb, 9 June 2004).

Many people in Ghana who admire Nkrumah are not necessarily Nkrumaist; there those who are. One does not have to be Nkrumaist to admire Nkrumah and acknowledge his contributions to Ghana and to Africa as a whole.

There are even some members in the New Patriotic Party which produced President John Kufuor who admire Nkrumah and acknowledge his contributions to Ghana and

Kwame Nkrumah with Empperor Haile Selassie

to Africa as Kufuor himself did, although their party is a lineal descendant of the United Gold Coast Convention (UGCC) which was the major opposition party when Nkrumah was prime minister and later president of Ghana until the country became a one-party state in 1964 dominated by Nkrumah's Convention People's Party (CPP); so were the United Party and Progress Party which produced Prime Minister Kofi Busia, equally steeped in the Danquah tradition, although without a long history like the UGCC as opposition parties.

But it is also true that there are some members in those parties, which can be described as conservative unlike Jerry Rawlings' National Democratic Congress (NDC) which can be described as liberal, who don't like and may be even hate Nkrumah; much of their dislike and hatred of Nkrumah being attributed to the way they believe Nkrumah mistreated their patriarch and political mentor Dr. J.B. Danquah who died in prison in February 1965 – almost exactly one year before Nkrumah was overthrown, just three weeks short of that – after being detained by Nkrumah under the Preventive Detention Act. Their hatred of Nkrumah is also attributed to their belief that Nkrumah also mistreated Dr. Kofi Busia, who later fled into exile claiming his life was in danger, when he was the main opposition leader in the country.

Yet, in spite of all that – there are people who will always denounce Nkrumah and try to dismiss his achievements as failures – nothing has diminished Nkrumah's stature among many Ghanaians and other Africans across the continent and beyond. As Fuller states:

"Ironically, the Kwame Nkrumah Memorial Park and Mausoleum, which was commissioned some two decades after Nkrumah's death, came to serve the purpose that the Nkroful museum-shrine, which was built at the site of Nkrumah's birth, did not fully get a chance to fulfill. It now serves as a pilgrimage site for people from Ghana, Africa, and the African Diaspora who have a personal or academic interest in the life and legacy of Nkrumah.

The Rawlings regime gave the Kwame Nkrumah Memorial Museum and Mausoleum the status of a national museum, governed by the National Commission on Culture.

Guided tours of the museum showcase a variety of Nkrumah memorabilia and personal effects, including furniture that he owned, books that he authored, audio-visual and written material on Nkrumah's life, a photo archive with official photographs of Nkrumah and other world leaders, and the metal coffin given by Sékou Touré in which he was buried in Nkroful.

Government functionaries also hold official state events there, including Emancipation Day – an African Diaspora holiday marked on August 1, annually – and wreath laying ceremonies to commemorate Nkrumah." – (Ibid., p. 177).

The redemption of Nkrumah also necessitated the rehabilitation of other Ghanaian leaders of national stature who were suppressed under Nkrumah. They included Dr J. B. Danquah who was considered to be the doyen of Ghanaian politics, having preceded Nkrumah in leading the struggle for independence. They were also accorded the status of founding fathers. But it is Nkrumah, because of his status as Ghana's first prime minister and first president, who has commanded attention surpassing his colleagues.

His contributions to Ghana are also unsurpassed. He not only led Ghana to independence; he also gave Ghana a true and solid national identity transcending ethno-regional differences. He also shaped that identity, and national character, to become an embodiment of the African personality he cherished so much throughout his life.

He made Ghana a microcosm of Africa in terms of ideals and aspirations for the betterment of all Africans; of what we ought to be as a people, united and strong and in control of our destiny instead of being playthings, as mere toys, in the hands of others.

He also had enemies, not only in Ghana but in other African countries where some of his colleagues saw him as an overly ambitious person, a megalomaniac, who wanted to rule Africa.

And he remains a controversial figure – yet highly respected – half a century after he was overthrown. His stature as a great African leader is also acknowledged and symbolised by his statue – with his right arm stretched up – erected in front of the headquarters of the African Union (AU) in Addis Ababa, Ethiopia, as a symbol of African unity. He is the only leader, among all African presidents, prime ministers and kings, to be so honoured by the AU.

Nkrumah's statue at the African Union (AU) headquarters, Addis Ababa, unveiled by Ghanaian President John Atta Mills. Also in attendance, former Ghanaian President Jerry Rawlings and Nkrumah's daughter Samia Nkrumah, and son Francis Nkrumah (wearing a badge)

There is no other statue, of another leader, on the grounds of the African Union, except Nkrumah's.

The statue was unveiled on 28 January 2012 by Ghanaian president John Atta Mills in the presence of two of Nkrumah's children, Dr. Francis Nkrumah and Samia Nkrumah, as well as Ghanaian ex-president Jerry Rawlings and other African leaders and dignitaries.

Not even Emperor Haile Selassie of Ethiopia has a statue there, an omission that angered many Ethiopians who argued that it was their emperor, not Nkrumah, who was the symbol of Pan-Africanism and continental unity; a sentiment that was harshly dismissed by Ethiopian Prime Miniser Meles Zenawi:

"The arrival of Ghanaian great Kwame Nkrumah in the Ethiopian capital Addis Ababa 40 years after his death has been met with notable local resistance.

Ethiopians are signing a petition demanding that a statue of the pan-Africanist leader which was recently unveiled outside the new African Union headquarters be joined by one of the late emperor Haile Selassie or removed.

As well as the signatures, a group of Ethiopian elders, opposition politicians and scholars have written to the AU Commission voicing their disappointment at its decision to 'ignore' the deposed emperor.

The golden statue of Nkrumah was erected to commemorate his founding role in the Organisation of African Unity, the AU's predecessor.

The late Ethiopian monarch's supporters have argued that their man, who became internationally famous for his resistance against the Italians under Mussolini, was a longer-standing supporter of African liberation than Ghana's founding president.

'It is Haile Selassie who is described by African leaders as the father of Africa not Nkrumah,' said Yacob Hailemariam, an opposition politician who has spoken out against the choice of the Ghanaian.

The campaign has, however, infuriated Ethiopia's current leader Meles Zenawi who said it was 'crass' to question Nkrumah's choice as an African symbol and has repeatedly denounced Selassie, who died in 1975, as a 'feudal dictator.'

'It is only Nkrumah who is remembered whenever we talk about pan Africanism,' Mr Meles told local media. 'It is a shame not to accept his role.'

The AU confirmed that it had received a letter signed by prominent Ethiopians, many of them living abroad, but declined to comment. The protest letter says that Selassie who ruled Ethiopia for 40 years had 'the legal, moral, historical and diplomatic legitimacy to have his statue erected next to Kwame Nkrumah.'" – (Daniel Howden, "Ethiopians give lacklustre welcome to Nkrumah statue," *The Independent*, London, 14 February 2012).

All that has added to Nkrumah being a highly controversial figure of continental and international stature who also commands great respect in his home country Ghana:

"In 2009, during the Nkrumah birth centennial, President Mills declared September 21st as Founder's Day. Nkrumah's birthday finally became a national holiday in Ghana.

Moreover, Ghanaians and tourists flocked to the Nkrumah Memorial Park to pay tribute to him and to revel in traditional and modern Ghanaian entertainment and culture. Fabric with the colors of the Ghanaian flag was draped over the forward-pointing arm of Nkrumah's statue at the mausoleum. Festive crowds also gathered at his mausoleum during Ghana's Golden Jubilee of Independence as well as the centennial of his birth to pay homage to Nkrumah.

Since September 2009, there have also been several academic conferences held in Ghana, Europe, and North America to commemorate and debate the centennial of the birth of Kwame Nkrumah as an important icon of Pan-Africanism and nationalism. The Ghanaian government and the African Union sponsored one such conference in Accra.

Even members of the United State Senate (of a country which played the biggest role in overthrowing him) passed a bill to commemorate Nkrumah – on the occasion of his birth centenary – something that Nkrumah had done philatelically, when his government issued stamps commemorating the birth and death of Lincoln and JFK.

This symbolic-diplomatic reconciliation between

Ghana and the United States is significant, given their informal break in relations toward the end of Nkrumah's presidency.

Undoubtedly, scholars will continue to debate the legacy of Kwame Nkrumah's almost two-decade long premiership of the Gold Coast/Ghana, as well as the implications of this legacy for the Diamond Jubilee of Ghanaian nationhood.

With the revaluation of the Ghanaian Cedi; plans to institute a regional, West African common currency (the Eco); the continual utilization of Ghanaian and African postage stamps to express nationalism; the building of new monuments of Nkrumah and other Founding Fathers and common citizens; the exhibition of museum objects to reinterpret Ghana and Africa's past; and the changing symbolism of Ghanaian and African national emblems and insignia, scholars will have more opportunities to analyze the changing role of symbolic nationalism in the continuous and contentious project of nation-building in Ghana, Africa, and the 'Third World.'

At the mark of his birth centenary, and despite some legitimate criticisms of Nkrumah's imperfect but important record as premier of Ghana and an international statesman, the *Osagyefo* has been overwhelmingly redeemed by history – at least symbolically. Gocking, in his final appraisal of the legacy of Nkrumah, stated:

'Undoubtedly the most important indication of Nkrumah's enduring stature is how much better he has done in retrospect than those who overthrew and succeeded him. He left a stamp on Ghanaian history that continues, long after his death, to fascinate and inspire many of his countrymen as well as people all over the world of African descent...his countrymen continue to 'render homage' to his 'immortal memory,' even to the point that his weakness and failures have largely been forgotten.'" – (Ibid., pp. 187 – 188).

He was denounced as a visionary who pursued Utopian ideals of continental unification under one government even if it was for altruistic reasons, not for his own benefit to make history. His critics said African countries can not unite and will never unite under one government. He said they can and they must. Otherwise we are going to perish. He has been vindicated by history. As Dr. K.B. Asante who was secretary (of state) to Nkrumah and later diplomat, stated in an interview with CCTV Africa, "Faces of Africa," in a documentary about Nkrumah:

"To him African union was a passion. And I think he is right. Look at what is happening in Africa now. Congo, the richest country, what is there now? Warlords all over, with these private enterprises from outside. They do what they like. I mean, look at what is happening. He foresaw that if we didn't come together, we would be in our present state....He could be charming when he wanted to but normally, as someone who worked with him, he was what I would call a charming hard task master." – (See also Kwame Nkrumah, *Challenge of the Congo: A Case Study of Foreign Pressures in an Independent State*, London: Panaf, 1967; Godfrey Mwakikagile, *Congo in The Sixties*, Dar es Salaam: New Africa Press, 2014).

Professor Mike Ocquaye, a former member of parliament, said the following about Nkrumah in the same documentary:

"His smile was infectious. That was the charm of Nkrumah, a man who was very committed to Africa. Nkrumah lived and died Africa."

He once said if African countries unite day, the name of the new giant nation should simply be "Africa." It would be a nation which would be able to protect her people and her resources. As he stated in *I speak of Freedom: A Statement of African Ideology*:

"For centuries, Europeans dominated the African continent. The white man arrogated to himself the right to rule and to be obeyed by the non-white; his mission, he claimed, was to 'civilise' Africa. Under this cloak, the Europeans robbed the continent of vast riches and inflicted unimaginable suffering on the African people.

....We must find an African solution to our problems, and that this can only be found in African unity. Divided we are weak. United, Africa could become one of the greatest forces for good in the world.

Although most Africans are poor, our continent is potentially extremely rich. Our mineral resources, which are being exploited with foreign capital only to enrich foreign investors, range from gold and diamonds to uranium and petroleum. Our forests contain some of the finest woods to be grown anywhere. Our cash crops include cocoa, coffee, rubber, tobacco and cotton. As for power, which is an important factor in any economic development, Africa contains over 40% of the potential water power of the world, as compared with about 10% in Europe and 13% in North America. Yet so far, less than 1% has been developed. This is one of the reasons why we have in Africa the paradox of poverty in the midst of plenty, and scarcity in the midst of abundance.

Never before have a people had within their grasp so great an opportunity for developing a continent endowed with so much wealth. Individually, the independent states of Africa, some of them potentially rich, others poor, can do little for their people. Together, by mutual help, they can achieve much. But the economic development of the continent must be planned and pursued as a whole. A loose confederation designed only for economic co-operation would not provide the necessary unity of purpose. Only a strong political union can bring about full and effective development of our natural resources for the benefit of our people.

The political situation in Africa today is heartening and at the same time disturbing. It is heartening to see so many new flags hoisted in place of the old; it is disturbing to see so many countries of varying sizes and at different levels of development, weak and, in some cases, almost helpless. If this terrible state of fragmentation is allowed to continue it may well be disastrous for us all.

....Critics of African unity often refer to the wide differences in culture, language and ideas in various parts of Africa. This is true, but the essential fact remains that we are all Africans, and have a common interest in the independence of Africa. The difficulties presented by questions of language, culture and different political systems are not insuperable. If the need for political union is agreed by us all, then the will to create it is born; and where there's a will there's a way.

The present leaders of Africa have already shown a remarkable willingness to consult and seek advice among themselves. Africans have, indeed, begun to think continentally. They realise that they have much in common, both in their past history, in their present problems and in their future hopes. To suggest that the time is not yet ripe for considering a political union of Africa is to evade the facts and ignore realities in Africa today.

The greatest contribution that Africa can make to the peace of the world is to avoid all the dangers inherent in disunity, by creating a political union which will also by its success, stand as an example to a divided world. A Union of African states will project more effectively the African personality. It will command respect from a world that has regard only for size and influence. The scant attention paid to African opposition to the French atomic tests in the Sahara, and the ignominious spectacle of the U.N. in the Congo quibbling about constitutional niceties while the Republic was tottering into anarchy, are evidence of the callous disregard of African Independence by the Great Powers.

We have to prove that greatness is not to be measured in stockpiles of atom bombs. I believe strongly and sincerely that with the deep-rooted wisdom and dignity, the innate respect for human lives, the intense humanity that is our heritage, the African race, united under one federal government, will emerge not as just another world bloc to flaunt its wealth and strength, but as a Great Power whose greatness is indestructible because it is built not on fear, envy and suspicion, nor won at the expense of others, but founded on hope, trust, friendship and directed to the good of all mankind.

The emergence of such a mighty stabilising force in this strife-worn world should be regarded not as the shadowy dream of a visionary, but as a practical proposition, which the peoples of Africa can, and should, translate into reality. There is a tide in the affairs of every people when the moment strikes for political action. Such was the moment in the history of the United States of America when the Founding Fathers saw beyond the petty wranglings of the separate states and created a Union. This is our chance. We must act now. Tomorrow may be too late and the opportunity will have passed, and with it the hope of free Africa's survival." – (Kwame Nkrumah, *I speak of Freedom: A Statement of African Ideology*, New York: Frederick A. Praeger, 1961, pp. xi – xiv).

Tragically, the same Western powers who played a major role in overthrowing Nkrumah are the same ones who are now busy exploiting Africa as Africans watch helplessly because Africa is not united, unable to protect herself from ruthless exploitation by foreign powers. The continent's resources are exploited ruthlessly, mostly by Western countries led by the United States, as if they belong to nobody. Multinational corporations, owned by the West, have taken over African countries in this era of globalisation.

In almost all the countries in sub-Saharan Africa, vast tracts of land – hundreds of thousands and even millions of acres in a number of countries – have been acquired by foreigners. The land does not belong to the people anymore:

"One of the most critical areas where we face the danger of losing our continent to foreigners, and where conflicts between the indigenous people and foreign investors could destabilise our countries, is land ownership.

We have a phenomenon – land grab or land grabbing – that has evolved into what can rightly be called the second scramble for Africa. It involves foreign investors, including multinational corporations, who are acquiring land across Africa on a scale never seen before, often by dubious means, and dispossessing rightful owners of millions of acres in collusion with unscrupulous politicians and bureaucrats who are in every government, in every country, on the continent.

Tanzania's minister of foreign affairs and international cooperation, Bernard Membe, conceded in an interview with Voice of America (VOA) in 2011 that we have lost hundreds of millions of acres of land to foreigners. He went on to say, collectively, the amount of land Africans have lost is equal to the size of Germany. The land does not belong to us anymore, he emphasised.

Yet, the government of Tanzania itself, his own government, signed a deal with Saudi Arabia which gave the Saudis 500,000 hectares of land to grow food crops for their own consumption in Saudi Arabia. And they are not the only people who have acquired vast tracts of land in Tanzania on long tenure to grow different kind of crops for human consumption and for industrial use such as biofuel production.

Other African governments have signed similar agreements, with many foreign countries and investors, depriving their own people of arable. This has led to food shortages and even starvation in many parts of Africa. Land which belongs to Africans is used to grow crops to feed foreigners while Africans themselves are starving or do not have enough to eat in their own countries.

Even a desperately poor and traumatised country like Sierra Leone which went through a horrendous tragedy during its 10-year civil war in the1900s can not justify its enormous sale of land to foreigners. The government has sold a fifth of the land to British, Indian, Chinese and Belgian companies, according to a report by Africa Today, PressTV, London, in April 2013.

According to the same report, Sudan has sold more than 700,000 hectares of land to South Korea. And Liberia has sold 30 per cent of its land to foreigners; some reports say it has sold 50 per cent of its land.

India is one of the biggest investors in Africa. It has acquired hundreds of thousands of hectares of land in Ethiopia, Kenya and Madagascar to grow food crops such as rice and maize to feed its people.

In the Democratic Republic of Congo (DRC), one of the largest, richest and most fertile countries in Africa and in the entire world, the government has sold 50 per cent of the land to foreigners. That land does not belong to the people of Congo anymore. When the land goes, so do the minerals underneath; everything goes to those who have bought the land: foreign investors.

And they hardly pay anything for it, compared to its value. For example, in Ethiopia, investors from India have leased some land for only one dollar per hectare. It's not much different in other countries on the continent where some investors have even acquired land for less than one dollar per hectare.

There is another very disturbing example of how Africans are losing their land on very "generous" terms. It has to do with South Sudan.

One Nigerian social activist, Nnimmo Bassey, former executive director of the Environmental Rights Action in Abuja, Nigeria, said in television interview with Henry Bonsu of Africa Today, PressTV, London, in April 2013, that there was an American company which, after speculating that South Sudan would become an independent country one day, bought 600,000 hectares of land there for only 25,000 US dollars. It is going to own the land for 50 years. The company bought the land not long before South Sudan won independence after seceding from Sudan on 9 July 2011.

There are similar and very disturbing reports from many parts of the continent on how Africans are losing their land to foreigners and at a very fast pace. African farmers, most of whom are poor peasants and whose only means of surviving is farming, virtually have no right to land ownership in their own countries if the government decides to taken land away from them.

Countless across Africa have been forcibly removed from their land, with many of them dying of starvation because they don't have arable anymore where they can grow food crops. Food security has not become a major concern across the continent because of land grabbing by corrupt and insensitive African governments working with foreign investors who are busy acquiring vast tracts of land at the expense of the indigenous people in this era of globalisation. This is the second scramble for Africa, a new invasion of Africa Julius Nyerere warned about more than 50 years ago, in 1960, even before Tanganyika became independent the following year under his leadership. As he stated at a conference on Dar es Salaam, Tanganyika, in a speech to the Pan-African seminar in August 1960:

'We are now entering a new phase. It is the phase of the second scramble for Africa.'– (Julius Nyerere, in a speech delivered to the Second Pan-African Seminar, World Assembly of Youth, Dar es Salaam, Tanganyika, August 1961, in *WAY* (World Assemby of Youth) *Forum*, No. 40, September 1961; reprinted in Paul E. Sigmund, Jr., editor, *The Ideologies of the Developing Nation*, New York: Frederick A. Praeger, 1963, p. 205. See also *Tanganyika Standard*, Dar es Salaam, Tanganyika, August and September 1961.

Multinational corporations and other foreign investors, in collusion with African leaders, are at the forefront of the second scramble for Africa. It is a new form of colonialism under the the guise of partnership for development, with Africans being at an enormous advantage in this partnership. Globalisation is the new imperialism.

Pleas by Africans who are losing their land have fallen on deaf ears. Even many who were most productive on their land before this new invasion have not been spared. As Justine Mutale, a Zambian social activist who was also involved in an international organisation to fight global hunger, stated in an interview with Henry Bonsu of Africa Today, PressTV, London, in April 2013:

'I am very concerned about land grabs and I do acknowledge that land grabs... some people might not be aware of this, but it is a wider segment of a wider policy by the international community starting all the way from the Washington Consensus that came into Africa and asked, or rather in a way imposed on Africa, to try and open their borders to international trade. It is part of the trade policy and it's a policy that benefits foreign investors.

Land grabs also started with colonization. Before that, Africans had a right to their land, we had customary land, land that we inherited from generation to generation for our own use.

To talk about trying to feed ourselves - there was a time

in some parts of Africa up til today you don't need to have money to eat because we have wild fruits we have wild vegetables we have wild game, all you need is to just go out to get that food.

But the moment that a certain way of life was imposed on us where you have to exchange your labor in order to eat, where you have to work to earn money as in notes and coins in order to eat rather than your labor to labor to go and hunt, to go and harvest so that you can eat the food that you directly harvest...

Even today we have capable Africans.

My own grandmother more than 5 generations ago, she owned a coffee farm in Zambia and she used to export her coffee to all over the world. And this coffee farm, at the time that title deeds and foreign land ownership was introduced has been taken away from our family.

It is something that I could have carried on, or one of my children or even my nieces and nephews could have done, but we found that this coffee farm, this land that my grandmother used to farm coffee and export - she even came to England on a trade fair to display her coffee - That land has been taken away from our family because we didn't have title deeds.

Remember we had the right and access to use the land it was a customary or social contract.

I am totally against any foreigners coming into our land to take our land....

Even to do a deal I'm totally against that.

My Grandmother fifty years ago she managed to feed the country, we used to export her coffee, it's just that the land was customary inherited so she didn't own title deeds and when the title deeds were introduced to our countries and to Africa we found that our country lost out on that.

I could have done it, my children could have done it or even any of my cousins... could have carried on feeding the country with coffee.

We believe that this is a scandal and it's a scandal that

needs to be stopped because land grabs render people refugees, they make people become refugees in their own God-given land.

They make people go hungry and making people go hungry is a violence against those people. You take away their rights of livelihood from the people; you take away their rights to shelter to food to clothing to anything they can do with the land that they have. You take that away from them and that is what the IF campaign is about is to stop land grab so that indigenous people can have their own dignity; can go back and use their land as they see fit.

All these generations we have been able to feed ourselves – until somebody comes and says you can't feed yourself. We know we can feed ourselves. If these people they come and purchase the land in which natural resources – underneath we've got copper or diamonds - they buy it and then they suddenly own the copper and diamonds, which should have belonged to my family or to the family that lived on that land.'

The people are completely left out. They do not take part in any negotiations involving such sales because they are not even invited by the leaders. African governments do what they want to do. They are ones who negotiate with the foreign investors, and they are the ones who sell the land to them, ostensibly for the benefit of the indigenous people.

The problem is compounded by the terms, unfavourable to the indigenous people, under which land is acquired by foreign investors reminiscent of what happened during the colonial era when long leases – for example, the 99-year leases in colonial Kenya – were common, enabling white settlers to acquire tens of thousands of acres of land at the expense of the indigenes who were not only barred from those vast tracts of land leased to white settlers; countless were forcibly removed from their ancestral lands which were then given to whites.

Just remember the Kikuyu and the Mau Mau uprising against the white settlers in central Kenya, the homeland of the Kikuyu.

The land question was one of the most volatile issues – if not the most incendiary – not only in Kenya during Mau Mau but also during the liberation struggle in the countries of southern Africa under white minority rule.

It is still a major problem today, as the conflict over land in Zimbabwe, has clearly demonstrated, and as the ethnic conflicts in the Rift Valley Province and elsewhere in Kenya – ignited and fuelled by unfair acquisition of land by the ruling elite since independence – also clearly show.

The only way to avert such catastrophes is to redistribute land fairly. Otherwise expect more eruptions and conflagrations over the central question of land.

Also, long tenures of ownership – all this nonsense about half-century and 99-year land leases to foreigners and even to local investors – should never be given. Those already given should be renegotiated to take into account the interests of the indigenous inhabitants who have been victimised by the land grabbers in these nefarious schemes in collusion with government officials who take bribes from foreign investors to grab land from the local people.

Land should be leased for no more than 20 years. After that, the terms of the lease should be renegotiated, taking into account the interests of the local people, how the land has been used, and what benefits the indigenes have been able to get from the investments in their area during that period. Shorter land leases will make investors more accountable, unlike 50 – 99-year leases.

The indigenous people should never be expelled from their land, deprived of ownership, to give room to investors. Never. Otherwise foreign investors are going to take over the continent and we will become slaves in our own land, owning nothing." – (Godfrey Mwakikagile, *Post-colonial Africa: A General Survey*, Dar es Salaam:

New Africa Press, 2014, pp. 409 – 415).

If Nkrumah were alive today, he would denounce globalisation as a new form of imperialism, a danger he foresaw coming and which he wrote about with so much passion in *Neo-Colonialism: The Last Stage of Imperialism*, a book that infuriated the United States so much that the American government decided to overthrow him for that reason alone even if there was no other to justify his ouster.

The book, published in October 1965, was preceded by another book by Nkrumah with an equally urgent message: *Africa Must Unite*.

When Nkrumah wrote *Africa Must Unite*, a book that was published to coincide with the establishment of the Organisation of African Unity (OAU) in May 1963 to emphasise the imperative need for unity, hardly anyone paid any attention to him. Now more than 50 years after he was removed from power, it is the enemies of Africa who are rejoicing. The continent is still weak and divided, and easy to exploit, which would have been impossible had African countries united under one strong government as Nkrumah advocated. He would say today: "I told you!"

But it's never too late. Regional economic blocs which exist today are a step in the right direction, eventually leading to formation of regional federations or confederations and possibly continental unity under one government as advocated by Nkrumah. As Nyerere stated in his speech, "Without unity, there is no future for Africa," in Accra on Ghana's 40th independence anniversary on 6 March 1997:

"In May 1963, 32 independent African states met in Addis Ababa, founded the Organisation of African Unity (OAU), and established the Liberation Committee of the new organisation, charging it with the duty of coordinating the liberation struggle in those parts of Africa still under colonial rule. The following year, 1964, the OAU met in Cairo [Egypt]. The Cairo Summit is remembered mainly for the declaration of the heads of state of independent Africa to respect the borders inherited from colonialism. The principle of non-interference in internal affairs of member states of the OAU had been enshrined in the [OAU] Charter itself. Respect for the borders inherited from colonialism came from the Cairo Declaration of 1964.

In 1965, the OAU met in Accra [Ghana]. That summit is not as well remembered as the founding summit in 1963 or the Cairo Summit of 1964. The fact that Nkrumah did not last long as head of state of Ghana after that summit may have contributed to the comparative obscurity of that important summit. But I want to suggest that the reason why we do not talk much about [the 1965] summit is probably psychological: it was a failure. That failure still haunts us today.

The founding fathers of the OAU had set themselves two major objectives: the total liberation of our continent from colonialism and settler minorities, and the unity of Africa. The first objective was expressed through the immediate establishment of the Liberation Committee by the founding summit [of 1963]. The second objective was expressed in the name of the organisation –the Organisation of African Unity. Critics could say that the [OAU] Charter itself, with its great emphasis on the sovereign independence of each member state, combined with the Cairo Declaration on the sanctity of the inherited borders, make it look like the "Organisation of African Disunity". But that would be carrying criticism too far and ignoring the objective reasons which led to the principles of non-interference in the Cairo Declaration. What the founding fathers – certainly a hardcore of them – had in mind was a genuine desire to move Africa towards greater unity. We loathed the balkanisation of the continent into small unviable states, most of which had borders which did not make ethnic or geographical sense.

The Cairo Declaration was promoted by a profound realisation of the absurdity of those borders. It was quite clear that some adventurers would try to change those borders by force of arms. Indeed, it was already happening. Ethiopia and Somalia were at war over inherited borders.

Nkrumah was opposed to balkanisation as much as he was opposed to colonialism in Africa. To him and to a number of us, the two – balkanisation and colonialism – were twins. Genuine liberation of Africa had to attack both twins. A struggle against colonialism must go hand in hand with a struggle against the balkanisation of Africa. Kwame Nkrumah was the great crusader of African unity. He wanted the Accra Summit of 1965 to establish a union government for the whole of independent Africa. But we failed. The one minor reason is that Kwame, like all great believers, underestimated the degree of suspicion and animosity which his crusading passion had created among a substantial number of his fellow heads of state. The major reason was linked to the first: already too many of us had a vested interest in keeping Africa divided.

East Africa

Prior to the independence of Tanganyika, I had been advocating that East African countries should federate and then achieve independence as a single political unit. I had said publicly that I was willing to delay Tanganyika's independence in order to enable all the three mainland countries to achieve their independence together as a single federated state. I made the suggestion because of my fear – proved correct by later events – that it would be very difficult to unite our countries if we let them achieve independence separately.

Once you multiply national anthems, national flags and

national passports, seats of the United Nations, and individuals entitled to a 21-gun salute, not to speak of a host of ministers, prime ministers and envoys, you would have a whole army of powerful people with vested interests in keeping Africa balkanised. That was what Nkrumah encountered in 1965. After the failure to establish the union government at the Accra Summit, I heard one head of state express with relief that he was happy to be returning home to his country still head of state. To this day, I cannot tell whether he was serious or joking.

But he may well have been serious, because Kwame Nkrumah was very serious and the fear of a number of us of losing our precious status was quite palpable. But I never believed that the 1965 Accra Summit would have established a union government for Africa. When I say that we failed, that is not what I mean; for that clearly was an unrealistic objective for a single summit.

What I mean is that we did not even discuss a mechanism for pursuing the objective of a politically united Africa. We had a Liberation Committee already. We should have at least had a Unity Committee or undertaken to establish one. We did not. And after Kwame Nkrumah was removed from the African scene, nobody took up the challenge again.

Confession and plea

So my remaining remarks have a confession and a plea. The confession is that we of the first generation leaders of independent Africa have not pursued the objective of African unity with vigour, commitment and [the] sincerity that it deserved. Yet that does not mean that unity is now irrelevant. Does the experience of the last three or four decades of Africa's independence dispel the need for African unity?

With our success in the liberation struggle, Africa today

has 53 independent states, 21 more than those which met in Addis Ababa in May 1963. [With South Sudan's independence in 2011, Africa now has 54 independent states.] If numbers were horses, Africa today would be riding high! Africa would be the strongest continent in the world, for it occupies more seats in the UN General Assembly than any other continent.

Yet the reality is that ours is the poorest and weakest continent in the world. And our weakness is pathetic. Unity will not end our weakness, but until we unite, we cannot even begin to end that weakness. So this is my plea to the new generation of African leaders and African peoples: work for unity with the firm conviction that without unity, there is no future for Africa. That is, of course, assuming that we still want to have a place under the sun. I reject the glorification of the nationstate [that] we inherited from colonialism, and the artificial nations we are trying to forge from that inheritance. We are all Africans trying very hard to be Ghanaians or Tanzanians. Fortunately for Africa, we have not been completely successful.

The outside world hardly recognises our Ghanaianness or Tanzanian-ness. What the outside world recognises about us is our Africanness. Hitler was a German, Mussolini was an Italian, Franco was a Spaniard, Salazar was Portuguese, Stalin was a Russian or a Georgian. Nobody expected Churchill to be ashamed of Hitler. He was probably ashamed of Chamberlain. Nobody expected Charles de Gaulle to be ashamed of Hitler, he was probably ashamed of the complicity of Vichy. It is the Germans and Italians and Spaniards and Portuguese who feel uneasy about those dictators in their respective countries.

Not so in Africa. Idi Amin was in Uganda but of Africa. Jean Bokassa was in Central Africa but of Africa. Some of the dictators are still alive in their respective countries, but they are all of Africa. They are all Africans, and all perceived by the outside world as Africans.

When I travel outside Africa, the description of me as a former president of Tanzania is a fleeting affair. It does not stick. Apart from the ignorant who sometimes asked me whether Tanzania was in Johannesburg, even to those who knew better, what stuck in the minds of my hosts was the fact of my African-ness.

So I had to answer questions about the atrocities of the Amins and Bokassas of Africa. Mrs [Indira] Ghandi [the former Indian prime minister] did not have to answer questions about the atrocities of the Marcoses of Asia. Nor does Fidel Castro have to answer questions about the atrocities of the Somozas of Latin America.

But when I travel or meet foreigners, I have to answer questions about Somalia, Liberia, Rwanda, Burundi and Zaire, as in the past I used to answer questions about Mozambique, Angola, Zimbabwe, Namibia or South Africa.

And the way I was perceived is the way most of my fellow heads of state were perceived. And that is the way you [the people of Africa] are all being perceived. So accepting the fact that we are Africans, gives you a much more worthwhile challenge than the current desperate attempts to fossilise Africa into the wounds inflicted upon it by the vultures of imperialism. Do not be proud of your shame. Reject the return to the tribe, there is richness of culture out there which we must do everything we can to preserve and share.

But it is utter madness to think that if these artificial, unviable states which we are trying to create are broken up into tribal components and we turn those into nation-states we might save ourselves. That kind of political and social atavism spells catastrophe for Africa. It would be the end of any kind of genuine development for Africa. It would fossilise Africa into a worse state than the one in which we are.

The future

The future of Africa, the modernisation of Africa that has a place in the 21st century, is linked with its decolonisation and detribalisation. Tribal atavism would be giving up any hope for Africa. And of all the sins that Africa can commit, the sin of despair would be the most unforgivable.

Reject the nonsense of dividing the African peoples into Anglophones, Francophones, and Lusophones. This attempt to divide our peoples according to the language of their former colonial masters must be rejected with the firmness and utter contempt that it richly deserves.

The natural owners of those wonderful languages are busy building a united Europe. But Europe is strong even without unity. Europe has less need of unity, and the strength that comes from unity, than Africa.

A new generation of self-respecting Africans should spit in the face of anybody who suggests that our continent should remain divided and fossilised in the shame of colonialism, in order to satisfy the national pride of our former colonial masters. Africa must unite! That was the title of one of Kwame Nkrumah's books. That call is more urgent today than ever before.

Together, we, the peoples of Africa will be incomparably stronger internationally than we are now with our multiplicity of unviable states. The needs of our separate countries can be, and are being, ignored by the rich and powerful. The result is that Africa is marginalised when international decisions affecting our vital interests are made. Unity will not make us rich, but it can make it difficult for Africa and the African peoples to be disregarded and humiliated. And it will, therefore, increase the effectiveness of the decisions we make and try to implement for our development.

My generation led Africa to political freedom. The current generation of leaders and peoples of Africa must pick up the flickering torch of African freedom, refuel it with their enthusiasm and determination, and carry it forward."

Nyerere strongly condemned the coup against Nkrumah and the forces behind it. He said there was not a single African leader who was more committed to the liberation of Africa than Nkrumah was. Now that he was gone, colonial and neo-colonial forces were jubilant. As he stated at a press conference in Dar es Salaam, Tanzania, soon after Dr. Nkrumah was overthrown:

"What is happening in Africa? What are the coups about? The last few months have seen changes of governments in many African countries. The latest has been in Ghana. What is behind all this? Are these 'revolutions' intended to remove humiliation and oppression from Africa?

Let us take the latest in Ghana. The enemies of Africa are now jubilant. There is jubilation in Salisbury and Johannesburg. Even a fool could begin to wonder whether these 'revolutions' would help Africa.

What was Kwame trying to do? He stood for the liberation of Africa. There is not a single leader in Africa more committed to this than Kwame. Whom did he anger with his commitment to freedom? Certainly not Africa. He was committed to true independence. He was not merely against ordinary colonialism; he was against neo-colonialism – against a colonial power going out through the political door and controlling the country through the economic door." – (Nyerere, quoted by Nkrumah, *Dark Days in Ghana* (New York: Monthly Review Press, 1968). See also *The Nationalist*, and the *Standard*, Dar es Salaam, Tanzania, February 25, 1966; and Godfrey Mwakikagile, *Africa after Independence: Realities of Nationhood*, Dar es

Salaam: New Africa Press, 2009, pp. 61 – 62).

Nkrumah was overthrown after most African countries had won independence in rapid succession, but the entire southern Africa was still under white minority rule when he was ousted. That was also where the toughest, and bloodiest, struggle for freedom was waged in the following years.

But in spite of his short tenure on the African political scene as president, he remained a formidable political personality of continental and international stature because of the awe and admiration he inspired among millions of Africans and people of African descent around the world. And decades after his death, he continued to have great influence among Africans of all generations as he still does today. But there is something missing in Africa today: good leadership.

Africa needs leaders with a Pan-African vision Nkrumah and a few other leaders of the independence generation had in order to unite the continent. We don't have leaders of that kind anymore fifty years after independence. When Nkrumah was overthrown in 1966, the strongest voice for continental unity faded into oblivion; so did the passion. But there is still hope for Africa.

Appendix I:

American ambassadors to Ghana: Excerpts from interviews

Ambassador Robert P. Smith, interviewed by Charles Stuart Kennedy, 28 February 1989, The Association for Diplomatic Studies and Training, Foreign Affairs Oral History Project.

Smith: When I left (Nigeria), I was reassigned to the Department. I had been abroad then for almost ten years and they pulled me back to the Department, having me in mind for the Nigeria desk. That was filled, initially, though, so I took the Ghana desk for the first year.
Q: This is 1965?
Smith: I came back in 1965 and from 1965 until 1966 I handled the Ghana desk. And toward the end of 1966 things in Nigeria went from bad to worse. It fell to my successor, Bob Barnard, to evacuate American citizens because of the war. There were massacres of Ibos in the North. I mean real massacres, they were killed in the streets.

Q: This is in Nigeria?

Smith: Yes. 1965 and 1966. So the civil war broke out. The Eastern Region tried to peel off, seceded from the Federation and declared itself the Republic of Biafra. By this time Ambassador Palmer had come back as Assistant Secretary for African Affairs, so I worked very closely with him during the war years.

Q: I'd like to come back to that but, first, why don't we talk about the Ghana time. You were, again, dealing with Ghana at a difficult time. Could you explain what our relations were in 1965 and 1966, how you saw it from the desk?

Smith: Before coming back and taking over the desk I drove overland from Enugu, west to Lagos, and then all the way across the west coast into Accra for a week's visit there with the embassy staff in Ghana. I'd been there before but only briefly. We had a very fine staff there, one of whom, a junior political officer on the staff then, is now our ambassador in Moscow, Jack Matlock. That was where I first met Jack.

Kwame Nkrumah was still in power in 1965. And to say that he was difficult for the embassy and the United States Government would be the understatement of the year. He seemed to be, at times, almost losing his mind. Ghana had been left--Ghana was the first to come to independence--in really excellent shape by the British--myths to the contrary notwithstanding. They had a very favorable balance of payments. They had millions and millions in foreign reserves, hard currency. And Nkrumah simply ran the country into the ground by his tortured anti-Western, Socialistic, anti-capitalist attitudes.

The strange thing about that initial visit to Ghana was, even though I was being briefed on the idiosyncrasies of Nkrumah, at the same time individual Ghanaians, even senior civil servants, to say nothing of the man on the street, couldn't have been nicer or more blatantly pro-American to the extent of their saying at times that, "You mustn't pay too much about what Osaygefo says." Osaygefo was a name he was called by the Ghanaian people. Ghanaians, perhaps second only to the Ibos, from whom I had just come, are among the most likeable, pleasant, nice people in all of Africa. They are simply an enormously likeable, warm, generous, outgoing people. I can't find enough adjectives to use with respect to the Ghanaians.

It was tragic for us to sit back and see Nkrumah running this country into the ground the way he did, and it was happening right before our eyes. When I went there in 1965, there were still a number of hotels in downtown Accra that served excellent meals. I remember having lunch on the patio of one of those hotels. By the time I went back years later as ambassador, none of them could do that. There was nothing to be had. There was nothing to eat, et cetera. And almost all of it was attributed to Nkrumah's madness. I don't mean that literally.

Q: Was there concern that there might be a mental problem there?

Smith: I don't think seriously, no.

Q: This was an attitude?

Smith: An attitude, yes. It was fascinating to deal with it. He was concentrating on the urban areas. And this is an age-old story in Africa where African leaders tend to concentrate on keeping their urban populations happy at the expense of their rural populations. And Nkrumah did this with respect to his cocoa farmers, cocoa being the largest source of foreign exchange. And as a result, they couldn't get people to man cocoa farms and the country just spun out of control.

So much so that, while I was on the Ghana desk nine or ten months later, they had had enough and Nkrumah was overthrown in a coup. They did this in relatively bloodless fashion. While Nkrumah was in the air flying to Red China, he was met on the ground in Peking by his Chinese host and it fell to them to inform him that he was no longer

Head of State in the Republic of Ghana. So that was a fascinating time in a fascinating country.

Q: Was our feeling one of passivity towards Nkrumah? I'm talking about the time that you were dealing with it. Were we trying to say enough is enough because the man was attacking us, at least verbally, all the time.

Smith: He certainly was. We tried for years to get along with Nkrumah. We would turn the other cheek at times and do everything we could to assuage his anger. Nothing worked with him, however. And, again, while I was on the Desk, I think Nkrumah dropped the straw that broke the camel's back, so to speak, in that he published a new book called *Neo-Colonialism*. I've forgotten the subtitle (*The Last Stage of Imperialism* – added by Godfrey Mwakikagile), which was simply outrageous. It accused the United States of every sin imaginable to man. We were blamed for everything in the world.

The book was so bad that I remember the then Assistant Secretary, G. Mennen Williams, called me up and gave me that book and said, "Bob, I know this is bad. I don't know how bad. I want you to take it home tonight and read it. You're not going to get any sleep and I apologize for that, but on my desk, by eight o'clock tomorrow morning, I've got to have a written summary of this because I have called the Ghanaian ambassador in at ten o'clock tomorrow morning. We're going to protest this book." There had already been advance publicity so we knew it was bad, but we hadn't had our hands on a copy. And it was everything we feared it would be. It was awful.

And the next morning--of course, he had me in on this meeting as the note taker—a lovely, old man, Michael Ribiero, was the Ghanaian ambassador. Hated Nkrumah privately, but was a good soldier trying to put the best face on this, a career officer in their foreign service and very respected here and in Ghana. Governor Williams, of course, was a relatively mild-mannered man. I had never heard Soapy Williams raise his voice until that conversation. Neither have I ever heard an ambassador get a tongue lashing like Ribiero got from Assistant Secretary Williams that morning. He, unfortunately, tried a couple times to interrupt the governor when he was making a point. He had my notes in front of him. And at one point, when Ribiero interrupted him, said, "Just a minute, Mr. Ambassador, don't interrupt me. I'm not through." And he continued to go on. He was raising his voice. He was shaking his finger in the ambassador's face. And it was a very painful, hour-long interview. To put it mildly, he protested vigorously the contents and publication of this book.

I think the publication of that book might also have contributed in a material way to his overthrow shortly thereafter. The Ghanaian people, as I say, did not share Nkrumah's views on many things. The Ghanaians have always had a warm relationship with the United States. Nkrumah simply, as the British say, went round the bend and they got a belly full of it and booted him out of office.

I also remember, the morning of the coup, I got the call about 2 a.m. here at the house and went into the Department and immediately set up a little task force in the Operations Center. Later in the same morning, about 8 or 8:30, Secretary Rusk wandered down the hall and came in and said, "I've seen the early reports, but I just want to hear it firsthand. What's going on in Ghana?" When I related how Nkrumah had landed in Peking and had been informed by his Chinese hosts of what had happened in Ghana, Dean Rusk broke into an ear-splitting grin. I've never seen him look so happy.

Q: Enough was enough, I guess.

Smith: Enough was enough, yes.

Q: Again, this is an unclassified interview, and I know there's been accusations. I think, actually, while you were in Ghana they came out to the fore again that the CIA had been involved. Did you have any feel towards that while you were there?

Smith: Yes. We had been accused of that all along. There was nothing to it. I mean, it was obvious that we were not among his legions of supporters, but neither were we involved because there was no reason to be involved. The Ghanaian military were quite capable of dealing with this on their own, as they did. Unfortunately, the government that followed was, in its own way, almost as bad as Nkrumah's. We had high hopes for it, but it didn't materialize.

In just a few years that civilian, truly democratic government, elected in a free election, was itself overthrown by the military because they hadn't been able to correct the economic imbalances and so forth, and there was corruption, which just seemed to be endemic. So Ghana then went on without any direct involvement on my part until I later went back as ambassador years later.

Q: Well, let's move on to Nigeria. You became the head of the Nigerian Desk in 1966. For somebody who was looking at this record, what does it mean to be the head of a desk or a desk officer for Nigeria, for example?

Smith: I think, perhaps, the simplest way of putting this is that the State Department desk officer for any given country is the point man for that country within the United States Government. And any questions, almost without exception, having to do with that country, that desk officer, if he doesn't have the answer, is supposed to be able to put his finger on it right away. He is the action officer on the incoming telegrams from that post and is expected to know a great deal about the country.

Ideally, he will, of course, have served in that country. So I was in an ideal situation, having just finished three years in Nigeria. I was also blessed by the fact that Governor Williams had been replaced by Joseph Palmer as Assistant Secretary, with whom I had a very close personal relationship.

Q: And who had been ambassador.

Smith: And who had been ambassador in Nigeria for four years. So the war came as a terrible, personal blow both to Assistant Secretary Palmer and to me because we had so thoroughly enjoyed our service in Nigeria, and we were so fond of the Nigerian people. Conscious as we were of the tribal problems which rent the country apart, we were very sad to have it happen.

In my own personal case, and I guess Foreign Service Officers have this kind of problem from time to time, I was in personal agony because my heart was pulling me in one direction in that my personal friends, my closest friends, in Nigeria, were all rebels overnight. They called themselves Biafrans. And very dear friends, my children's teachers, the entire cabinet of Premier Okpara, and so forth, and many of the army officers that I knew were suddenly rebels.

Instinctively, therefore, in my heart I had a certain latent sympathy for them because I knew what they had gone through the last few years. I knew how mistreated they felt, how put upon. So I couldn't avoid a personal feeling of sympathy. And yet, our policy, which I must say, I helped formulate and adhere to over those years, was one of clear-cut support for the federal government. We felt very strongly that the worst things that could happen was to see Nigeria torn apart.

Had that happened, I think we would have seen a real domino effect in Africa in that there isn't a single country in Black Africa that doesn't have similar tribal divisions. If you once start down the road of tribes being able to secede from the national government, it would be utter chaos and you'd have a Balkanization such as the world has never seen before.

Q: We'd already been facing this problem in the Congo.

Smith: Yes, that's true. And we had a similar policy there.

Q: Did you feel that the Congo example was very

much before you?

Smith: I don't remember Congo being much of an example. I'm sure it may have been in the back of our minds. On the other hand, and, again, I will confess to some prejudice here, the Nigerians were simply a great deal more civilized. When the Belgians left Kinshasa, there wasn't a single graduate engineer in the country. Nigeria was full of Rhodes Scholars, engineers, doctors, lawyers. The British, in short, did a much better job, so we had higher expectations for Nigeria, much higher. But I had this ambivalence in that I was sympathetic to the Biafrans on the one hand, but our policy was to support to the federal government.

Q: Let me ask a bit about this. All of a sudden all hell was breaking loose in Nigeria. How did policy develop? I mean, all of a sudden did everyone say, "Okay, let's sit down. We've got to have a policy."

Smith: No. I think it was not a question so much of formulating a new policy as continuing the old one. We have always taken the position that tribalism was one of the problems and that African states must have a strong central government and they must have a feeling of oneness, of unity. We had contributed to this all the time. When the secession came, we had strongly advised the Ibos not to go down this road.

I think, in their heart of hearts, they really felt that we would support them. They felt so close to us. The Ibos, I think, more than other tribes in Nigeria, felt close to Americans. They fancied themselves like Americans in their attitude toward work, and their gregariousness, and so forth. I think it came as a real shock to many of them that we did not support them. Now mind you, many private Americans did. Indeed, one of the most painful mornings I spent during those early years of the Biafra War was one Saturday morning when Joe Palmer and I drove out to Senator Kennedy's residence in McLean.

Q: This was Robert Kennedy?

Smith: No, Teddy Kennedy. We briefed him on the war and our policy there. Senator Kennedy made no bones about his sympathies lying with the Biafrans because the Biafrans had mounted an enormous and very successful propaganda campaign about their suffering.

Q: You said you went to see Senator Teddy Kennedy.

Smith: I should back up by mentioning how successful the Biafran, or Ibo, propaganda campaign was. I hadn't, at that point, seen anything quite equal to it except, possibly, the Israelis. They managed to get cover stories in *Time*, in *Newsweek*, *Life*, with the cry of "genocide," that these horrible northern Moslems in Nigeria were trying, literally, to wipe out the Ibos as a people, all eight or ten million of them, however many there were. This was not true. We never thought it was true.

Ambassador Palmer, of course, knew Balewa, Azikiwe, and the others much better than I did. And later, when Balewa was assassinated, General Gowon became the Head of State. He was a hymn-singing, practicing Methodist, although from one of the small Northern tribes, not the major tribes. We never really thought for a minute that genocide was the intention of anyone.

Q: Let me ask a question that there was a hint of in what you are saying. Do you think that there was a parallel between this and, you might say, the media looking at the problem of Israel? In other words, here is an outgoing people and here are these Moslems. Maybe it wasn't the Israeli lobby, but the supporters of Israel saw a parallel here.

Smith: Absolutely.

Q: And if you let one go, the other might go.

Smith: Absolutely. The Ibos, with great pride, called themselves in those years, "the Israelis of Africa." They milked that for all it was worth.

Q: So this is much of the reason for the success of this?

Smith: Yes. Yes. They raised enormous amounts of money here and in Israel, and elsewhere. The Israelis flew in military equipment, and so forth. Several other states did, too, the French and others. In short, the Biafrans almost succeeded, especially, in Britain because of their British ties, but elsewhere in Western Europe, and in Israel, and in the United States. They developed an enormous reservoir of good will and support. Our policy was not to do that, of course. So this became very awkward for us.

Also, because the Ibos are so Christian, they managed to enlist the support of Catholic Relief Services. The major hierarchy of the Catholic Church here was strongly supportive of Biafra. That, of course, impacted on Senator Kennedy. They also enlisted the support of the World Council of Churches, and the American Jewish Committee. And I can best illustrate the point by relating that Catholic Relief Services, the World Council of Churches, and the American Jewish Committee, and several other religious organizations all got together and demanded a meeting with Secretary Rusk on the Biafran War, demanding that we change our policy and stop the "genocide" going on in Biafra.

So I arranged this meeting. Assistant Secretary Palmer and I accompanied the Secretary. And for an hour or an hour-and-a-half, these distinguished religious leaders of all the major faiths were ripping into Secretary Rusk, whom we had prepared, obviously, as best we could, to answer these questions. And I must say, the Secretary responded beautifully, keeping his eye on the U.S. interests down the road. "We didn't want to see the country fall apart and, indeed, we did not believe for a minute the charge of genocide. Any civil war is horrible, brother against brother, et cetera, et cetera." And the Secretary handled this beautifully. But I don't think we satisfied these gentlemen.

I'll never forget what happened then. The meeting

broke up and we saw the religious leaders out the door. We left the conference room and started walking down the hall. I was sort of lagging behind the Secretary and Ambassador Palmer. I remember Mr. Rusk put his arm around Joe's shoulder and looked at him as they were striding down the hall, and he said, "Joe, congratulations." He said, "You've succeeded in getting the Catholics and the Jews and the Protestants all mad at us at the same time. What do you do in your spare time?" And he laughed. [Laughs] These were difficult times, and we needed to keep our sense of humor.

Q: Well, after all, when you look at it, we have a policy that makes sense, but Nigeria, or even Africa, is not at the top of our plate or what have you.

Smith: No, but Nigeria was at the top of our African plate.

Q: At the same time, looking at it at as a practical measure, one can say that, in the Middle East, Israel is a political entity because of support within the United States, rather than looking at it as in our real strategic interests. I mean, there's a strong case to be made there. But because of political pressure we give it our unqualified support. Now here you have almost the same pressures, albeit not over a long period of time, but rising up. The State Department and the Administration often gives in to expediency, particularly, political expediency. Why didn't we give in on this one?

Smith: Well, I take great pride in that. I think I helped contribute to it because I know Ambassador Palmer would often refer to me as illustrating his point that, however sympathetic we might be to Biafrans on a personal basis, here is my desk officer who lived there for three years and knows them intimately, but even he understands that we can't let the secession succeed, not that we would lift a finger militarily to prevent it. We had a very firm policy of providing neither arms nor ammunition to either side in this dispute. Unfortunately, a lot of the other countries didn't follow this, so they were getting arms from the Soviets and some of the NATO countries, as well.

I would also attribute it to what I have already referred to, and that is the enormous success of the Biafrans' public relations effort. It was skillfully done. They retained high powered firms both in California and New York, and there was a steady drumbeat in the press. But I think, certainly, Ambassador Palmer, and the Secretary, and the President never wavered in their support. Indeed, one of the first national decision memoranda put before the new President Nixon was on the Biafran War. Nixon, too, came down firmly on the side of maintaining our policy.

But you are quite right, we were under enormous domestic political pressure. I will not identify this congressman, but I got an angry phone call one day from a congressman who demanded that we change our policy. I explained as best I could why we could not. I got a call from some Jewish leaders in New York who demanded the same thing. I had to refuse, there was just no way, this policy was firm and fixed. He said, "Well, I think you're going to be hearing from some of our friends on Capitol Hill." And within a week, the Department was inundated with irate telegrams, letters, and so forth, from representatives and senators on this.

Some of them, otherwise intelligent men and women, would have gotten us involved militarily, I'm sorry to say. Some U.S. senators, and I won't identify them, were actually pressuring us to use U.S. Air Force transport aircraft to drop food, supplies, and equipment behind the front lines into Biafra. And, of course, we kept refusing.

Going back to my personal agony on this, to reflect our support of the federal government, we would not receive or meet with Biafran officials. We didn't recognize it as an independent country. They built a clandestine air strip in Eastern Nigeria and managed to fly out on these various fund raising missions, and so forth. I remember on one occasion Sir Francis Ibiam, himself, the Governor of Eastern Nigeria, got to the States, got to Washington and asked to see me. What to do? Ambassador Palmer said, "Bob, there's no way you can receive him in the Department." And I said, "Well, right. But we need to know what he has to say."

To make a long story short, I found myself, literally, climbing up the backstairs of a Washington Hotel to a virtually clandestine meeting with the distinguished Sir Francis Ibiam, the Governor. And it was painful because he said, literally, "Bob, you know us. How can you let this happen to us? They're killing my people." So it was a difficult time for me.

Q: Were you there when the war was over or had you left?

Smith: Yes. And it ended in the way that we anticipated. That is to say, the federal government finally prevailed and crushed the secession. But what made us happiest was not that so much as the way they handled the defeated Eastern Region. Like Lincoln, they were very generous in their victory. There was no genocide or anything approaching that.

Q: I think this surprised so many of us because we had been hearing the drumbeats, and all this, and thought, "Oh, my God, here it comes." And it didn't.

Smith: Never happened.

Q: Which shows that you all knew what you were talking about.

Smith: It made honest men out of us. And I must say, it was a sigh of relief, in a way. Ambassador Palmer and I went out to Nigeria several times during the war, of course, and we would meet with General Gowon in Lagos. I had great confidence in him. I still think it was tragic that he was later assassinated (Gowon was not assassinated. He was overthrown by Murtala Muhammed who was later assassinated). He was one of those military leaders who was genuinely skilled in the art of governments, which is a rare thing, I think, in Africa.

Q: In your time on the desk you dealt with both Governor Mennen Williams, Soapy Williams, and with Joseph Palmer. I wonder if you could do a little of, as we used to say in school, compare and contrast their styles, and interest, and the way they dealt with matters in the Department, as you saw it from your point?

Smith: I admired both men enormously. Governor Williams, of course, came out of the American domestic political scene, a very popular four-term governor in Michigan. And I think what impressed many of us, as you may recall, was that President Kennedy appointed Soapy Williams as Assistant Secretary for Africa before he appointed Secretary Rusk, attaching, thereby, the importance to the job that Kennedy felt. And Soapy certainly shared that. He was genuinely interested in Africa. He was an indefatigable traveler, like a politician must be. He was a very fine listener, and so forth.

I don't think he was an intellectual heavyweight, but he was bright. And he, above all, knew to listen to his people. I think there was some naivete on Soapy William's part in that he expected too much too soon from Africa and was, I think, disappointed, as he was, of course, with Nkrumah, in the case of Ghana.

Joseph Palmer, on the other hand, brought to the job 20 to 25 years experience in Africa and elsewhere. He was a consummate professional foreign service officer. He was very, very bright, out of Harvard, was a very polished, intelligent, hard-working diplomat and knew Africa very well. He was cautious, conservative in his approach.

I didn't mention this before and I was very negligent not to have done so. We had a very fine professional in Lagos who replaced Ambassador Palmer there in the form of Elbert G. Matthews as ambassador. He was another seasoned professional. He'd been ambassador to Liberia before and knew Africa very well. He was a strong supporter of the federal government.

I guess I had a closer, personal relationship, for obvious reasons, with Ambassador Palmer. And, of course, then we were dealing with a crisis situation--12, 15 hour days. Many times Ambassador Palmer and I would be there until 10 o'clock at night, getting instructions out to the embassy, or something of that sort. I liked them both and they were both very effective in the job, very effective.

Q: Speaking from a somewhat removed perspective, not having dealt with African affairs, but the impression of many of the people in the foreign service was that Mennen Williams was a man whose heart was in the right place, but you mention this naivete, that it was hard to report from some posts in Africa if you said, you know, this country is falling apart, or this is a lousy leader, or something like this. He didn't want to hear this, particularly, if we were talking about native leaders. There was a certain amount of caution in how one reported because of this advocacy of the new independence movements in Africa.

Smith: Well, there may be something to that. I have no direct experience of that because I was in a consulate, reporting through the embassy, most of the time.

Q: And in a successful area, too.

Smith: Yes. Nigeria was successful. Certainly, there was nothing like that under Ambassador Palmer. With Williams I would simply leave it with naiveté. I think his heart certainly was in the right place, but he expected rather too much, I think.

Q: I think he reflected how many people in the United States felt. Certainly, you might say the liberal wing, and I include myself in this, wished Africa all the best.

Smith: Indeed, we all did. Sure.

Q: I'd like to move on. You then went from this rather agonizing place to quite a different world, but at the same

time, as difficult a world, when you were assigned from 1970 to 1974 to South Africa.

Smith: Yes. My last year in Washington, after I closed out the Nigerian Desk, I was a student at the National War College for a year. I was assigned from there as deputy chief of mission and minister counselor in the embassy in Pretoria, South Africa.

Q: Could I ask just a little about the War College? Did you find the War College a good year as far as professionally, or not?

Smith: Absolutely delightful year. I learned a great deal but, most of all, it was a delight to get out from under the pressure I had been working under for the previous four years. I still refer to it as, perhaps, my favorite year in my career. I didn't have to work nearly as hard.

South Africa, again, was a choice assignment for me, particularly since the ambassador, who was named just a few weeks before I was named, was a political appointee with no Foreign Service experience whatever. I was, therefore, the senior career State Department officer in the embassy.

Q: His name was John Hurd?

Smith: John Hurd, from Texas. A delightful man, warm, generous, outgoing, but with a considerable bit of naiveté, both with respect to Africa and even, indeed, the civil rights movement here in the United States.

Q: Why?

Smith: He had been Chairman of the Texas Republicans or Texas Republicans for Nixon, I forget exactly. He always insisted he was not a heavy, major contributor, but he was active in Republican politics in Laredo and San Antonio, Texas, and it was, admittedly, a political assignment. But John Hurd was enormously popular with the South Africans.

Q: When you say South Africans, what do you mean?

Smith: With white South Africans. Your point is well taken. He was popular among the embassy staff, too, in terms of John Hurd as a man, as an individual, because he looked every inch of the American ambassador, tall, handsome, distinguished, and without a mean bone in his body. He was just a warm, generous guy.

But in a way, I think he felt then, and perhaps he still feels now, that I pushed him awfully hard a lot of the time to do things that were "nasty" as far as the South African government was concerned. I had very strong views then and do now about this institutionalized racism that permeates the scene out there.

So those four years as DCM (Deputy Chief of Mission) to John, in one way, were delightful in the sense of our personal relationship and the beauty of the country and the people that we liked, black and white. At the same time, it was a real strain because I was always regarded by the South African government as the guy who the State Department sent out to keep John Hurd from being John Hurd and letting his normal instincts run; i.e, let the South Africans handle their own problem. "It's an internal problem and why should we be butting into their business. We wouldn't like it if they were butting into our business, et cetera, et cetera."

And the whole human rights equation didn't loom that large in Ambassador Hurd's mind. I say this, despite the way it may read, without any rancor whatever. He's very conservative. But to me and, happily, to the overwhelmingly majority of my embassy staff, the South African government was simply anathema in many respects.

Q: But in a way, you can say, "Okay, but you represent the United States Government's policy and, being the principal professional there, you wouldn't be giving guidance or pushing according to your predilections but more because this is American policy towards Africa and such and so, and Mr. Ambassador, you should do such and so even if you don't want to."

Did you feel, maybe, you were giving a little extra twist or something because of how you felt?

Smith: Perhaps at times I did. But on the other hand, our policy was all right. Our policy was one of open condemnation of apartheid, even then and that was during the Nixon years. There was no getting around that, but there are different ways of looking at a policy and then implementing it on the ground, as you very well know. Or you can wink and nod at a policy and simply not put your back into it. I guess the basic difference between us is I really wanted to put my back into it to a greater extent than the ambassador.

Having said that, it was under our regime, the Hurd-Smith regime in South Africa, that the first black foreign service officer was appointed to our staff in the embassy in Pretoria. He was a young economic officer named Jim Baker, no relation to the current Secretary. While Ambassador Hurd made all the right noises, he did have to swallow hard on this because I think he thought that was really going too far and rubbing the white South African noses in it a bit, whereas I didn't share that view.

Q: Whose initiative was this assignment made because, obviously, it was a policy initiative? It was in the papers of the day. I mean, it wasn't something that was unnoticed.

Smith: I, privately, had been pushing it for some time and I think Assistant Secretary David Newsom and Bev Carter, his principal deputy and later my predecessor in Liberia, probably were instrumental in pushing that appointment through. Mind you, not that there was vociferous opposition to it. I don't know what John Hurd said privately on the telephone, perhaps, to someone back in Washington, but he never really opposed us in any open fashion at all. He would make veiled references to it to me, privately. He'd say, "Bob, is this really necessary? And isn't he going to be ostracized?" He would come up with reasons. "Where are we going to house him? Will he be able to go into the same restaurant and eat with us?" I would have to keep reassuring him. So he was sort of dragged into this a bit. He couldn't have been nicer to him when it happened.

I don't mean to say for a minute that John Hurd is in any way, shape, or form a racist or anything approaching that. It's just that one brings different perspectives to this and he felt strongly that we shouldn't be pushing the s South Africans quite so hard.

Q: To finish up on this, how did the Baker assignment work out?

Smith: It worked out very well. For one thing, the South African government leaned over backwards to show us that they were not racist and that they did not put American blacks in the same category with their own Africans. Therefore, he was lionized. When Jim Baker arrived, this young officer, his picture was in every paper in South Africa.

I remember once when we went to lunch with the ambassador, Jim, and I, and our political counselor and a few others, the *maitre d'* (headwaiter) in this restaurant pointedly ignored Ambassador Hurd and walked up to Jim Baker, this young black officer, shook his hand, and gave him the seat of honor at the table, which gave us all a roar, including Ambassador Hurd.

The South Africans worked very hard to make it work. This is not to say that there wasn't real pressure and strain on Jim, as there has been on every black officer since.

Q: I was going to ask that. How did this work out personally?

Smith: It was a great strain on him but he had the moxie to handle this, and the intelligence, and the emotional stability. He handled it very well. He also, obviously, provided another entree into the black community which, while we had it before, we didn't have it to the same extent as we did with a black officer.

Q: We're talking about the 1970 to 1974 period. What were the United States' concerns in South Africa?

Smith: We had genuine human rights concerns there. Our concern was that the country was going to explode some day unless they took their figurative foot off the neck of the black man. A position, by the way, I still hold because I still think we may have a blood bath in South Africa one of these days. And we did not want to see that happen.

In those early 1970s, I'm sorry to say, some senior South African officials, I think, really thought that, if a race war were to actually occur in South Africa, that we would come militarily to their rescue, that we could not stand idly by and see white South Africans slaughtered in their beds by Africans. I think only now are they beginning to realize that that was never the case, that we would not lift a finger.

Q: Was this a question that would come up and that you would try to scotch?

Smith: Very hard.

Q: How about our military attachés?

Smith: The military attachés, in those days, had very close relations with the South African military. I don't think that's the case anymore. I think their presence contributed to that feeling. Also, the fact that, for instance, the head of the South African Navy and my ambassador, John Hurd, were tied up alongside each other as Navy commanders during World War II at some point during the war in the Atlantic someplace. The South Africans would keep reminding us that they fought with us in several wars, that they were vehemently anti-communist, and so forth. They made all the right noises.

If you could leave the race question aside, which in my judgment, is absolutely impossible, the South Africans would be the strongest allies we have anywhere in the world, if you look at in those terms. But you can't put the race questions aside, in my judgment.

Q: Did you find that the communist menace was raised every time?

Smith: Oh, yes. Oh, yes.

Q: Was this having any real effect on our policy? I mean, were you getting concerns from Congress or from other American business interests and all this saying, well, let's not push too hard because if we do this the communists are going to take over?

Smith: I would have to say we got very little of that. On the other hand, we were getting pressure from the liberal side in Congress, particularly members of the Black Caucus who were critical that we were too close to the South Africans and that we should take a tougher policy towards that country. Actually, it's remarkable when one looks back on it.

The last eight years our policy has been called constructive engagement. In point of fact, I think that would be a fair characterization of the Nixon-Kissinger policies in the early '70s because, when I look back on it, that's about what we were doing. We were engaged and our leverage was then and is now quite limited. But we felt that, by continuing to whittle away at them and hammer these points home, we would slowly get them to come to their senses. But that was not to happen and has not yet happened.

They continue to think that American blacks are not blacks. They're colored, as far as the white South African is concerned, because there's a mixture of white and black. And, therefore, when we talk about their race problem, they simply say, "Bob, you just don't understand blacks. You just don't understand. Congressman Diggs is not black. Look at him. He's colored." To them, that changes the whole picture. It's really quite pathetic.

I had discussions with Prime Minister Vorster and so many others. But we felt it was sort of a one step forward, two step back thing, and that they would continue to do outrageous things. Our closest white South African friends, of course, tended to be in the progressive liberal community, people like Helen Suzman and Colin Eglin, who remain some of our closest friends today. And they fought the good fight for a long time, but it's far from over.

Q: Did you find that you had much relations with the Dutch element?

Smith: Yes. It was somewhat more strained. The current president, P. W. Botha, we used to call "Guns" Botha because, in our day, he was the Minister of Defense. Ambassador Hurd had him to the residence for dinner, as we tried to do with all the cabinet. But the Afrikaner was always much more suspicious of us and of our motives, particularly of me. There was less of that with Ambassador Hurd. They genuinely liked Ambassador Hurd. But the career officers in the State Department, they were quite suspicious of them. Too liberal, too protective of black rights, et cetera.

Q: Did you have any contact with the black community?

Smith: Oh, yes. That had been started even before I arrived but I certainly intensified it. I had a terrific political section staff and we worked very hard at it.

We were somewhat circumscribed. There were certain places where you couldn't go, or they couldn't go, and so forth, but yes, we would have lunches and dinners. We had more success in that we could easily have, and did have, a great number of functions with black South Africans. Where you got into trouble, where you had to be very, very careful, was trying to mix them with white South Africans.

I remember once the Minister of Police Affairs had a suspicion that I was going to have a black South African at our residence. He happened to be a very distinguished doctor. And he asked me flat out before coming were there going to be black South Africans there. I said, "Well, yes,

Jimmy, there will be." And he said, "Aw, come on. I can't come, Bob. Don't do that to me. I can't come." Private Afrikaners would and there are a number of progressive, liberal Afrikaners. They're not all Neanderthals by any means. But the government, the ministers in particular, some of them were just beyond the pale. They just were and are hopeless, some of them, and they wanted nothing to do with them.

I think you'd have small successes in that I've had a number of Afrikaners, after a mixed function at our home or one of the other embassy homes, come up to me and say, "Bob, I want to thank you because this is the first time I have ever eaten with a black man and talked with him as an equal. I want to thank you for that." But this is just such a small thing compared to the enormity of the problem.

Q: What about the American business community? This has become such a focal point. This is the one place where we can sort of show our policy by trying to get people to disinvest, American firms, from not putting money into South African firms. Was this much of an element at that time?

Smith: With some exceptions, I think the average attitude of the American business community in those years was, don't rock the boat, don't fiddle with the status quo. I must say, in more recent years, I think they've become far more enlightened. We were constantly pressuring them to do what they could to upgrade the working conditions, salary, et cetera, of their black employees. Many of them tried hard but I think most of that has happened in the last few years.

Q: At your time it was, "We're here to do business and we'll do what we have to."

Smith: Yes. We stay out of politics, don't talk to me about politics. So they took sort of a standoff attitude. But we've leaned on them, I think, more strongly in recent years with some success.

....Q: We just finished with your time eating lotus in Malta.

Smith: That's a good way to put it.

Q: As a matter of fact, that's around that area where they ate lotus. Then you moved to another difficult assignment, and that was Accra, Ghana.

Smith: Yes.

Q: We're talking about 1976 to 1979 when you were ambassador there. How did this come about?

Smith: I was on home leave after two years in Malta. I was in the West visiting relatives. The Department tracked me down in a motel in Boulder, Colorado and it was Bill Schaufele calling, who was then Assistant Secretary for Africa, saying, "Bob, would you be interested in Ghana?" And oh, boy, would I. I loved Ghana despite all the trauma. So I jumped at that and said, "Yes, go with it." They put my name forward and we went back to Malta to pack up. We only stayed there another couple of months, I guess, before we left.

Q: You went back to Malta?

Smith: To Malta, that's right, to say good-byes and so forth. So we went on to Ghana. I was very, very glad to get back in Africa. I felt a little bit out of it in Europe, frankly, delightful as it was from a physical standpoint. I went on to Ghana and found that the country had just gone from bad to worse in the intervening years since I had been there. Nothing in the stores; indeed, many of them were boarded up. Only one operating restaurant worthy of the name in the whole city of Accra, which is a very large city. The economy was in a shambles.

By the time I got there, of course, they had been through a number of coups and a General Acheampong was the Head of State and Chairman of the Supreme Military Council, a rather unprepossessing military type who was struggling along. But I had so admired the Ghanaian people, and still do, because they had retained their wit, and charm, and humor despite all the privations piled upon them. They have, in short, been badly served by every government they've had since Nkrumah.

Q: Is it somehow endemic within this charming people or is it just fate?

Smith: I don't know. It's difficult to answer because the Ghanaians, like the Ibos, were among the best educated in Africa, again, a plethora of lawyers, doctors, engineers, even scientists, and so forth, most of whom now are working and living abroad. There may be some dribbling back now, but most of them got out while they could, further running down the economy. Nkrumah quickly went through the British reserves I alluded to earlier.

Under the Acheampong regime, which was a military regime, I was greeted with open arms, literally with open arms, most warmly, our relations with it were very good. But corruption was rampant in the country, as it is in many places in Africa. We had a modest AID and Peace Corps program there. And again, because of the greed and the corruption, there were, not one, but two coups during my three years stay in Ghana leading to still other military regimes, each one no better than the last.

As I say, even the civilian regimes have not been able to repair the damage and really put the country back on its feet. The only hopeful sign I can point to is that the current regime, headed by Jerry Rawlings, seems to have finally gotten its act together, despite his early rhetoric of anti-Americanism, *a la* (in the style of) Nkrumah.

He has reached agreements with the International Monetary Fund and World Bank, and the Ghanaian Cedi, the currency, is again worth something, I gather. He is making it worthwhile to be a cocoa farmer again. He's making it easier for foreign businessmen to do business there. And in short, this young ex-flight lieutenant in the Ghanaian Air Force now seems to be doing a much better job than he did at first.

Q: When you came there what was American policy towards Ghana? We're talking about 1976.

Smith: Our relations have traditionally been warm and close. There were a number of Americans living there, in fact. Huge numbers of Ghanaians had immigrated to the United States either legally or illegally. Our policy was to try to help Ghanaians do what they could to get the country back on its feet and make it economically viable through our Peace Corps, and AID programs, and so forth. But again, the needs were so great and our means were so limited there wasn't a great deal we could do.

Q: What were we doing in AID at that time?

Smith: Largely in agricultural development, economic development in general, health, the Peace Corps, in education.

Q: How do you deal with the problem? You've got an AID project and, obviously, this is, in one way, funneling equipment, or money, or something to a place that is full of corruption. I mean, people must have come up and said, "Look, we can't do this unless we pay off so and so."

Smith: Then we didn't do it. Then we just didn't do it. We monitored the AID programs closely to prevent that sort of thing on a virtually daily basis. I have no hesitancy in saying that none of our AID money was siphoned off.

Q: How effective was it? I mean, if the atmosphere was corrupt, how do you operate in those circumstances?

Smith: Well, you operate through non-corrupt officials or you design the projects in such a way so that it doesn't lend itself to that sort of thing. I think most of the money was made off commercial enterprises, commercial deals, certainly not our AID programs, perhaps with others. Difficult, difficult years, a tragedy.

I think our AID programs were making some impact in the short run. But if I take the long view, if I go back to

1960-1961 and look at what I found in Africa then and look at what I find in Africa today, I have got to be terribly depressed. Our AID program has not really worked that well, in my judgment, in Africa or, indeed, elsewhere in the world. The Ghanaian people are, in fact, worse off today than they were at the time of independence. The same thing is true in many other African states.

Q: Well, I mean, in the first place, it's obviously the fault of people not getting their act together. But looking at our AID, when you were looking at these programs, were we doing the right thing or the wrong thing?

Smith: I thought, at the time, we were doing the right thing. I think, in retrospect--and I don't want to single out the particular projects--unfortunately, they were not self-sustaining to a sufficient extent or self-perpetuating.

Q: Could you give some examples?

Smith: Well, I mean by that, simply that we didn't have enough projects that were sustainable over the long haul after the American technicians departed. Now there are a lot of exceptions to that and there are a lot of projects operating in Africa today, I'm sure, under purely African direction with no American technician in sight.

So I don't mean this to be a blanket condemnation, far from it. But I have to say I'm terribly disappointed when I look at the status of African countries and their peoples today from what I anticipated it would be back in 1960 and 1961 because, given their human and natural resources, many of these countries should be much further ahead. So I don't think Western aid programs--I shouldn't even single out the West--aid programs, in general, have not been nearly as effective as they should have been, sad to say.

Q: Again, maybe there are certain things that aid can't do unless there is the proper infrastructure to support it. I'm talking about the human infrastructure to support it.

Smith: Yes, perhaps not. I'm reminded of a conversation I had with Premier Okpara in Eastern Nigeria early on in the '60s, who was also the head of the political party in Eastern Nigeria. I remember him slamming his big fist down on the table once and saying, "Mr. Smith, please, no more feasibility studies. You send people out and they do a study. Then three months later you send another team of Americans out and they do a study of that study, all of which is designed to come up with a feasibility study. You're studying us to death and nothing gets done."

He was ranting and raving, but all in good fun. He was grinning as he was saying this, but there was a barb in it because our AID programs were excruciatingly slow and hemmed in with all sorts of bureaucratic restrictions and caveats. It was a tremendous frustration to African leaders to deal with our AID people.

I don't have the answers. I know now, in 1989, they're looking at the whole AID program again. I think they've reached the same conclusion that I just articulated; that it has not been as effective worldwide as we wanted it to be. I think we bit off more than we could chew in many of these places. You can't undo it. I'm not saying we did any damage, it's just that they were not self-sustaining and viable in the long run, which is very sad.

Q: Were we concerned with Ghana as being an African leader? Or by the time you got there, had Ghana's role become less important?

Smith: Ghana, until recent years, certainly through the Nkrumah years, always had a leadership role in Africa quite disproportionate to its relatively small size. You have to give Nkrumah credit for that because they led the way to independence. They were the first independent black Africans, other than Liberia and Ethiopia. So they did have a major leadership role.

Therefore, we paid a great deal of attention to it even while I was there because their voice in the councils of the OAU, Organization of African Unity, and others was quite loud and often strident while Nkrumah was in power. So yes, they very definitely had a leadership role and we took cognizance of that.

Also, they had been blessed with an excellent foreign service and civil service all these years who had managed to hang on and survive these various regimes that were doing them such damage. And they've got tremendous human resources. If we could get all the Ghanaians living abroad, especially in England and the States, to go back and put their talents to use, they could turn it around in a hurry. But you're going to have to have the right government in power to make that happen.

Q: Speaking of governments and power, when you were there you said there were several coups. Could you describe what happened, and what you saw and did, and what the embassy did?

Smith: Strangely enough, and this is a source of great amusement with some of my colleagues, I happened to be in the States, either on medical leave or consultations, when both those coups happened. I got back on the first commercial flight but I was not physically there for the coup. It had very little impact on the embassy or the American population. This was an internal squabble among the military in the case of Ghana, and having to do with corrupt practices and not sharing the wealth with the right people. Each new man pledges to correct these wrongs and it doesn't happen. Liberia was a very different case. We should get to that in a moment, I think.

Q: Were there any particular problems that you had in Ghana that come to mind?

Smith: No. No. It was a most enjoyable tour of duty except for the privations being suffered by the Ghanaian people themselves. And, indeed, because of our insistence that Peace Corps volunteers live as their indigenous counterparts live, we had real food problems, almost amounting to malnutrition, among some of our Peace Corps volunteers. We had to start shipping sardines and other canned goods up country to some of our Peace Corps volunteers just to keep body and soul together. Things were that bad in Ghana and that was a source of great concern.

But politically, no. Ghana, during my tenure there, was behaving itself on the international scene and they didn't have the voice in international councils that they once had. We had very friendly relations. It was just the frustration of being unable to cut through the graft and corruption internally. Not that we were affected by it, but it just prevented a lot from getting done. It prevented American firms from coming in and investing there. The economy just kept going downhill while I was there.

Q: Were you getting any pressure? While you were there the Ford Administration went out and the Carter one came in with a new emphasis on human rights and all that. Did this cause you any turnaround or reactivate you on things?

Smith: No turnaround, certainly. I welcomed this new thrust and it gave me a lot of additional ammunition to use in various conversations with the head of state, with the foreign minister, and other cabinet ministers who would give me a very polite, even cordial, hearings and make all the right noises, but very little real change.

Q: What sort of things were we concerned about in the field of human rights?

Smith: In Ghana there were some political prisoners and that sort of thing. I can't remember many others. Most of that came in the years in Liberia, as a matter of fact. Why don't we go on to Liberia?

Q: All right. Why don't we go on to Liberia. In a way, it's rather remarkable in this day and age, where ambassadorial assignments are getting scarcer and scarcer as far as professional officers, that you had three.

So many people have had distinguished careers and they are tossed a year and a half in Rwanda or something like that to end off their career and they're supposed to depart the scene as quietly as possible. And this was your third ambassadorial assignment.

Smith: Yes. I was very fortunate, indeed, and I think it was just the question of, quite literally, being in the right place at the right time.

First of all, let me back up to Ghana just a minute. I forgot one major thing. I followed Shirley Temple Black but there was about a six-month interregnum. We pulled Mrs. Black out in anger when the Ghanaians, to show their displeasure over some American policy--I forget now what it was--at the last minute would not let Secretary Kissinger land in Ghana. So my marching orders in Ghana were to go back in there and patch things up, which didn't take long because the Ghanaians were already predisposed to resume friendly and close relations.

Q: How effective had Mrs. Black been?

Smith: Quite effective. She's not the dilettante that some, at least, would have you think she is. She was popular, very popular not only among the Ghanaians, but among our own embassy staff. And the fine DCM (Deputy Chief of Mission) I inherited from Shirley was very high on her.

There are obvious limitations on any political appointee who knows little or nothing about the foreign service. But Shirley was very, very bright, and dedicated, and sincere. She had had experience at the UN. Even if she didn't, I'd have to give her very high marks. As a matter of fact, because she then came out of Ghana and was made chief of protocol, she swore me in when I went out there.

To go back to Liberia, the shift over there was simply "good luck," because Bev Carter had left some time before.

Q: He had been ambassador?

Smith: Yes, he had been ambassador in Monrovia. And Liberia, like Ghana, is a class two mission, or was a class two mission. I don't know whether you even use the phrase anymore. And the Department and AF, the African Bureau, felt very strongly they did not want a rookie ambassador in Liberia, but rather someone who had had African ambassadorial experience. My number was just coming up. I was then about two and a half years into my Ghana tour, so it worked out most fortuitously.

We went on to Liberia very happily. Very different from Ghana. To be blunt about it, I never found the Liberians, with all their American ties, nearly as charming as the Ghanaians or, indeed, the Ibos. This isn't to say I disliked the country or the people.

Q: Well, it has that reputation. It seems like it always has been the exception or the side show and something that is basically overlooked when you think about Africa.

Smith: Yes. Of course, they were the exception to the rule, too, in that they had been independent for so long. They are widely regarded by other Africans as kind of an appendage to the United States or, indeed, a colony of the United States. That may be a bum rap but there's enough of a grain of truth in it to make one uncomfortable at times, particularly when I arrived there and found the Monrovia Police Department dressed in uniforms that could only have been hand-me-downs from the Los Angeles Police Department, the black shirt and trousers, caps, and so forth. All the armed forces uniforms were also our own secondhand stuff.

But I was greeted very warmly by a very distinguished African leader, President Tolbert, and we got along famously. I had a few squabbles with the foreign minister, Cecil Dennis, largely on human rights issues, and so forth, because, while a democratic nation, they also ruled with a pretty heavy hand.

The indigenous people up country did not fare too well under this, what we called, Americo-Liberian regime--the descendants of American slaves that went back to Liberia to found the country.

But the relationship, basically, was one of warmth and cordiality. The president went out of his way to be personally cordial to me, even taking me up with him on a week-long jaunt through the provinces in Northern Liberia as his honored guest, riding with him every step of the way in his limousine.

Q: What were our interests there?

Smith: Many. We had certain rights that remain in the classified area concerning the use of Roberts Field, the international airfield there. We have our largest communications set up anywhere in Africa at the embassy in Monrovia, large numbers of communications technicians, and other interests, as well, strategic and otherwise. And, of course, a long, long history of ties to the United States. Many Liberians did, in fact, consider themselves sort of the 51st state, like it or not. And because of corruption that was rampant there, that often was downright embarrassing at times.

But President Tolbert was very nice. At the same time, we would have to fuss at the foreign minister or the president several times about human rights violations, imprisoning people and then keeping them without charge, that sort of thing. But the main problem was that the Americo-Liberian clique, and they were a small minority in the country, in fact, ruled the country. They controlled the court system, the police, the armed forces, the parliament, everything about life in Liberia.

And, again, inevitably perhaps after my experience in Ghana, I had come back to the States on a medical evacuation and was an outpatient at the Mayo Clinic in Rochester, Minnesota, when I got the inevitable call at one o'clock in the morning from the desk officer in Washington saying, "Mr. Ambassador, the Secretary would like you back in Liberia like yesterday. There's been a coup." And we did not anticipate that coup. I would like to be able to say we saw it coming. We did not. We knew there was great unhappiness.

In this case, in April of 1980, a group of enlisted men in the armed forces were down on the beach near the presidential palace drinking beer and they had their weapons with them. One thing led to another and, to make a long story short, they got a group together and went into the presidential palace and murdered President Tolbert. They tracked down virtually the entire cabinet, senior parliamentary leaders, and other prominent Americo-Liberians, and it was a bloodbath.

I got back in the next day on the first flight in. The young man who had taken over the country was a 29-year old master sergeant named Sammy Doe. He was semi-literate, could barely read and write his own name. Could, in fact, barely speak proper English. I literally, at times, would resort to pidgin English to communicate with Sergeant Doe after he became head of state.

It was a real body blow, not because we had anything against the indigenous peoples of Liberia, and we knew the faults of the old regime, but at the same time, the bloodbath that followed was inexcusable.

There were a few frantic days, and they were frantic because this unleashed this latent hatred which was there on the part of the enlisted men in the armed forces, and the first order Doe gave was that you no longer have to obey the orders of your officers either in the police force or in the army. You can imagine the kind of chaos that resulted from that.

So they were stopping people on the street, dragging people from their beds and murdering them. In the case of the cabinet, tying them to stakes on the beach and executing them by firing squad.

This, despite the fact that in the morning I had again gone to see Sergeant Doe and given him a personal appeal from President Carter to spare their lives. He heard me but made no commitment. That afternoon my public affairs officer burst into my office and said, "Mr. Ambassador, my God, they have done it. They've shot all of them. They've killed all of them, eight or nine lined up on the beach tied to a stake." So it was a bloody mess.

Worse yet, we had the obvious concern about these ignorant, poorly educated, almost illiterate enlisted men being gotten to by the other side and being turned around and having Liberia wind up as a communist state.

Q: Who were the other side?

Smith: Well, the Soviets were there and very interested in all this, although they were completely nonplussed by the coup. But they immediately saw an opportunity here and tried to move in on it. And I must say, I think one of the major things that saved us there was not, certainly, the charm or good looks of the American ambassador, but rather the presence of a U.S. military mission that had been there for decades, headed, in my tenure, by a tough, charming Texas full colonel in the Army named Bob Gosney who was the head of the U.S. Military Mission and who, in that capacity, had helped train Master Sergeant Doe.

Master Sergeant Doe adored Colonel Gosney, and called him "Chief." He referred to him always in the third person as "the Chief."

I very quickly became cognizant of this and I started taking Colonel Gosney with me when I went to see Sammy Doe. This helped enormously because he respected and had total confidence in Colonel Gosney.

He knew little and cared less about communism and the Soviet Union. There was nothing ideological. This was a genuine tribal upheaval to get rid of the hated upper classes and to bring more privileges to the underprivileged.

So Sammy Doe was not then and is not now a politically ideological person.

But I can't emphasize strongly enough how helpful it was to have this small group of American Army officers, consisting of a group of lieutenant colonels and majors who had, instead of lording it over the enlisted men of the armed forces as their Liberian counterparts did, the Americans, being Americans, would learn these fellows names, including Sergeant Doe, and so forth, and they were warm and cordial to their underlings. And, as a result, Sergeant Doe quickly passed the word that whatever the chief says, goes.

So I had the members of my military mission out in their vehicles literally patrolling the streets. And when they would see a drunken or doped up Liberian soldier holding a group of civilians at gunpoint or something, trying to rob them, or rape them or whatever, one word from one of my American officers would stop that dead in its tracks. They would stop, salute, and say, "Yes, sir," and go on about their business.

It saved lives, literally saved lives, this personal relationship that they had established. And that really sustained us for a very lengthy period before their government got formed and Sammy Doe came up with a foreign minister who was bright and well educated that we could deal with.

The problem was that Sammy Doe and his immediate cohorts, to me, were, of course, in a very personal sense, murderers. They had murdered William Tolbert, who was a very dear friend of mine, and the other members of the cabinet with whom I had been very close. And yet, here they were, the new government. It was clearly not in our national interest to see the country go down the tubes, so it fell to me to do what we could to sustain this young man in steering along a certain course, which we managed to do with great difficulty.

But that led to a situation in which he came to lean on me and the embassy almost too much. He would summon me at all hours of the night to say, "Mr. Ambassador, we have a problem." He would state the problem and wait for me to come up with a solution. So at times it came very uncomfortably close to running a country that you really don't want any part of, and always putting out fires and fears that he had.

He had a fear that Houphouët-Boigny, President of the Ivory Coast, whose daughter was married to Tolbert's son, with the help of French troops was going to invade Liberia.

So it was a question of hanging in there and doing what we could to moderate the behavior of Sergeant Doe and his government. And I think we were relatively successful, as was my successor, Bill Swing, who had a long tenure there, about five years, pumping in a great deal of American aid, especially to the military, since the unhappiness of the military with their lot in life was one of the main causes of the coup.

It was an exciting time. The Secretary ordered me to evacuate American dependents. We had to get them out of the country right after the coup when the troops were running wild. So it was, perhaps, the most exciting time in my Foreign Service career, but not the most satisfying.

Q: Were you under any other pressures? You found the situation repugnant to you, I mean, dealing with people whom you had to deal with, but there had been Pulitzer Prize winning photographs of these leaders being executed and all this, there must have been a lot of pressure from Congress, and from the news press, and all that. Did this translate to you at all?

Smith: Yes. We felt we were really operating in a goldfish bowl or under a microscope, I should say. Human rights pressure inevitably came into this picture after the coup. But strangely enough, not a great deal of congressional pressure. Everyone was sickened, of course, by what happened out there.

But you can't reverse that and I think everyone saw that what we had to concentrate on was where do we go from there. And I had to keep reminding people of some of the things that the previous government had done and why the depths of anger being felt by these people was quite genuine.

Q: Were you getting any pressure from the black caucus one way or another?

Smith: I had a number of visits out there. Congressman Bill Gray came out, Julian Dixon, those two members. I had Andy Young, then at the UN, come out a couple of times before the coup. He also visited me in Ghana a couple times. But not undue congressional pressure. I had more congressional pressure in South Africa than anyplace else, in particular from Charlie Diggs. He did not like our policy in South Africa. Indeed, he would not have been happy unless we had broken relations, I think.

But I've talked long enough. It's been a fascinating and very satisfying career. I retired in January of 1981, sort of in the middle of all this, but I felt, for a number of reasons, that I had to. One, the Department offered a monetary incentive to do that. Secondly, I developed a medical problem which was beginning to worry me.

After a couple of times when I stumbled going up the steps to the presidential mansion I realized, hey, I've really got to do something about this. These trips back to Mayo didn't get to the bottom of it. My right leg was deteriorating. To make a long story short, only after I retired and got back here and started running the African Wildlife Foundation did they discover that I, in fact, have multiple sclerosis. So it's just as well I retired when I did because I just didn't have the stamina.

Q: And strain is a major factor.

Smith: Stress, as the doctor says, is contraindicated for MS patients. And in those last two posts, particularly Liberia, I had more than my share.

Q: In these interviews we try to ask two questions. One, what do you consider your greatest achievement

or what did you do that gave you the greatest satisfaction?

Smith: I would have to say, I guess, in my last post, keeping Liberia, quite literally, from going down the tubes. I know countries don't go bankrupt but Liberia came about as close as any country could, I think. We had to resort to some pretty imaginative policy initiatives to keep that from happening in Liberia. To keep Liberia from going down the tubes and basically, to retain the feeling that Liberians continue to have toward the United States despite all that happened out there. I think to keep that ship on a steady keel was perhaps the greatest achievement.

Source:

Ambassador Robert P. Smith interviewed by Charles Stuart Kennedy, 28 February 1989, pp. 7 – 26, 29 – 39.
Foreign Affairs Oral History Collection, Association for Diplomatic Studies and Training (ADST), Arlington, Virginia, USA, www.adst.org
Copyright 1998 ADST.

Robert E. Fritts ambassador to Ghana, interviewed by Charles Stuart Kennedy, 8 September 1999, The Association for Diplomatic Studies and Training (ADST), Foreign Affairs Oral History Project.

Q: Well, in around '83, you left. Whither?
Fritts: To Ghana as ambassador.
Q: From when to when?
Fritts: 1983 - 1986.
Q: Before you went out to Ghana, what were you getting from the Department, from the African Bureau, about our interests in Ghana and what needed to be done?
Fritts: Ghana had a very long history of a close relationship with the United States. It was the first country in Africa to become independent, in 1957. It was the first country to receive American Peace Corps Volunteers. Ghana under its first prime minister, Kwame Nkrumah, had become what was called the "Black Star of Africa."

During those early years of promise, he had attracted many of the best and the brightest of the American African community to look upon a new day in Africa with Ghana as the potential leader of a unified Africa. None of that came to pass, of course.

By the time I was preparing to go out, there had been a number of governments in Ghana, often short-lived, led by military generals, and even under occasional parliamentary processes, there had been endemic corruption and malfeasance. That had led to a coup earlier in the year by Flight Lieutenant Jerry Rawlings, who had taken power briefly and then turned it back over to a civilian government.

A few months later, in Rawlings's view, that government had also not measured up, so he staged a second coup on the same grounds as the first. He then executed two previous military presidents and imprisoned the latest elected president.

He was embarked upon a revolution under what was called the Provisional National Defense Council (PNDC). It was radical socialist in its approaches to the country's economic, social, and political problems. Rawlings saw Libya and Cuba as models. The Soviet Union had rising influence. Rawlings was intrigued by radical revolutionary regimes in Africa and the world.

So our previous ambassador…

Q: Who was that?

Fritts: Tom Smith. He had worked very closely with the previous parliamentary government overthrown by Rawlings. Tom was crestfallen over developments. He waited and waited for the opportunity of a normal farewell call on Rawlings as the new head of state/head of government, but it never happened. He even missed his daughter's graduation from his alma mater, Harvard. U.S.-Ghanaian relations were at a very low point.

Q: What did you see as what you were going to do when you went out there in '83?

Fritts: Well, there's a process of developing an ambassador's mission statement with goals and objectives, but I didn't want to develop a whole new policy approach before even stepping foot in the place. The situation was also volatile as Rawlings in his "second coming" had only been in power for several months. As you know, ambassadors try to write their own instructions, which they then seek to implement. I thus gave myself some breathing room, saying essentially that I wanted to assess the situation on the ground first and would report in 90 days or so with a prescription as to what policies we might pursue.

I was very fortunate that the assistant secretary for African affairs, Chet Crocker, whom I didn't know, was more than amenable. I wrote up a formal memo of instructions within a conceptual policy framework. Of course, I had worked it out within the African Bureau and incorporated those aspects which made sense to me with other bureaus, departments and agencies.

When I saw Crocker shortly before departing, he gave a cursory scan of the document and then gave me orally the absolutely best instructions any American ambassador could ever desire. His words were, "I don't think much can be done in Ghana. But go out, see what might be done, and don't take any guff." And he used a word other than *guff*. In other words, I had *carte blanche* to do my thing.

He also said that if I concluded the situation was hopeless, then draw down the embassy staff and maybe close the embassy. If I thought something could be done, come up with proposals. In the interim, do what I thought was necessary and maybe just tell the Department afterwards. One could not ask for more. Going back to our earlier conversation – for me, another ship was about to get underway and with some independence. Real responsibility.

Q: Well, now, I take it that at this time, Ghana did not rank very high in American policy. It had been, since the late '50s, as you say, that the "Black Star" was there, but by this time, did it have any real constituency in the United States? Were we concerned about it? Did we have any strategic concerns?

Fritts: Naturally we had the usual concerns we had

throughout Africa during the Cold War. Under the PNDC, one could anticipate that Ghanaian votes in the United Nations would be primarily with our adversaries. We knew that the climate for American investment was now even worse.

There was no rule of law worth much. There were major human rights considerations, because there had been killings and purges and shutting down of a free press. Supreme Court judges had been murdered in suspicious circumstances. We were concerned over an expanding wedge of Russian, Chinese, Libyan and Cuban influences and that Ghana could become a platform to destabilize West Africa.

Key members of Rawlings's entourage, including his chief of security, had fought with Samora Machel in Angola (Mozambique). The idea of radical revolution expanding in Africa and affecting our access to strategic resources and to military bases was all part of Cold War tensions.

We also thought that Ghana had a special history and Ghanaians proven skills, which if freed and supported, could reverse its downward economic spiral and create a more open political system. Ghana was thus an integral part of U.S. interests in Africa.

Q: When you arrived in Accra, what was your impression of the embassy?

Fritts: The embassy staff, frankly, was only a skeleton. Staff had been pulled out without replacements, who would not come in for some months. The carry-over DCM overlapped only 10 days and then departed early with prior Dept. approval. The few FSOs were, in general, inexperienced.

It was one of those cyclical dips that affect many posts in the developing world. I felt singularly alone in trying to figure out who was who, what was going on, and what we should be doing. It seemed incredible that the world's superpower had such a dysfunctional disinterest, particularly at smaller posts in difficult places where, in fact, there are no back-ups. State was the problem. USIA, AID and DOD did better.

Over time the State quality also improved as FSO bidders learned in corridor gossip that Ghana was not a pit. I helped recruit persons by saying we had career opportunities in an improving situation. My premise was that in Ghana, you could have impact. At the end of the day and tour, you could say, "Yes, this is what I/we sought to achieve and this is what was accomplished (or not)." You wouldn't get lost in a larger embassy where individual achievement was muddled, professional growth diffuse and psychic reward lacking.

Q: Watch officers on a destroyer again.

Fritts: Maybe. In addition, the embassy location was in downtown Accra. Given the increasingly politically hostile environment, Ambassador Smith had made the correct decision to relocate to our more defensible and underutilized USAID building. We had thus begun to quietly renovate that building on the Ring Road outside of downtown. I accelerated the plan. Much of the work was by our own efforts with technical specialists rotating in and out. In essence, we built an embassy inside the AID building without the Ghanaian Government being alert to it.

After several months, we delivered a note to the Foreign Ministry after it had closed on Friday, indicating we would reopen for business on Monday in the new location. Over the weekend, we moved the embassy lock, stock, and barrel from the chancery downtown to the renovated building. We had dropped off the note late assuming no Ghanaian official would read it until Monday and thus be unable to interfere or interrupt the movements of our vehicles carrying classified equipment and files.

We probably made a hundred sorties using motor pool vehicles and our personal cars. There was no incident, but we had Marines in civilian clothes riding along in case the convoys were challenged. We were proud of the accomplishment. We felt there was some danger in it all.

Q: Why would there be opposition? Why did it have to be done surreptitiously?

Fritts: I didn't trust the Ghanaian Government at that time. They'd been in office less than six months. There were some very unsavory folk in the "Castle" – the seat of government – who were ideologues, impulsive and armed. Anti-American vitriol was official. I knew Rawlings had contempt for the Reagan Administration and my predecessor. The U.S., wrongly, was considered opposed to the PNDC. There was a wide-spread Ghanaian belief going back to the old Nkrumah period that somehow the CIA was the arbiter of U.S. policy in Ghana and that we were involved in seeking to overthrow the PNDC.

My concerns were based on intelligence and other sources, that for us to give the Ghanaian Government advance notice could be twisted by their security group's paranoia into temptations to interfere, such as by detaining our vehicles which were carrying cryptographic equipment, classified material and so on.

Q: Did we also feel that our embassy had been pretty well exposed to listening devices and that sort of thing?

Fritts: Sure. The embassy had received a design prize at one time in the '50s, I guess, as one of the then-new embassies, which reflected an idealized host-country architectural style and used local products. Our offices fronted onto a second-floor square veranda that overlooked an open courtyard. The walls were made primarily of local mahogany and plywood. We were enveloped by much taller government buildings. The logical assumption was that we had no communications security whatsoever, even for spoken conversations. So, yes, that was also one of the reasons we decided to relocate.

There was also an overall security issue as the

chancery grounds had been open and were now only fenced off with wire. Being in the heart of downtown, we were exposed to mass demonstrations, if ginned up by the government. We were also on the main track to and from the soccer stadium and thus an additional potential target for unruly crowds, which could be induced. Some Ghanaians were also intimidated to visit the chancery for fear of observation from the government offices. The list of concerns was long.

Q: What was your estimate, after your reading up and getting started, on Rawlings? Who was he? Where was he coming from? Could he be dealt with?

Fritts: Rawlings was an enigmatic figure. Over the course of my time there, I got to know him fairly well – to the degree that an official American could and, in truth, far better than any Western ambassador there.

He was a populist mystic – almost messianic. He had, as did many African revolutionary leaders, overtones of a prophet. Very nationalistic and patriotic. Quite idealistic, but through an anti-Western lens. Also sincerely desirous, I thought, of improving the lives of ordinary Ghanaians, but the models he then found appealing were Cuba and Libya. And he was feted by Castro and Qadhafi with whom he developed kindred relationships.

His was an unusual personality. There was no normal flow of conversation – a lot of in's and out's and elliptical phrases. I sensed he often held back as not trusting what he might say. He was emotional, unpredictable and quick to judge on what I thought poor or limited information. In short, someone to be careful with. I thought how difficult it was for his ministers and staff. They weren't sure when they might inadvertently offend him. None of them ever said that to me, of course, but I observed their nervous behavior if, for example, asked a question from out of the blue.

He detested forms of Western protocol as being artificial and imposed. That was okay by me, but bent

European ambassadors out of shape. For example, he generally would not receive credentials of new ambassadors and was choosy in whom he saw at departure. I presented my credentials to one of the members of his five or seven-person PNDC senior team, a Mrs. Annan, I think. A pleasant figurehead.

Q: So how did you get to know him?

Fritts: A well-connected Ghanaian businessman sought me out to suggest that it might be useful if I were to meet with the "Chairman." I knew the businessman was reliable, as he had been mentioned to me by former ambassador Shirley Temple Black, a predecessor twice removed.

He inferred there were those who felt a rapprochement with the U.S. was important. Naturally, I said "Sure." The result over some months was a series of meetings at the businessman's home in a close-by Ghanaian town and once at my residence. The sessions were always late at night and into the early morning. I sensed Rawlings was seeking to draw some measure of what I was while I did the same with him.

Sometimes I'd go to a location to meet him, spend four or five hours waiting around with a couple of ministers, and he wouldn't show. During the wait, several of his cabinet and security people would bounce in and out using hand-held radios to contact him as he and entourage prowled the night.

He operated a lot at night and was concerned, probably correctly, about counter-coups and assassination. A nighttime curfew was in force and getting home could be risky for us as the police and military at the roadblocks were scared and often fortified their courage with drugs and beer. Because of that, on occasion he's escort us in his armed vehicle. Scared our guards, but also helped us in the Ghanaian street rumor mill. If he didn't show, I'd get word several days later of a rescheduled rendezvous.

From the very first, my wife, Audrey, was specifically

invited to those sessions. I think it was because Rawlings didn't quite trust his own reactions and thought a woman's presence would have a calming influence. He had a sense of obligation towards women and could be quite charming at times – almost boyish. I felt her presence helped facilitate the discussions and also kept some of the potential thugs in check.

After getting back to the residence, Audrey and I would use separate typewriters and write up inputs, which I would combine for my cable report. We would finish about dawn. Audrey's independent analyses of the meeting and participants were invaluable. Hers was absolutely the kind of contribution Foreign Service spouses make to the conduct of American foreign policy.

By the way, the first meeting did not begin well. He arrived with a full panoply of bodyguards, gun on his hip, telling of having been delayed while attending the execution by firing squad of one of his former military friends who had been convicted – so-to speak – of fomenting a counter-coup. Rawlings had personally recorded his last words with a hand tape recorder. In fact, he did it twice as the first time he hadn't pushed the "On" button.

His interest had been to get a possible deathbed confession of who had previously murdered several Supreme Court justices, but no success. He commented that the condemned man had made a last request that Rawlings look after the man's widow and children financially. Rawlings said he agreed. That's when I first noted his colleagues being nervous in his presence.

Q: Sounds like this personalized Rawlings government with a ruling clique would have had the country living in considerable fear.

Fritts: Well, fear for some, but just uncertainty for most. Rawlings first coup had involved considerable bloodshed in Ghanaian terms, but not much compared to other African countries then and now. As I said, he had executed two of his presidential military predecessors on grounds of corruption and imprisoned the elected president, who had only been in office for several months.

The three murdered Supreme Court justices, including a woman, had been found in a forest, their bodies partially burned. Several journalists were murdered or disappeared. Some scores, official or personal, were settled with an occasional body in the early morning streets. It was relatively mild in African terms. That all preceded my tenure.

When I arrived, the second Rawlings coup was over and he was well into establishing the PNDC structure with borrowings from Cuban and Libyan models, such as neighborhood Committees for the Defense of the Revolution (CDR). Purges were continuing, particularly members of professional groups, such as lawyers, journalists and past politicians, who were arrested and imprisoned without trial.

Although denied by the PNDC, the anti-American, anti-imperialism media line was run out of the Castle.

There were still some murders in ambiguous circumstances. His close associates had begun to talk about drafting some kind of Basic Law. The view in the street was that he'd only be in charge a short while. Either be killed or get bored.

Q: Sounds grim.

Fritts: It was, but after a time I decided the previous government, although elected, had been corrupt and elitist. Some of Rawlings' populist instincts were compatible to degrees with American values.

He believed, I think sincerely, that the mass of Ghanaians had not only been exploited by their leaders, but also by their own faults. He believed he was fated to restructure society more equitably. He believed in forms of simplistic participatory democracy. He wanted to improve the lot of the average Ghanaian and restore Ghana to its golden age of immediate post-independence international image. He was embarrassed by what Ghana had become. The economy was a shambles. There had been years of decreasing GDP. But there had been no mass bloodletting and no intertribal atrocities. Ghanaians have a societal sense of decorum and personal respect, which inhibited the worst.

After a few months, I decided it would be possible to work with Rawlings and some of the people around him, who saw the prospect for economic recovery through rational Western concepts. If successful, I thought in time economic progress and American/Western influence could support or induce favorable political adjustments, including human rights. With careful, judicious initiatives, we might be able to make something of the situation.

Q: You mentioned the economy. Ghana was pointed out at one time as being a fairly self-sustaining country - it had solid crops like peanuts and cocoa and other things of this nature - that it should be able to do fairly well. Were we involved in that or concerned about their economy?

Fritts: The economy and its infrastructure – roads, ports, railroad and communications were a complete, utter shambles. All the worst kinds of problems endemic elsewhere in Africa.

In 1957, Ghana had been the first African colony to become an independent country. It had been generally prosperous with a reasonably well-educated middle-class. The "Black Star" had been the leader of Africa and its first prime minister, Nkrumah, among other disastrous views, saw himself as a pending "President of a United States of Africa". He even built an African presidential compound in Accra for the first meeting of the Organization of African Unity (OAU).

In 1957, Ghana and South Korea had been virtual twins in economic and demographic data. Now in 1983, South Korea was an upward Asian "Tiger" and Ghana had only spiraled downward.

The cocoa producer smallholder had been squeezed almost out of existence. Bloated state corporations controlled the economy. Marginal employment and over staffing were six to ten times what was required. The budget was broken. There was hyperinflation. The economy functioned primarily by smuggling and small traders. The infrastructure had deteriorated. There was no foreign exchange for spare parts or to replace equipment. Railroads to carry bulk products had stopped functioning. Telephone wires had been stripped to use to tie bundles or smelted down. Roads were awful. And to top it off, drought and mismanagement had caused a serious food shortage. Malnourishment was rampant up-country and starvation had begun.

To most observers, it all looked hopeless, particularly with a radical Marxist PNDC in charge.

Q: And the positives?

Fritts: As I noted, there were several in the PNDC who viewed the economy rationally. One was Kwesi Botchwey, minister of finance and economic development. He and a few others favored a disciplined approach using the International Monetary Fund (IMF) and the World Bank IBRD). They recognized that to have any hope of inducing those institutions and any Western consortia, they had to have at least the acquiescence of the United States. That's what I came to believe caused my late night meetings with Rawlings. To see if they could get him to overcome his visceral distaste for dealing with the United States, which, in their shoes at that time, meant me.

Interestingly, I had served in Indonesia and seen first-hand how a small group of American-trained Indonesian economists, the "Berkeley Mafia", could be successful economically in a situation very similar to what existed in Ghana, even if Indonesia had been on a much larger scale. And there had been associated political improvements, including on human rights.

As for Rawlings, I felt many of his concerns were

sincere and that over the course of time and experience, he could be brought to welcome progress if packaged appropriately – multilateral, basic human needs, export infrastructure, grass roots projects etc. I though his humanistic instincts could be directed, not by me probably, but by pragmatics around him.

Thus, in Ghana, I saw a chance.

Q: Why was there this distaste for the United States? I wouldn't think that we'd had a particularly heavy hand there. Was it coming from the London School of Economics socialism? Or was it Marxism, or what?

Fritts: There was a belief among much of the Ghanaian populace that the United States and the CIA had been instrumental in the overthrow of Nkrumah, who was the founding father of the nation. It had become part of the historic fabric, even for those who believed Nkrumah had betrayed his promise and become a disaster.

Nkrumah's role was resurrected by the PNDC; his grave was buffed up, etc. Soviet Bloc, Cuban and Libyan anti-CIA diatribes and disinformation were common in the media. Philosophically, much of the PNDC brain trust adhered to socialist or communist theory, including the standard analyses of former Western colonialism and current "neo- colonialism."

The U.S. was depicted as the capitalist-imperialist center of the world. The Reagan Administration was looked upon as a cowboy renegade racist group whose concern was to overthrow non-puppet governments in the developing world. All this mythology and cant was constantly promulgated by the government-controlled press.

Q: Were there elements of the population - I'm talking about within the capital city, maybe, intelligentsia that you could deal with that had a more rational view?

Fritts: Absolutely. For most Ghanaians, the anti-U.S.

anti-Western cant just flew over their heads. They had "been there, done that" before. Now they just wanted a functioning economy, employment, education, money to travel, a stable currency and goods in the stores. And political peace. The CDRs (Committees for the Defense of the Revolution), for example, never amounted to much. Ghanaians were masters at only pretending to participate.

The general public regarded the U.S. and Americans highly. The U.S. had done much for Ghana since independence, many Ghanaians had studied in the U.S., almost all knew that the first Peace Corps group was sent to Ghana, and many knew or had seen Americans firsthand.

I often said to visitors that while we had a difficult political environment, we also had, in my view, the best human environment in Africa. And, frankly, there was no doubt in my mind that if the PNDC collapsed in some way, some of the PNDC officials who were most vociferously anti-American, would vie to be first in line for an American visa. I had to bite my tongue on that more than once.

I mentioned there were many Ghanaians, lawyers, professionals and politicians, who'd been involved in the parliamentary system. But I felt their leaders were discredited, fairly or unfairly.

Still, I wanted to encourage potentially independent institutions. The first goal was damage control, try to keep a few functioning and support a few new ones. For example, I did a lot of discreet work directly with the Chief Justice of the Supreme Court, which the PNDC had not abolished, but just ignored.

Some times at the most basic, such as providing stationery and typewriter ribbons out of our own stocks.

I worked with the lawyers' society in similar ways, looking toward a day when they might be able to function, although some of the persons in that organization were suspect in my own view concerning their personal integrity.

We worked at trying to maintain women's and other professional organizations, to help keep them viable and quietly demonstrate some support.

But we had to be careful, because if support were too much or too open, it would just reinforce the PNDC in-house paranoia that we were in the coup business.

As part of political image, I no longer wore coat and tie, except for the most formal functions even at my own embassy, as coats and ties were looked upon by the PNDC as Western bourgeois affectations, even though the Ghanaian Oxford-Cambridge elite had been among the best Western dressed Africans in the past. Their threadbare London suits were now seldom worn, but carefully retained.

The PNDC and the government wore safari suits. Frankly, I also wore safari suits in part because the European ambassadors didn't. When serving in Africa, I always wanted to show that while many of us looked like Europeans, we weren't and, indeed, had once been revolutionaries ourselves. In that and other ways, I tried to indicate that I was not the representative of that great mythical ogre of the United States, but was willing to have an open mind and look for ways in which we could cooperate rather than ways to confront. But if the PNDC confronted us, we would confront them back – as Chet Crocker had directed.

That reminds me that sometime in my first year the PNDC renovated the home where W.E.B. Dubois had lived and worked for some years. There was an outdoor ceremony for the diplomatic corps where Rawlings gave a speech of praise, which also ripped the U.S. for slavery, bigotry and racial oppression.

He then said he would call on an ambassador to talk about W.E.B. Dubois' life. The diplomatic corps froze. Of course, he tagged me, so I stood in place and winged some minutes on W.E.B. Dubois and U.S. progress in civil rights. Going out later, a Rawlings's associate whispered, "It was a test. You passed."

....Q: What about American exiles - maybe they weren't exiles –but American expatriates who'd gone to Ghana during the halcyon days. Was there such a community?

Fritts: Yes, it was a poignant group. A number of African Americans had come to Ghana in the first flush of African independence to welcome a new world for Africa and for Africans led by Ghana and Kwame Nkrumah, now president of Ghana, but also expected to be the future president of a united States of Africa headquartered in Accra. They had also fled racial bias and discrimination in the U.S.

But their dreams were unfulfilled. The unified Africa vision died and Ghana deteriorated politically and economically. Some had denounced their American citizenship. Many had married Ghanaians and their children were now adult. Their lives and futures as Ghanaian rather than American citizens had not worked out as they wished. They were still loyal to Ghana, but wistful that their hopes and dreams when young had been dashed.

Q: How was life – for you, your wife and embassy colleagues?

Fritts: The infrastructure – roads, phones, water, and electricity was extremely run down. There were no functional Western hotels or restaurants. Stores and shops were dark and empty, with a few canned goods from Eastern Europe. We were dependent upon the local markets for seasonal foods and our small commissary for basic items plus quarterly shipments of stuff from Denmark. We had brought paper products and other consumables sufficient for two years. Audrey was a great planner. It worked.

I played tennis at a local club, which had fallen on hard times, and several embassy houses had basic tennis courts.

There was a rocky golf course with sand "browns" rather than grass "greens." We had a small embassy club with a pool and basic amenities. A major outlet for us and other diplomats was Sunday family beach parties more or less potluck. The embassy also had a lease on a beach cove, which we used when security permitted and sometimes when it didn't. But the undertows were fierce and dangerous. I found a spot about ten miles outside of Accra where I could surf fish occasionally from a jetty, but I went as incognito as I could at dusk, because it was near a main highway and my face was well known.

We traveled upcountry whenever we could, visiting local officials, chiefs, including the Asantehene of the Ashanti who kept still impressive court and American missionaries plus AID and Self Help projects. We would stay with our hosts or in basic government guest houses, as there were no local hotels we could really use. Travel was difficult. We carried our own gasoline in 50-gallon drums in the backseat, which always bounced, leaked and smelled from the rutted roads.

The defense attaché plane was very useful. It would arrive every three months or so and enable us to fly to certain parts of the country and show the flag with local officials. And we had incidents. Even though we'd inform the Foreign Ministry of the itinerary, communications were difficult. Usually, local Ghanaian officials would adapt with their usual cheer. But the ideologues could be trouble.

In one particular instance I was most incensed when we arrived to pay a call on a regional governor, who was paranoid about an American military airplane, pilots in uniform and a so-called American ambassador and USAID officials. Under several dissembling guises, we were effectively detained under guard at gunpoint.

I had everyone put the best face on it for a while, but the governor became increasingly insulting and unbuttoned his pistol holster in speaking to me. After several hours, I was at the point of organizing a walkout past the armed guards, when he received word from Accra that we were legitimate. But I canceled the meetings (it was then too late anyway) and we returned to Accra where I sent a protest the next day. He later became the secretary of agriculture. I never called on him officially.

There were a number of American missionaries in Ghana as Ghanaians are very religious. As I may have said before, while we had a difficult political climate, we also had what I thought was the best human climate in Africa. Average Ghanaians warmly welcomed us. The political stuff went over their heads.

The country doesn't suffer from the degree of ethnic and tribal conflicts that many other African countries do. Nkrumah was successful in welding a sense of Ghanaian nationhood out of it all. Many educated Ghanaians, even some of those who would speak about the United States in most difficult terms publicly, on a personal level were very astute, accommodating and frequently witty.

Q: How about American academics? Was there much of an academic flowing back and forth, and was it of value and interest?

Fritts: Practically none. At independence in 1957, American scholarship on Ghana was widespread. In reading up before going to post, I found a vast amount of scholarly work, but all outdated – political and sociological work from the early '50s into the mid- '60s and after that nothing. Ghana went off the academic scope as the economic and political climate deteriorated, the grant funds dried up and the scholars left.

Indeed, my successor, Steve Lyne, asked me at one point to recommend books he might read to prepare for Ghana. I replied that the only good stuff had been done during the Nkrumah period and was outdated. Instead, I suggested, not wholly tongue-in-cheek, to be sure to re-read two books, neither one on Ghana nor Africa – *The Prince* by Machiavelli and *The Annals of Rome* by Tacitus.

The former was insightful as to how Rawlings often operated, even had to operate at times, and the latter on how the group in the Castle operated.

Q: What was your impression of the academic system, the university and the schools leading up to it?

Fritts: At independence Ghana had possibly the best educational system in Africa. The University of Ghana at Legon, was recognized within the British Commonwealth as a prestige institution. Its degrees were accepted as equivalents with Oxford or Cambridge. By my tenure, that had not been true for over a decade. Legon and the other universities were frequently closed, classrooms and buildings had deteriorated, furniture, phones, desks and books had been stolen and sold, and electricity was problematic. Even paper and pencils were unavailable. The situation was similar even in the formerly prestigious private secondary schools.

Professors and teachers were unpaid or received barter. Some teachers would not teach in classrooms, preferring to tutor the same students outside of class for cash. Many professors, Ghanaian and foreign, had gone abroad, some to Saudi Arabia and the Middle East. The professional classes in general, especially medical doctors, had deserted Ghana. Intellectual flight accelerated during the initial year or so of the PNDC. Hospitals barely functioned. The educational system was a mere shell. But Ghanaians value education highly, and many students persevered. Indeed.

Q: Hadn't there been in Ghana an American aluminum plant or something?

Fritts: Yes, the major American investment in Ghana was the Volta Aluminum Company (VALCO) aluminum plant in the southern part of Ghana, a joint venture of Kaiser Aluminum and Reynolds Metals. The dam on the Volta River was the largest earthen dam in the world. It had been a major aid project by the U.S. and the World Bank. Nkrumah had lobbied for it personally with Presidents Eisenhower and Kennedy.

The project was controversial at the outset and considered even more so as time went on. In this day and age it would not have been built because of the environmental impact and the relocation of massive numbers of people whose farms and houses were drowned by the reservoir.

The company was under great pressure from the ideological PNDC for allegedly previous sweetheart deals, which were raping Ghana of its resources, underpaying its taxes, falsifying import documents, using foreign rather than Ghanaian bauxite, etc. While certainly exaggerated, I suspect VALCO may have done what it had to do to survive corrupt Ghanaian governments. Eventually, after much stress, the PNDC and Reynolds successfully renegotiated the basic agreement to a balance they both could live with.

Actually, in my time, I found VALCO quite a straightforward operation with enlightened American and Ghanaian management. It was progressive in its personnel policies, while operating a major industrial plant in a part of the world whose infrastructure and workforce were difficult in terms of education, quality and consistency.

For example, it had by far the best literacy and vocational training program in the country. I've mentioned that a major drought existed. The lake level had fallen so far that the plant kept decreasing production and finally stopped entirely, generating only a fractional amount of electricity for national use – a single turbine. While most of the workers were laid off, the company used its duty-free privilege to import agricultural implements, fertilizers and seeds and other tools not then available in Ghana so its former employees could try to earn a living until such time as they could be rehired. That's not a usual American corporate practice anywhere that I know of.

Q: Wasn't VALCO concerned that it would be taken over or looted by undisciplined people?

Fritts: It was always under PNDC pressure and media

attacks for being part of a neocolonialist conspiracy. There were also labor strikes stirred up by agitators or simply general worker concerns over layoffs and shutting down. There were occasional concerns over worker violence and/or provocations by PNDC zealots.

At the embassy, we had the usual kinds of early warning arrangements with VALCO with other American entities, such as up-country missionaries. But VALCO had some very accomplished Ghanaians in top jobs and recognized its best protection was as a Ghanaian corporate citizen, rather than an American-owned firm.

The government was also heavily dependent upon the foreign exchange earned from aluminum and electricity exports. So as time went by, the PNDC and its increasingly sophisticated negotiators became increasingly pragmatic, despite PNDC-controlled media rhetoric. I generally kept out of the discourse and only worked in the background when VALCO thought the embassy shoulder patch might be useful.

Q: So when you left Ghana in 1986, did you feel things had really moved in the right direction?

Fritts: Absolutely. U.S.-Ghanaian relations had been turned around, Ghana was embarked upon an increasingly effective economic recovery program, and its ideological bark was worse than its bite. Then the bilateral relationship collapsed dramatically.

Q: What happened?

Fritts: A first-class spy flap. And I can talk about it because I think I'm one of the very few American ambassadors ever authorized to discuss a CIA Station publicly. The crisis also had major media coverage internationally.

A support person in our CIA station, Sharon Scranage, was turned to spy against us. Her male cohort, Michael Sousouides, was a close relative of Rawlings. A foreign power aided and abetted the affair and Ghanaian internal security was in up to its ears Scranage had left post on reassignment and received the usual polygraph test at CIA Headquarters. I understand the needle went off the chart. She then confessed her activity and cooperated in setting up a sting to entice and meet her Ghanaian lover and handler in the U.S. He was arrested at Motel 50, just down the street here on Arlington Boulevard. It was kept quiet and I knew nothing about it.

Several days later I was playing tennis with Ghanaians when the CIA Station Chief and several visitors came and sat courtside. I assumed it was not to admire my backhand. During a set break, I was informed they needed to speak with me urgently. Back at the residence, I was briefed on the arrests and that the USG (United States Government) would announce them shortly. I knew all hell would break loose. It wouldn't be a routine event such as with the Soviet Union.

Q: What did you do?

Fritts: The first priority was to get our CIA people and compromised Ghanaians out of Ghana. Scranage had reportedly identified many of them as well as some innocents to her handlers. I couldn't take chances with lives and there was already a Ghanaian FSN in prison on spy charges.

I think we had about a week. We progressively evacuated all the Americans associated in any way as well as those not associated if Scranage said she had mentioned them. The exodus was an all-hands embassy effort. There's always chit-chat about State-CIA tensions and rivalries, but in this case everyone really pulled together. We had the CIA folk and their families gone quickly – maybe 72 hours.. They pulled their kids out of school and left their pets, household effects and full refrigerators behind.

Over the following weeks, State, USAID and other Country Team members, including Audrey, fed the pets, packed and shipped additional suitcases, took in and protected heirlooms, and helped pack up effects. Real

Foreign Service cohesion. We staggered the CIA departures to avoid raising suspicions. I'd occasionally go and hang out at the airport on some pretext in case any incident developed, but none did.

We also arranged to inform many of the compromised Ghanaians, who also left the country precipitately. Some real human tragedies, of course.

Q: What else?

Fritts: I had to prepare the embassy in advance of the Washington statement.

In that regard, given potential Ghanaian government volatility, I had informed only DCM John Brims and another officer of why we were doing what we were doing. For the others I outlined only in general terms why the Station draw down was swiftly proceeding. I held several embassy Town Meetings at which I essentially said, "Trust me."

I believed strongly that if Tsikata and Ghanaian security tumbled to what we were up to, they would round up Ghanaians they suspected, have phony trials and execute them. There could also be incidents and attacks by thugs and PNDC stalwarts against the embassy, our American officers and staff, and even FSNs.

Safety lay in getting our people out first and then seeking to manage reactions with the Ghanaian government. If I were to be openly candid within the embassy before the Washington announcement, the situation would not be kept secret.

By the way, when the eventual months long crisis was finally successfully over, the Department sent one of its psychiatrists to post to interview everyone involved.

At the onset and over the weeks and months, several officers and staff had suffered from the continuing tension and two had been transferred. I suppose today it's called post-traumatic syndrome.

The psychiatrist faulted me for not initially bringing everyone into my confidence as it may have increased mental stress. She stated she was "sure" that if faced with a similar situation in the future, I would be open and inclusive from the beginning.

I said, "Absolutely not." I was sorry for the stress, but my responsibility was to save lives and I would do it again if faced with what I thought was the same choice. She was shocked. So be it.

Q: How did you inform the Government?

Fritts: The top task was to forestall any intemperate reaction from within the Castle or zealot supporters by giving Rawlings a brief advance alert. That meant I had to see him on short notice, which was always difficult. Only an unconventional approach might do.

So the next morning at dawn I camped outside the home of a government cabinet member along with the usual levee of Ghanaian relatives and others seeking jobs or favors. It's part of Ghanaian culture. I was moved to the head of the queue, invited in and sat down at his breakfast. I apologized for the intrusion and said I had to see Rawlings that very day. That I had an issue of major importance to the future of U.S.-Ghana relations.

When I saw Rawlings later that morning, I informed him of what had occurred, that an announcement of the arrests of Scranage and Sousouides would be made in Washington in a few hours, that unless we managed the matter wisely, there could be serious repercussions, and that I expected, of course, the fullest government protection for our embassy and personnel.

He didn't do much batting of his eyes and I don't know how much he may have known. I think he gave me the right answers, but his speech was often elliptic. I then returned to the embassy to finally open up with the Country Team and prepare to hunker down. That afternoon, I learned that the Ghanaian security was making arrests in town.

Q: What was the reaction after the announcement?

Fritts: Given the time differential between Washington

and Accra, the full story was emblazoned in the Ghanaian media with a heavy overlay of the U.S. and the CIA attempting to overthrow Rawlings and the PNDC. We had an urgent Country Team meeting, issued public statements, briefed the FSNs with the facts, sent them home, and shut down the embassy to await further developments.

Audrey and I were to attend a diplomatic corps activity the next day hosted by the Ghanaian Army. It was to observe a shooting competition at the main military base. I'd been busy most of the night and early morning, of course. And the army event had already started. Once the embassy was buttoned up, should we go?

We decided we weren't going to slink around. After all, it was the Ghanaians and their friends who had spied on the U.S., which had no interest or intention of overthrowing the PNDC.

So later that morning we got into the car, drove into the military base, and then across a broad field up to the stands, with the flags flying on the fenders and every eye in the place upon us. Our stomachs were tight. But we got out and walked in with our heads high as if it were a normal day. The Ghanaian officers didn't know whether to shake hands with us or whether they'd be punished if they did. I put my hand out to General Quainoo and the usual Ghanaian politeness carried the day. But, of course, the adulation days of "best ambassador" and easy access were over.

Q: Well, let's go to what was done. What was this all about?

Fritts: Scranage had been at the embassy several years in a support job. She appeared capable and was quite popular and good for morale. Evidently this Ghanaian, who became her lover, had captivated her. He had money and gave lavish Ghanaian parties with an in-crowd. She was seduced physically and morally by the glamour of being selected to go where no other Western foreigner went.

They also worked on her gripes. She provided detailed inside information to him and thence to the Ghanaian Government and what I have to call a "foreign power." It was a very extensive and serious compromise, including far beyond just Ghana.

Q: When you say the foreign power, is this something we can –

Fritts: Not really as I'm not sure if we ever stated it publicly.

Q: Well, why would this cause such problems in Ghana? I mean, this was, you know, our problem, not theirs. It strikes me as a self-induced tempest in a teapot on the side of the Ghanaians. With the Soviets, for example, we both go through the exercises and move on.

Fritts: You're correct about recurrent spy incidents with the Soviets, the then East Germans and others being flash-in-the-pan routine. But in the Third World, nationalism, paranoia and sensitivity are much more volatile. As I mentioned earlier, most Ghanaians believe that the CIA instigated the overthrow of Nkrumah. It's part of local lore and even those who had no love for Nkrumah believe and resent it. The PNDC, having a radical Marxist, anti-colonialist and anti-imperialist mantra, always saw a presumed CIA hand in world events.

A number of its true believers and Rawlings as well, believed or were led to believe, that the CIA was working with Ghanaian exiles in Togo to overthrow the PNDC. I was regularly called in on the carpet or the Ghanaian media would carry reports on CIA connivance from Togo. It was all delusional.

As I frequently said, my task with Washington was to get anyone in any agency to pay attention to the U.S.-Ghana relationships, not beat back budding coup attempts.

I remember a cabinet secretary reading me the riot act one day. I asked him to cite one single shred of evidence to support his view. His reply was classic, "The absence of evidence is proof of the conspiracy!"

In some conversations, Rawlings would state that I couldn't know what the CIA was really doing. Once he even added, "Even me. Intelligence agencies have more in common with each other than they do with their own governments". In his world, that was certainly true at least some of the time. And maybe elsewhere as well. He could be quite insightful.

The PNDC itself had come to power in a coup and executed two former presidents. And given what many of them believed to be an Nkrumah precedent, they saw a mirror image. I'm also sure the Cubans, Libyans, Soviets and others were egging the issue on and reinforcing it.

All part and parcel of the challenges in the developing world.

Q: Well, the fact that we had a CIA station within the embassy couldn't have been a great shock to anyone.

Fritts: Of course not. In fact, some persons on both sides had worked on liaison matters under the previous government. The government knew we had a station, but probably felt it could live with it and didn't want to jeopardize the evolving overall U.S. relationship, which it needed.

Q: When you say the Government of Ghana, Rawlings must have known that this was going on.

Fritts: Sure. After all, we knew they were watching us. I was aware of surveillance at times.

Q: Well, did this happen as you left post?

Fritts: No, during my last year. Both we and the Ghanaians began trials of our respective arrestees; the Ghanaians matching us step for step. Thus, the issue was in the news all the time – photos of Sousouides in shackles, etc. Vignettes of CIA skullduggery in Ghana. On and on. A constant hemorrhage.

We eventually began prolonged negotiations for an exchange of "spies." We would hand back their man in the

U.S. – Sousouides – for all our "persons of interest." There were also a number of side issues. The negotiations were tortured, extended, and broke off on several occasions. At one time there was a semi-official threat against me personally when the Ghanaian chief negotiator said he would not guarantee my continued safety. To their credit, AF Assistant Secretary Chet Crocker and DAS Jim Bishop called in the Ghanaian ambassador, who was a very good man, and laced in to him. I think one of Crocker's comments to the ambassador was "If a small country like Ghana wants to make an enemy of the U.S., let it." It got their attention and the chief negotiator was switched to the foreign minister, Obed Asamoah. With him the process remained difficult, but professional.

By the way, AF DAS Jim Bishop was superb as the Washington focal point. He handled the Washington end on a real-time basis and I had no second-guessing from Langley or elsewhere on my game plans. Just support and constructive ideas.

After about six months and many perils of Pauline, we reached agreement for the exchange and related matters. On a particular day, they took their arrestees to the border with Togo and the convicted Sousouides came across to Ghana. In order to positively identify the Ghanaians, the CIA had brought along several of the people we had gotten out previously. The Ghanaian press took telescopic photos of the exchange, including the exiles hugging the newly exchanged. It was not a good press day for the United States in Ghana. Naturally, I wasn't there, but was in touch with embassy officers who kept me informed in case any glitch occurred or the exchange was aborted.

I thought the crisis was finally over, but it wasn't.

Q: Why was that?

Fritts: It had been agreed that the Ghanaians and we would announce the agreement and exchange at the same time, but the Justice Department violated the agreement and jumped the gun by several hours. The PNDC and

Rawlings were furious when they heard the news on VOA and the BBC. Again, CIA and U.S. perfidy. We hunkered the embassy down again and took a break for Thanksgiving. I sent a cable saying that the Justice action had undone months of efforts and placed the embassy and my colleagues again in jeopardy. Actually, the night before the affront I had seen the Foreign Minister at a reception and we had agreed on "no more surprises" and to get on with our bilateral business.

Audrey and I hosted a large Ghanaian group for Thanksgiving dinner. As the specially imported turkeys were being served, I was summoned to call at the Foreign Ministry urgently. I delayed until dessert. Asamoah said the PNDC had decided the USG had not dealt in good faith and read the names of four embassy officers named *persona non grata*. They were to be out in forty-eight hours for interfering in Ghana's internal affairs. All blameless. I remonstrated conceptually and individually, but he said the PNDC decision was final. We responded, of course, by expelling the same number from their embassy in Washington and suspending – temporarily - our aid programs. Obviously, our new "surprise" had been answered.

A sidebar. After returning to the residence and finishing dessert with the guests, I called a Country Team meeting where we did the necessary. I remember sending the Defense Attaché to Gen. Quainoo to tell him informally that I would keep the Ghanaian Army out of this. I then began a reporting cable.

Alone in the embassy, the phone rang from Washington midway though the cable. In those days phoning Accra wasn't easy. It was a State Operations Center watch officer saying the BBC was carrying an item that American embassy officers were being expelled from Ghana. What was going on? I didn't want him to be the purveyor of interpretative comment, so I said I didn't know, but the ambassador was preparing a cable as we spoke. "Fine", he said.

Q: So now what? Was it finally over?

Fritts: Yes and no. This was November and I was due to leave the following June. During my tenure the bilateral relationship had gone from a pit to a pinnacle and was now back in a pit. Neither my status nor credibility were the same. Some people thought we had been interested in overthrowing a Ghanaian government – again. It was also apparent that Rawlings no longer considered me esteemed. That complicated access to the government as it meant officials felt some risk in too close an association or not having it cleared by the Castle in advance. Also, international economic aid programs were expanding and the PNDC didn't need me or the U.S. as much.

We had really been of critical importance to the Ghanaian Government at a formative period. The U.S. decision to work with the PNDC, build a relationship and convince others to do so through an economic stabilization program had been essential. Recovery was underway. There were now established alternatives to a singular role with the U.S.

The government also reverted to petty harassments and vitriolic media attacks, which had marked earlier days, despite *pro forma* statements of putting the issues behind us. Meanwhile, I was determined to uphold the honor and dignity of the U.S. and that meant not trying to ingratiate myself personally. As long as we were pilloried, we would be correct and business like, but I was also back to Report Cards. It would set the stage for my successor to be a good guy.

I never saw Chairman Rawlings again personally, although I did receive a letter from him some months after I had left Ghana, apologizing for not meeting with me on departure. But it was an exercise by the Ghanaian ambassador in Washington.

I've often commented that the role of an ambassador is not to be well loved or liked, although that's preferable, but to pursue hopefully enlightened U.S. national interests. That's our professional responsibility, not always shared, to my observation, by political appointees who covet abstract bilateral relations and local popularity.

Q: Just on that, who took your place in Ghana?

Fritts: Steve Lyne, a career FSO. It was almost a year before he went out. The GOG (Government of Ghana) wrongly interpreted the delay as a further expression of our displeasure. In reality, it was just one of those variants of the personnel process.

Q: Sometimes something of this nature, such as problems in a country, whether or not it's your fault, can be induced – sort of like being the captain of a destroyer –as happening on your watch and thus responsible. Did you think the system was saying, Well, I don't know about Fritts, there was trouble out in Ghana while he was there? I mean, you didn't feel that –

Fritts: No, not at all. I received a personal commendation from the Acting Secretary of State and glowing evaluations by Chet Crocker and others plus a CIA award. I understand that to this day I hold some kind of record for negotiating the most one-sided exchange of "spies" – their one for our multiple – in the history of U.S. diplomacy. A few years later, I was the Department's selectee at the White House to be an assistant secretary, but a political appointee was chosen.

Q: Did you feel that the Central Intelligence Agency appreciated what you did?

Fritts: Very much so. A lot of working level attention plus an award and lunch with the Acting CIA Director, Bob Gates, I think. It also created a corridor reputation, which served me well in some other tasks.

In retrospect, some CIA officers opined that they expected me as an FSO to be less cooperative and to care more about safeguarding State's image in the country. Sort of opt out with a low profile. I didn't see that as an option.

Whatever status I had was to be used. In this case, negotiating an exchange and saving lives was not only humanitarian, but also a message that the USG, which includes the CIA, will not abandon those who, for whatever reasons, have placed their trust in it. Kind of a professional duty thing, I guess.

Q: Well, while you were going through this, were you at a certain point getting ready to get a new job? Did you know what you were going to do?

Fritts: I had expressed interest in a diplomat–in-residence slot and Director General George Vest was kind in his praise of my work in Ghana and gave me first choice among the fifteen he had. I chose the College of William and Mary in Williamsburg, Virginia.

Source:
Ambassador Robert E. Fritts, interviewed by Charles Stuart Kennedy, 8 September 1999, pp. 99 – 124, and 126.
Foreign Affairs Oral History Collection, Association for Diplomatic Studies and Training, Arlington, Virginia, USA, www.adst.org
Copyright 2004 ADST.

Appendix II:

Nkrumah's speech to the first conference of the Organisation of African Unity (OAU) when the OAU was formed in Addis Ababa, Ethiopia, 25 May 1963. His book, *Africa Must Unite*, was also published in May 1963 to coincide with the formation of the OAU as an attempt to encourage his fellow leaders to agree with his plan for immediate continental unification under one government.

Your Excellencies, Colleagues, Brothers and Friends,

At the first gathering of African Heads of State, to which I had the honour of playing host, there were representatives of eight independent States only. Today, five years later, we meet as the representatives of no less than thirty-two States, the guests of His Imperial Majesty, Haile Selassie, the First, and the Government and people of Ethiopia. To His Imperial Majesty, I wish to express, on behalf of the Government and people of Ghana my deep appreciation for a most cordial welcome and generous hospitality.

The increase in our number in this short space of time is open testimony to the indomitable and irresistible surge of our peoples for independence. It is also a token of the revolutionary speed of world events in the latter half of this century. In the task which is before us of unifying our continent we must fall in with that pace or be left behind. The task cannot be attached in the tempo of any other age than our own. To fall behind the unprecedented momentum of actions and events in our time will be to court failure and our own undoing.

A whole continent has imposed a mandate upon us to lay the foundation of our Union at this Conference. It is our responsibility to execute this mandate by creating here and now the formula upon which the requisite superstructure may be erected.

On this continent it has not taken us long to discover that the struggle against colonialism does not end with the attainment of national independence. Independence is only the prelude to a new and more involved struggle for the right to conduct our own economic and social affairs; to construct our society according to our aspirations, unhampered by crushing and humiliating neo-colonialist controls and interference.

From the start we have been threatened with frustration where rapid change is imperative and with instability where sustained effort and ordered rule are indispensable.

No sporadic act nor pious resolution can resolve our present problems. Nothing will be of avail, except the united act of a united Africa. We have already reached, the stage where we must unite or sink into that condition which has made Latin America the unwilling and distressed prey of imperialism after one and a half centuries of political independence.

As a continent we have emerged into independence in a different age, with imperialism grown stronger, more ruthless and experienced, and more dangerous in its international associations. Our economic advancement demands the end of colonialist and neo-colonialist domination in Africa.

But just as we understood that the shaping of our national destinies required of each of us our political independence and bent all our strength to this attainment, so we must recognise that our economic independence resides in our African union and requires the same concentration upon the political achievement.

The unity of our continent, no less than our separate independence, will be delayed if, indeed, we do not lose it, by hobnobbing with colonialism. African Unity is, above all, a political kingdom which can only be gained by political means. The social and economic development of Africa will come only within the political kingdom, not the other way around. The United States of America, the Union of Soviet Socialist Republics, were the political decisions of revolutionary peoples before they became mighty realities of social power and material wealth.

How, except by our united efforts, will the richest and still enslaved parts of our continent be freed from colonial occupation and become available to us for the total development of our continent? Every step in the decolonisation of our continent has brought greater resistance in those areas where colonial garrisons are available to colonialism.

This is the great design of the imperialist interests that buttress colonialism and neo-colonialism, and we would be deceiving ourselves in the most cruel way were we to regard their individual actions as separate and unrelated. When Portugal violates Senegal's border, when Verwoed allocated one-seventh of South Africa's budget to military and police, when France builds as part of her defence policy an interventionist force that can intervene, more especially in French-speaking Africa, when Welensky talks of Southern Rhodesia joining South Africa, it is all part of a carefully calculated pattern working towards a single end: the continued enslavement of our still dependent brothers and an onslaught upon the independence of our sovereign African States.

Do we have any other weapon against this design but our unity? Is not our unity essential to guard our own freedom as well as to win freedom for our oppressed brothers, the Freedom Fighters?

Is it not unity alone that can weld us into an effective force, capable of creating our own progress and making our valuable contribution to world peace? Which independent African State will claim that its financial structure and banking institutions are fully harnessed to its national development? Which will claim that its material resources and human energies are available for its own national aspirations? Which will disclaim a substantial measure of disappointment and disillusionment in its agricultural and urban development?

In independent Africa we are already re-experiencing the instability and frustration which existed under colonial rule. We are fast learning that political independence is not enough to rid us of the consequences of colonial rule.

The movement of the masses of the people of Africa for freedom from that kind of rule was not only a revolt against the conditions which it imposed.

Our people supported us in our fight for independence because they believed that African Governments could cure the ills of the past in a way which could never be accomplished under colonial rule. If, therefore, now that we are independent we allow the same conditions to exist that existed in colonial days, all the resentment which overthrew colonialism will be mobilised against us.

The resources are there. It is for us to marshal them in the active service of our people. Unless we do this by our concerted efforts, within the framework of our combined planning, we shall not progress at the tempo demanded by today's events and the mood of our people. The symptoms of our troubles will grow, and the troubles themselves become chronic. It will then be too late even for Pan-

African Unity to secure for us stability and tranquillity in our labours for a continent of social justice and material well-being. Unless we establish African Unity now, we who are sitting here today shall tomorrow be the victims and martyrs of neo-colonialism.

There is evidence on every side that the imperialists have not withdrawn from our affairs. There are times, as in the Congo, when their interference is manifest. But generally it is covered up under the clothing of many agencies, which meddle in our domestic affairs, to foment dissension within our borders and to create an atmosphere of tension and political instability. As long as we do not do away with the root causes of discontent, we lend aid to these neo-colonialist forces, and shall become our own executioners. We cannot ignore the teachings of history.

Our continent is probably the richest in the world for minerals and industrial and agricultural primary materials. From the Congo alone, Western firms exported copper, rubber, cotton, and other goods to the value of 2, 773 billion dollars in the ten years between 1945 and 1955, and from South Africa, Western gold mining companies have drawn a profit, in the four years, between 1947 to 1951, of 814 billion dollars.

Our continent certainly exceeds all the others in potential hydroelectric power, which some experts assess as 42 per cent of the world's total. What need is there for us to remain hewers for the industrialised areas of the world?

It is said, of course, that we have no capital, no industrial skill, no communications and no internal markets, and that we cannot even agree among ourselves how best to utilise our resources.

Yet all the stock exchanges in the world are preoccupied with Africa's gold, diamonds, uranium, platinum, copper and iron ores. Our capital flows out in streams to irrigate the whole system of Western economy. Fifty-two per cent of the gold in Fort Knox at this moment, where the U. S. A. stores its bullion, is believed to have originated from our shores. Africa provides more than 60 per cent of the world's gold. A great deal of the uranium for nuclear power, of copper for electronics, of titanium for supersonic projectiles, of iron and steel for heavy industries, of other minerals and raw materials for lighter industries – the basic economic might of the foreign Powers – come from our continent.

Experts have estimated that the Congo basin alone can produce enough food crops to satisfy the requirements of nearly half the population of the whole world.

For centuries Africa has been the milk cow of the Western world. It was our continent that helped the Western world to build up its accumulated wealth.

It is true that we are now throwing off the yoke of colonialism as fast as we can, but our success in this direction is equally matched by an intense effort on the part of imperialism to continue the exploitation of our resources by creating divisions among us.

When the colonies of the American Continent sought to free themselves from imperialism in the 18th century there was no threat of neo-colonialism in the sense in which we know it today. The American States were therefore free to form and fashion the unity which was best suited to their needs and to frame a constitution to hold their unity together without any form of interference from external sources. We, however, are having to grapple with outside interventions. How much more, then do we need to come together in the African unity that alone can save us from the clutches of neo-colonialism.

We have the resources. It was colonialism in the first place that prevented us from accumulating the effective capital; but we ourselves have failed to make full use of our power in independence to mobilise our resources for the most effective take-off into thorough going economic and social development. We have been too busy nursing our separate States to understand fully the basic need of our union, rooted in common purpose, common planning and common endeavour. A union that ignores these fundamental necessities will be but a shame. It is only by uniting our productive capacity and the resultant production that we can amass capital. And once we start, the momentum will increase.

With capital controlled by our own banks, harnessed to our own true industrial and agricultural development, we shall make our advance. We shall accumulate machinery and establish steel works, iron foundries and factories; we shall link the various States of our continent with communications; we shall astound the world with our hydroelectric power; we shall drain marshes and swamps, clear infested areas, feed the under-nourished, and rid our people of parasites and disease. It is within the possibility of science and technology to make even the Sahara bloom into a vast field with verdant vegetation for agricultural and industrial developments. We shall harness the radio, television, giant printing presses to lift our people from the dark recesses of illiteracy.

A decade ago, these would have been visionary words, the fantasies of an idle dreamer. But this is the age in which science has transcended the limits of the material world, and technology has invaded the silences of nature. Time and space have been reduced to unimportant abstractions. Giant machines make roads, clear forests, dig dams, layout aerodromes; monster trucks and planes distribute goods; huge laboratories manufacture drugs; complicated geological surveys are made; mighty power stations are built; colossal factories erected – all at an incredible speed. The world is no longer moving through bush paths or on camels and donkeys.

We cannot afford to pace our needs, our development, our security to the gait of camels and donkeys. We cannot afford not to cut down the overgrown bush of outmoded attitudes that obstruct our path to the modern open road of the widest and earliest achievement of economic independence and the raising up of the lives of our people to the highest level.

Even for other continents lacking tile resources of Africa, this is the age that sees the end of human want. For us it is a simple matter of grasping with certainty our heritage by using the political might of unity. All we need to do is to develop with our united strength the enormous resources of our continent. A United Africa will provide a stable field of foreign investment, which will encourage as long as it does not behave inimically to our African interests. For such investment would add by its enterprises to the development of the national economy, employment and training of our people, and will be welcome to Africa. In dealing with a united Africa, investors will no longer have to weigh with concern the risks of negotiating with governments in one period which may not exist in the very next period. Instead of dealing or negotiating with so many separate States at a time they will be dealing with one united government pursuing a harmonized continental policy.

What is the alternative to this? If we falter at this stage, and let time pass for neo-colonialism to consolidate its position on this continent, what will be the fate of our people who have put their trust in us? What will be the fate of our freedom fighters? What will be the fate of other African Territories that are not yet free?

Unless we can establish great industrial complexes in Africa – which we can only do in united Africa – we must have our peasantry to the mercy of foreign cash crop markets, and face the same unrest which overthrew the colonialists? What use to the farmer is education and mechanisation, what use is even capital for development; unless we can ensure for him and a fair price and ready market? What has the peasant, worker and farmer gained from political independence, unless we can ensure for him a fair return for his labour and a higher standard of living?

Unless we can establish great industrial complexes in Africa, what have the urban worker, and all those peasants on overcrowded land gained from political independence? If they are to remain unemployed or in unskilled occupation, what will avail them the better facilities for education, technical training, energy and ambition which independence enables us to provide?

There is hardly any African State without frontier problems with its adjacent neighbours. It would be futile for me to enumerate them because they are already familiar to us all. But let me suggest to Your Excellencies, that this fatal relic of colonialism will drive us to war against one another as our unplanned and uncoordinated industrial development expands, just as happened in Europe.

Unless we succeed in arresting the danger through mutual understanding on fundamental issues and through African Unity, which will render existing boundaries obsolete and superfluous, we shall have fought in vain for independence. Only African Unity can heal this festering sore of boundary disputes between our various States. Your Excellencies, the remedy for these ills is ready to our hand. It stares us in the face at every customs barrier, it shouts to us from every African heart. By creating a true political union of all the independent States of Africa, we can tackle hopefully every emergency, every enemy and every

complexity. This is not because we are a race of superman, but because we have emerged in the age of science and technology in which poverty, ignorance and disease are no longer the masters, but the retreating foes of mankind. We have emerged in the age of socialized planning, when production and distribution are not governed by chaos, greed and self-interest, but by social needs. Together with the rest of mankind, we have awakened from Utopian dreams to pursue practical blueprints for progress and social justice.

Above all, we have emerged at a time when a continental land mass like Africa with its population approaching three hundred million are necessary to the economic capitalization and profitability of modern productive methods and techniques. Not one of us working singly and individually can successfully attain the fullest development. Certainly, in the circumstances, it will not be possible to give adequate assistance to sister States trying, against the most difficult conditions, to improve their economic and social structures. Only a united Africa functioning under a Union Government can forcefully mobilize the material and moral resources of our separate countries and apply them efficiently and energetically to bring a rapid change in the conditions of our people.

If we do not approach the problems in Africa with a common front and a common purpose, we shall be haggling and wrangling among ourselves until we are colonized again and become the tolls of a far greater colonialism than we suffered hitherto.

Unite we must. Without necessarily sacrificing our sovereignties, big or small, we can, here and now, forge a political union based on Defence, Foreign Affairs and Diplomacy, and a common Citizenship, an African currency, an African Monetary Zone and an African Central Bank. We must unite in order to achieve the full liberation of our continent. We need a common Defence system with an African High Command to ensure the stability and security of Africa.

We have been charged with this sacred task by our own people, and we cannot betray their trust by failing them. We will be mocking the hopes of our people if we show the slightest hesitation or delay by tackling realistically this question of African Unity.

The supply of arms or other military aid to the colonial oppressors in Africa must be regarded not only as aid in the vanquishment of the freedom fighters battling for their African independence, but as an act of aggression against the whole of Africa. How can we meet this aggression except by the full weight of our united strength?

Many of us have made non-alignment an article of faith on this continent. We have no wish, and no intention of being drawn into the Cold War. But with the present weakness and insecurity of our States in the context of world politics, the search for bases and spheres of influence brings the Cold War into Africa with its danger of nuclear warfare. Africa should be declared a nuclear-free zone and freed from cold war exigencies. But we cannot make this demand mandatory unless we support it from a position of strength to be found only in our unity.

Instead, many Independent African States are involved by military pacts with the former colonial powers. The stability and security which such devices seek to establish are illusory, for the metropolitan Powers seize the opportunity to support their neo-colonialist controls by direct military involvement. We have seen how the neo-colonialists use their bases to entrench themselves and attack neighbouring independent States. Such bases are centers of tension and potential danger spots of military conflict. They threaten the security not only of the country in which they are situated but of neighbouring countries as well. How can we hope to make Africa a nuclear-free zone and independent of cold war pressure with such military involvement on our continent? Only by counter-balancing a common defence force with a common defence policy based upon our desire for an Africa untrammelled by foreign dictation or military and nuclear presence. This will require an all-embracing African High Command, especially if the military pacts with the imperialists are to be renounced. It is the only way we can break these direct links between the colonialism of the past and the neo-colonialism which disrupts us today.

We do not want nor do we visualize an African High Command in the terms of the power politics that now rule a great part of the world, but as an essential and indispensable instrument for ensuring stability and security in Africa.

We need a unified economic planning for Africa. Until the economic power of Africa is in our hands, the masses can have no real concern and no real interest for safeguarding our security, for ensuring the stability of our regimes, and for bending their strength to the fulfilment of our ends. With our united resources, energies and talents we have the means, as soon as we show the will, to transform the economic structures of our individual States from poverty to that of wealth, from, inequality to the satisfaction of popular needs. Only on a continental basis shall we be able to plan the proper utilisation of all our resources for the full development of our continent.

How else will we retain our own capital for our development? How else will we establish an internal market for our own industries? By belonging to different economic zones, how will we break down the currency and trading barriers between African States, and how will the economically stronger amongst us be able to assist the weaker and less developed States?

It is important to remember that independent financing and independent development cannot take place without an independent currency. A currency system that is backed by the resources of a foreign State is *ipso facto* subject to the trade and financial arrangements of that foreign country.

Because we have so many customs and currency barriers as a result of being subject to the different currency systems of foreign powers, this has served to widen the gap between us in Africa. How, for example, can related communities and families trade with, and support one another successfully, if they find themselves divided by national boundaries and currency restrictions? The only alternative open to them in these circumstances, is to use smuggled currency and enrich national and international racketeers and crooks who prey upon our financial and economic difficulties.

No independent African State today by itself has a chance to follow an independent course of economic development, and many of us who have tried to do this have been almost ruined or have had to return to the fold of the former colonial rulers. This position will not change unless we have unified policy working at the continental level. The first step towards our cohesive economy would be a unified monetary zone, with, initially, an agreed common parity for our currencies. To facilitate this arrangement, Ghana would change to a decimal system. When we find that the arrangement of a fixed common parity is working successfully, there would seem to be no reason for not instituting one common currency and a single bank of issue. With a common currency from one common bank of issue we should be able to stand erect on our own feet because such an arrangement would be fully backed by the combined national products of the States composing the union. After all, the purchasing power of money depends on productivity and the productive exploitation of the natural, human and physical resources of the nation.

While we are assuring our stability by a common defence system, and our economy is being orientated beyond foreign control by a Common currency, Monetary Zone and Central Bank of Issue, we can investigate the resources of our continent. We can begin to ascertain whether in reality we are the richest, and not, as we have been taught to believe, the poorest among the continents. We can determine whether we possess the largest potential in hydroelectric power, and whether we can harness it and other sources of energy to our own industries. We can proceed to plan our industrialization on a continental scale, and to build up a common market for nearly three hundred million people.

Common Continental Planning for the Industrial and Agricultural development of Africa is a vital necessity.

So many blessings must flow from our unity; so many disasters must follow on our continued disunity, that our failure to unite today will not be attributed by posterity only to faulty reasoning and lack of courage, but to our capitulation before the forces of imperialism.

The hour of history which has brought us to this assembly is a revolutionary hour. It is the hour of decision. For the first time, the economic imperialism which menaces us is itself challenged by the irresistible will of our people.

The masses of the people of Africa are crying for unity. The people of Africa call for a breaking down of boundaries that keep them apart. They demand an end to the border disputes between sister African States – disputes that arise out of the artificial barriers that divided us. It was colonialism's purpose that left us with our border irredentism that rejected our ethnic and cultural fusion.

Our people call for unity so that they may not lose their patrimony in the perpetual service of neo-colonialism. In their fervent push for unity, they understand that only its realization will give full meaning to their freedom and our African independence.

It is this popular determination that must move us on to a Union of Independent African States. In delay lies danger to our well-being, to tour very existence as free States. It has been suggested that our approach of unity should be gradual, that it should go piece-meal. This point of view conceives of Africa as a static entity with "frozen" problems which can be eliminated one by one and when all have been cleared then we can come together and say: "Now all is well. Let us unite." This view takes no account of the impact of external pressures. Nor does it take cognizance of the danger that delay can deepen our isolations and exclusiveness; that it can enlarge our differences and set us drifting further and further apart into the net of neo-colonialism, so that our union will become nothing but a fading hope, and the great design of Africa's full redemption will be lost, perhaps, forever.

The view is also expressed that our difficulties could be resolved simply by a greater collaboration through cooperative association in our inter-territorial relationships. This way of looking at our problems denies a proper conception of their inter-relationship and mutuality. It denies faith in a future for African advancement, in African independence. It betrays a sense of solution only in continued reliance upon external sources through bilateral agreements for economic and other forms of aid.

The fact is that although we have been cooperating and associating with one another in various fields of common endeavour even before colonial times, this has not given us the continental identity and the political and economic force which would help us to deal effectively with the complicated problems confronting us in Africa today. As far as foreign aid is concerned, a United Africa would be in a more favourable position to attract assistance from foreign sources. There is the far more compelling advantage which this arrangement offers, in that aid will come from anywhere to Africa because our bargaining power would become infinitely greater. We shall no longer be dependent upon aid from restricted sources. We shall have the world to choose from.

What are we looking for in Africa? Are we looking for Charters, conceived in the light of the United Nations example? A type of United Nations organisation whose decisions are framed on the basis of resolutions that in our experience have sometimes been ignored by member States? Where groupings are formed and pressures develop in accordance with the interest of the group concerned? Or is it intended that Africa should be turned into a lose organization of States on the model of the organization of the American States, in which the weaker States within it can be at the mercy of the stronger or more powerful ones politically or economically or at the mercy of some powerful outside nations or group of nations? Is this the kind of association we want for ourselves in the United Africa we all speak of with such feeling and emotion?

Your Excellences, permit me to ask: is this the kind of framework we desire for our United Africa? And arrangement which in future could permit Ghana or Nigeria or the Sudan, or Liberia, or Egypt or Ethiopia for example, to use pressure, which either superior economic or political influence gives, to dictate the flow and the direction of trade from, say, Burundi or Togo or Nyasaland to Mozambique?

We all want a United Africa, united not only in our concept of what unity can connotes, but united in our common desire to move forward together and dealing with all the problems that can best be solved only on a continental basis.

When the first Congress of the United States met many years ago at Philadelphia, one of the delegates sounded the first chore of unity by declaring that they had met in a "state of nature" in other words, they were not at Philadelphia as Virginians, or Pennsylvanians, but simply as Americans. This reference to themselves as Americans was in those days a new and strange experience. May I dare to assert equally on this occasion, Your Excellences that we meet here today not as Ghanaians, Guineans, Egyptians, Algerians, Moroccans, Malians, Liberians, Congolese or Nigerians but as Africans. Africans united in our resolve to remain here until we have agreed on the basic principles of a new compact of unity among ourselves which guaranties for us and future a new arrangement of continental government.

If we succeed in establishing a new set of principles as the basis of a new Charter or Statute for the establishment of a Continental Unity of Africa and the creation of social and political progress for our people then, in my view, this Conference should mark the end of our various groupings and regional blocs. But if we fail and let this grand and historic opportunity slip by then we should give way to greater dissension and division among us for which the people of Africa will never forgive us. And the popular and progressive forces and movements within Africa will condemn us. I am sure therefore that we should not fail them.

I have spoken at some length, Your Excellencies, because it is necessary for us all to explain not only to one another present here but also to our people who have entrusted to us the fate and destiny of Africa. We must therefore not leave this place until we have set up effective machinery for achieving African Unity. To this end, I now propose for your consideration the following:

As a first step, Your Excellencies, a Declaration of Principles uniting and binding us together and to which we must all faithfully and loyally adhere, and laying the foundations of unity should be set down. And there should also be a formal declaration that all the Independent African States here and now agree to the establishment of a Union of African States.

As a second and urgent step for the realization of the unification of Africa, an All-Africa Committee of Foreign Ministers be set up now, and that before we rise from this Conference a day should be fixed for them to meet.

This Committee should establish on behalf of the Heads of our Governments, a permanent body of officials and experts to work out a machinery for the Union Government of Africa. This body of officials and experts should be made up of two of the brains from each Independent African State. The various Charters of the existing groupings and other relevant document could also be submitted to the officials and experts. A praesidium consisting of the Head of the Governments of the Independent African States should be call upon to meet and adopt a Constitution and others recommendations that will launch the Union Government of Africa.

We must also decide on allocation where this body of officials and experts will work as the new Headquarters or Capital of our Union Government. Some central place in Africa might be the fairest suggestion either at Bangui in the Central African Republic or Leopoldville in Congo. My colleagues may have other proposals. The Committee of Foreign Ministers, officials and experts should be empowered to establish:

1. A Commission to frame a Constitution for a Union Government of African States;

2. A Commission to work out a continent-wide plan for a unified or common economic and industrial programme for Africa; this plan should include proposals for setting up:

A Common Market for Africa
An African currency
African Monetary Zone
African Central Bank, and
Continental Communications System;

3. A Commission to draw up details for a Common Foreign Policy and Diplomacy;

4. A Commission to produce plans for a Common System of Defence;

5. A Commission to make proposals for Common African Citizenship.

These Commissions will report to the Committee of Foreign Ministers who should in turn submit within six months of this Conference their recommendations to the Praesidium. The Praesidium meeting in Conference at the Union Headquarters will consider and approve the recommendations of the Committee of Foreign Ministers.

In order to provide funds immediately for the work of the permanent officials and experts of the Headquarters of the Union, I suggest that a special Committed be set up now to work a budget for this.

Your Excellences, with these steps, I submit, we shall be irrevocably committed to the road which will bring us to a Union Government of Africa. Only a united Africa with central political direction can successfully give effective material and moral support to our Freedom Fighters in Southern Rhodesia, Angola, Mozambique, South-West Africa, Bechuanaland, Swaziland, Basutoland, Portuguese Guinea, etc., and of course South Africa.

Appendix III:

Nkrumah: A great African but not a great Ghanaian?

Nkrumah at 100: What Dr. Kwame Nkrumah did for Ghana

Sunday 6 December 2009

Kwame Osei writes a tribute to an Afrikan Colossus, Dr. Kwame Nkrumah

The month of September was a poignant one in Ghana and the Afrikan continent as a whole as it marked the centenary celebrations of the greatest Afrikan of the 20th century (BBC Afrika listeners' poll) Osagyefo Dr. Kwame Nkrumah.

There were major celebrations and events in Ghana and across the continent for the man who really launched the Afrikan renaissance in the 1950's with his Afrikan

Liberation drive.

Incidentally these celebrations will culminate in a grand finale to be staged on Afrika Day, May 25 2010.

In Ghana, Kwame Nkrumah's birthday which was on the 21st September was a national holiday with many events across the country in remembrance of the great man. The day was started by a national address by current Ghanaian president John Evans Atta-Mills signifying Dr. Nkrumah's significant contribution to Ghana's independence and development.

For this feature, as an Afrikan historian we will analyze and examine what Dr. Nkrumah did do for Ghana.

There has been an attempt, a pathetic attempt in my view, from some sections of Ghanaian society who for their own perverse reasons want to rubbish and downplay the colossal achievements of the great man.

In addition to this some in Ghana claim "what did Nkrumah do for Ghana?" Again because of the attempt by some in Ghanaian society to erase the achievements of Dr. Nkrumah from the annals of Ghanaian history, the vast majority of Ghanaian people especially the youth, have no idea of the colossal achievements of Dr. Nkrumah and what he did for Ghana.

Also respected Afrikan historian Ali Mazrui once said that "Nkrumah was a great Afrikan but not a good Ghanaian."

This feature seeks to identify and impart to Ghanaians and Afrikans at large what Dr. Kwame Nkrumah indeed did do for Ghana.

When one looks back Dr. Nkrumah was an excellent leader, despite the shortcomings that every leader has. If Ghanaians were to take a critical look at ALL of the state institutions that Ghana now has, they will see the handwriting of Dr. Nkrumah on those institutions.

In actual fact the majority of the infrastructure that is present in Ghana was built by the administration of Dr. Kwame Nkrumah.

Part of Osagyefo's grand vision for Ghana was to take it into the industrial age and make the country self-reliant and self-sufficient in all areas of nation building and development and take the country from an enslaved colonial economy to an economically liberated one.

It must be remembered that the British colonialists LEFT NOTHING in terms of infrastructure, development and industry. The only thing the British did do was to partly build railways to take the gold from Kumasi to Accra and another railway line from Kumasi to the port of Takoradi.

In 1962 in a radio address to the nation entitled "Work and Happiness: Ghana's Seven Year Development Plan" Osagyefo Dr. Kwame Nkrumah launched a massive industrialization drive.

Incidentally if this Seven Year Development Plan had reached its fruition, Ghana would have been a developed economy by 1970 and this was seen as a great threat to Western interests. This is why Kwame Nkrumah was overthrown in the CIA orchestrated coup of 1966.

This drive was launched because Nkrumah inherited a colonial economy in which the interests of the British and NOT the Ghanaians were served. An example of this is that the revenues from cocoa were invested in British banks instead of promoting local Ghanaian industry.

Kwame Nkrumah was also well aware that without industrialization, Ghana was going nowhere. The vision for this grand scheme was founded on the Volta River Project, a huge project that sought to exploit Ghana's vast bauxite reserves to process it into aluminum.

To do this required a smelter and a smelter cannot function without cheap electricity, and at that time hydroelectric energy was the cheapest form of electricity.

Therefore Dr. Kwame Nkrumah moved quickly and managed to convince then US president John F Kennedy (and Dwight Eisenhower) to help Ghana generate cheap electricity to supply the proposed Volta Aluminum

Company (VALCO) to smelt the bauxite and process it into aluminum by financing the project.

As such Nkrumah got the Akosombo Dam to be built which at the time was a colossal undertaking. The Akosombo Dam was not only meant to spearhead Ghana's industrial revolution, but it was also to supply other Afrikan countries in the sub-region with cheap electricity giving further credence to his Pan-Afrikan ideology.

The availability of electricity meant that other industries could take off. In effect Osagyefo Dr. Kwame Nkrumah foresaw the positive domino effect the construction of the Akosombo Dam would have on the economy of Ghana and other Afrikan states.

His end objective for VALCO was to be an engine to supply aluminum to a plethora of Ghanaian owned companies who would then process the aluminum into products like cooking utensils, roofing sheets and even solar panels so that Ghana would be a net exporter of value added aluminum products.

Dr. Nkrumah also established the GIHOC Industries (Ghana Industrial Holding Corporation) – again Nkrumah's grand vision meant that GIHOC had several subsidiaries that would provide Ghanaians with most of their needs and wants.

Dr. Nkrumah knew that industrialization was impossible without steel. He therefore established the Tema Steel Factory – more on Tema later.

Steel and glass go hand in hand so he established the Abosso Glass Factory.

In any nation building project cement is an imperative commodity and recognizing that cement was key to his development plans, GHACEM was established to provide cement for the massive construction work that was to take place both commercially and for private/residential use.

Osagyefo did not rule out agriculture in his development plan for he knew that a nation that could not feed itself was destined ultimately for failure.

Firstly Nkrumah wanted to revolutionize the cocoa industry. Cocoa was the cornerstone of the Ghanaian economy and still is. However, he was aware that Ghana was importing the sacks to package the cocoa. It was a complete waste of resources.

Therefore as part of his agricultural programme he established the Jute factory in Kumasi to manufacture cocoa sacks for our farmers. With this simple move he created employment for thousands of Ghanaians and at the same time reducing the importation bill – that is leadership, vision and doing what is in the national interest.

As far as the cocoa industry was concerned, Dr. Kwame Nkrumah's ultimate objective was for Ghana to eventually process our own cocoa beans and supply value-added products like chocolate bars, chocolate drinks to the world market and NOT just be a supplier of the raw material which is why he set up the West African Mills to process our cocoa beans.

Another agricultural development initiative that Nkrumah did was in the area of tomatoes. Tomatoes are a key ingredient in any Ghanaian dish. It is used in the preparation of stews, soups etc.

Ghana grew tomatoes but for part of the year Ghana had a huge shortage of the product in its markets. This was due to not having a place to store the excess tomatoes. As such Dr. Nkrumah sought to address this problem by the construction of two tomato factories in Northern Ghana namely in Wenchi and Pwalugu.

This was a very significant development for Dr. Nkrumah to start building factories and enterprises in Northern Ghana. This was so because Nkrumah was well aware that the TOTAL development of Ghana meant the development of every region in Ghana and not neglecting any of the regions.

It MUST be remembered that the British colonialists who ran Ghana, formerly the Gold Coast, DID NOT leave any manner of development in the North. This was because the British saw the Northerners as a peasant, uneducated, backward people whose lot in life was to be servants to other people.

As such the British deliberately underdeveloped the North (Northern Region, Upper East and Upper West) and failed to provide them with educational opportunities. This action by the British colonialists explains the problems in Northern Ghana especially in areas like Bawku.

So Nkrumah establishing these factories in the North was a strategic move as well as a nationalistic move to correct the injustices of British colonial rule by giving the North the opportunity to become economically viable and share in the nation's wealth. Again this demonstrated Nkrumah's vision, leadership and selfless desire to see the masses of the people have their daily bread.

A very crucial and innovative part of Nkrumah's agricultural policy was the establishment of the Agricultural Development Bank. This was set up to help finance agricultural projects and to support farmers with loans and financial assistance key for their development.

Another vital source of employment particularly in the agricultural sector that Nkrumah provided in the North was the establishment of the Meat Processing factory at Bologatanga to provide Ghana with a clean healthy source of protein to improve the health of our people.

Talking about health, Kwame Nkrumah realized that there can be no effective health care system without adequate supplies of medicines to treat the sick. Therefore under the GIHOC Industrial complex, he set up the GIHOC pharmaceutical sub-division that was established at Tema to meet this need by producing our OWN medicines.

It is a great shame that today when one goes to Korle Bu, Komfo Anokye and other clinics/hospitals up and down the country that medicines are either non-existent or in very short supply and that most of it is imported.

In the days of colonial rule, our security institutions like the Police Service, the Military etc, had to rely on imported shoes or boots to wear. When Nkrumah became prime minister, he thought we could do much better and so he established the Shoe Factory in Kumasi which manufactured shoes and/or boots for all Ghana's security institutions.

As Afrikan people, alcoholic drinks are a key feature of most of our social functions. However, even in the times of Nkrumah, Ghanaians were beginning to develop a penchant for foreign alcoholic beverages as they thought them to be more superior to the local stuff.

Again under the GIHOC Industries, Nkrumah established the GIHOC Distilleries to meet this demand and to produce alcoholic beverages that were as good as or even better than the foreign-produced liquor.

Again as part of the GIHOC Industries Dr. Kwame Nkrumah established the GIHOC Electronics sub-division to manufacture electronic devices such as radios (Sanyo) to the people and also to help Ghana gain technological know-how.

The Tema Project

As a showcase for what Nkrumah had planned for other strategic areas of the country, he launched the Tema project. The Tema project consisted of a huge industrial complex and housing project to house Ghana's increasing population.

This was a grand project by Nkrumah as the Tema industrial complex was meant to serve as an industrial hub to the country and become a gateway to West Afrika.

The Tema industrial complex consisted of key industries that would launch Ghana's industrial revolution. Such industries included:

Tema Oil Refinery

Tema Steel Company
Tema Food Complex, GIHOC
VALCO
GIHOC
Tema Harbour

The Housing Project at Tema was designed to give people affordable housing and somewhere to lay one's head after a hard day's work. Apart from this Kwame Nkrumah knew that the population was expanding and that is was only right and proper to provide housing for them.

As such he built residential communities in Tema from scratch – these housing communities had access to clean water, tarred roads, access to electricity, had a regular refuse collection and proper drainage systems that when it rained, did not lead to flooding.

These communities were also master-planned in that they also had schools, post offices, hospitals, shops and everything that befit a thriving community. These communities made Tema a showcase in Ghana.

This housing project that Kwame Nkrumah showcased in Tema was replicated in other areas of the country. Such housing projects included in Accra (Labone Estate, Kanda Estates, Osu Ringway Estates, Airport Residential Area) - in Kumasi (Patasi Estate, Kwadaso Estate, Buokrom Estates, North and South Suntreso).

Apart from this Kwame Nkrumah also established the Continental Hotel (now Golden Tulip) and the City Hotel in Kumasi (now Golden Tulip Kumasi City).

Conclusion

Osagyefo Dr. Kwame Nkrumah was a patriot unlike some who claim to be patriots. He was no looter of state resources nor cared about ex-gratias. He did not have any Swiss bank account or any other account for that matter.

He died a poor man.

Above all Kwame Nkrumah was a nationalistic person. He cared deeply about Ghana and her people. He could identify with the people; after all as one of our own kith and kin he wanted to make a difference to the people's lives – a huge difference!

The companies that I have listed here are but a tip of the iceberg for he built many, many more. Kwame Nkrumah wanted Ghanaians to work and be happy! There is nothing in this world than to enjoy the fruits of one's hard work.

The companies that Dr. Nkrumah set up provided REAL job opportunities for the people, a key component in any nation building programme. These jobs also afforded the opportunity for Ghanaians to develop invaluable managerial and entrepreneurial skills. For this Ghana shall be forever grateful to him for his leadership, vision and immense foresight.

For those Ghanaians and others who are still not convinced about the achievements of Kwame Nkrumah, please refer to the following list that highlights some of his vast contributions to Ghana.

1. Bank of Ghana
2. Bonsa Tyre Manufacturing
3. Cape Coast University
4. Cocoa Marketing Board (now Cocobod)
5. Cocoa research Institute, Tafo
6. Compulsory Free Education for ALL
7. Dairy Farms at Amrahia and Avatime
8. Farmer's Council
9. Free Medical Care for ALL
10. Ghana Airways Corporation
11. Ghana Black Star Shipping Line
12. Ghana Commercial Bank
13. Ghana Film Industries
14. Ghana Housing Corporation
15. Ghana Law School

16. Ghana Medical School
17. Gold Processing Factory, Prestea
18. Job 600
19. Komenda Sugar Factory
20. Kwame Nkrumah University of Science and Technology
21. National Cultural Center
22. National Investment Bank
23. National Research Council
24. Nsawam Prison
25. Okomfo Anokye Hospital
26. Polytechnics and Technical Schools in all regions
27. Social Security Bank (SSB now SG-SSB)
28. State transport Corporation
29. Trade Fair Center
30. University of Ghana (Legon)
31. University Scholarships for study abroad

Kwame Osei is an Afrikan historian, writer and broadcaster who contributes to various radio stations and writes for a number of newspapers in Ghana.

Copyright © 2000-2009 The Ligali Organisation

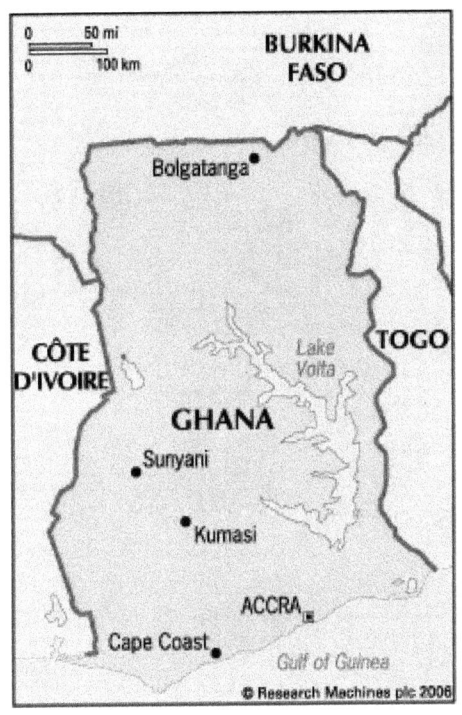

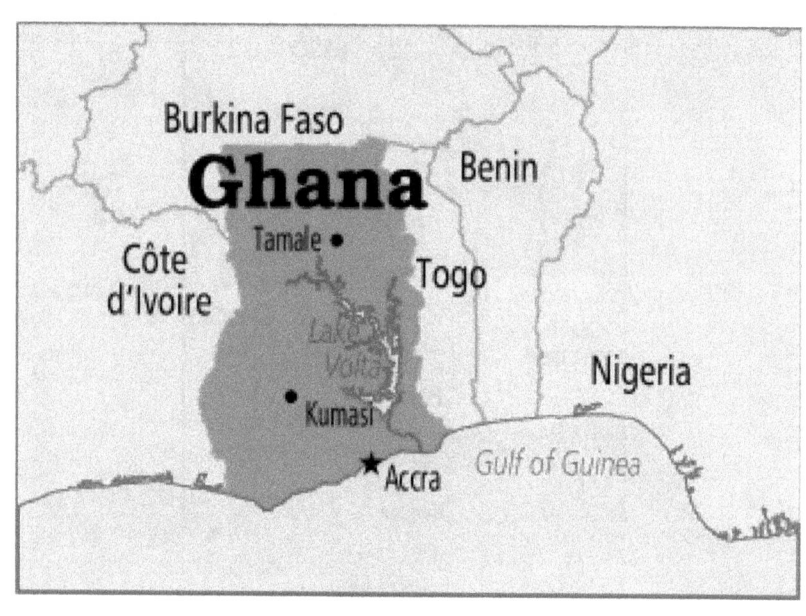

Nkrumah statue, African Union (AU) headquarters, Addis Ababa

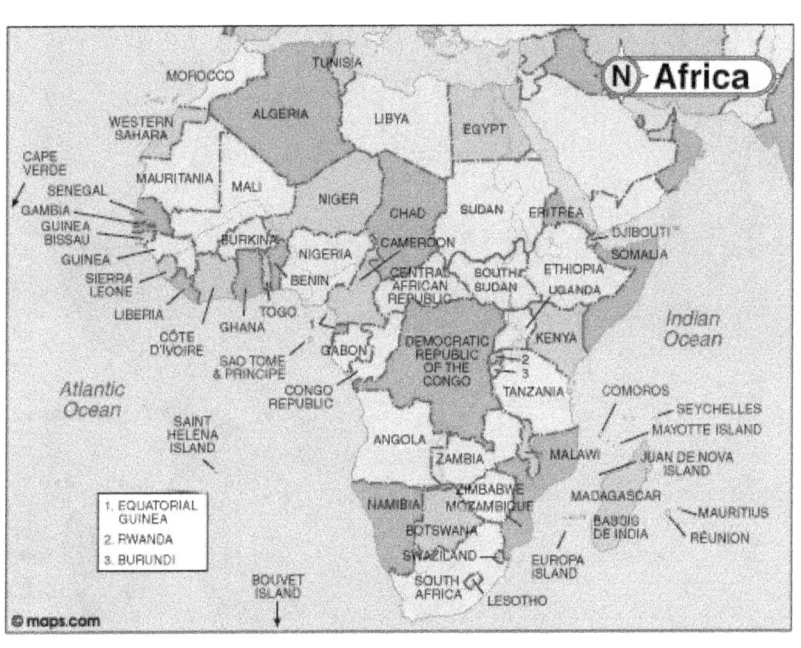

www.ingramcontent.com/pod-product-compliance
Lightning Source LLC
Chambersburg PA
CBHW070736170426
43200CB00007B/537